Praise for *Driving with Dead People*

"Holloway's strong voice and remarkable sense of humor . . . make this an unforgettable read."   —Hope Edelman,
New York Times bestselling author of *Motherless Daughters*

"The best child narrators, like Monica Holloway, create a portal through time. Their take on the world is so evocative that your own early memories start jostling for space with the scenes being described."
—*Telegraph*

"Holloway's [memoir] shines because of her deft handling of the small details, while painstakingly assembling the larger picture."
—*Booklist*

"*Driving with Dead People* certainly packs a punch, and will provide countless discussions for reading groups looking for emotionally challenging material."   —*Kirkus Reviews*

"A gripping read, [*Driving with Dead People*'s] conclusion will stay with you long after you finish the last page."   —*Woman's Way*

"*Driving with Dead People* is a heartbreaking story, but it's made entertaining and readable thanks to Monica's sharp, witty recollection of the eccentric characters and strange incidents that popped up throughout her early years."   —*Heat Magazine*

"This is a classic—and the honest, eloquent storytelling is a tribute to Holloway's resilience."   —*Glamour UK*

"Families don't come much more dysfunctional than this, yet Monica becomes the heroine of her own traumatic life story, resulting in a tale of resilience and self-sufficiency."   —*The Mail on Sunday*

"An extraordinary and sometimes humorous account of life in an eccentric and dysfunctional family. Holloway captures perfectly her childhood resilience and coming of age."   —*In Style UK*

"[*Driving with Dead People*] works well, the McGuffin of the mortuary moments giving living colour and black humour to her story."
      —*Times Online UK*

DRIVING WITH DEAD PEOPLE

Monica Holloway

A Memoir

SIMON SPOTLIGHT ENTERTAINMENT
New York   London   Toronto   Sydney

SĮSĮE

SIMON SPOTLIGHT ENTERTAINMENT
An imprint of Simon & Schuster
1230 Avenue of the Americas, New York, New York 10020
Copyright © 2007 by Monica Holloway
All rights reserved, including the right of reproduction in whole or in part in any form.
Also available in a Simon Spotlight Entertainment hardcover edition.
SIMON SPOTLIGHT ENTERTAINMENT and related logo are trademarks of Simon & Schuster, Inc.
Designed by Yaffa Jaskoll
Manufactured in the United States of America
First Edition 10 9 8 7 6 5 4 3 2 1
The Library of Congress has cataloged the hardcover edition as follows:
Holloway, Monica.
Driving with dead people / by Monica Holloway.—1st ed.
p. cm.
ISBN-13: 978-1-4169-4002-9 (hc)
ISBN-10: 1-4169-4002-2 (hc)
1. Holloway, Monica. 2. Problem families—Biography. 3. Undertakers and undertaking—Family relationships. 4. Interpersonal relations—United States. I. Title.
CT275.H6443A3 2007
977.2'043092—dc22
[B]
2006026316
ISBN-13: 978-1-4169-5512-2 (pbk)
ISBN-10: 1-4169-5512-7 (pbk)

Note to Reader

This book presents the story of my journey from childhood to adulthood. All incidents are portrayed to the best of my recollection, although the names of schools and people (with the exception of my first name) have been changed, as have some identifying details and place names. Some individuals are composites.

To my beloved husband, angelic son, and remarkable sister

with love

Part I

DEAD GIRL

CHAPTER ONE

It changed everything: a school picture printed on the front page of the *Elk Grove Courier*, the newspaper my father was reading. I was eight. Sitting across the breakfast table from Dad, I pointed. "Who is she?"

"She's dead."

He kept reading.

"What happened?" I asked.

No answer.

I leaned forward to get a closer look. She looked like me: same short cropped hair with razor-straight bangs, same heart-shaped face, same wool plaid jumper. I looked at Dad: bloated, smudged glasses slid halfway down his nose. Why wasn't he telling me what happened? He loved talking gore; lived for it; documented it, even.

Dad drove his Ford pickup with his Kodak movie camera sitting shotgun just in case he saw an accident. If he was lucky enough to come upon something, he'd jump out and aim his camera at whatever was crumpled, bleeding, or burning. And every Thanksgiving he lined up Mom and the four of us kids on the gold-and-brown-plaid studio couch, hauled out the Bell + Howell reel-to-reel, and rolled his masterpieces.

Images jiggled past, scenes from our tiny Ohio town of Galesburg. Christmas morning, four beautiful children in color-coordinated Santa pajamas, squinting; summertime, my older brother Jamie's first home run; a station wagon hideously wrapped around a telephone pole, blood dripping down the passenger door and plop, plop, plopping onto the road; my two older sisters and me in hats with wide ribbons hunting for Easter baskets; a dead cow smashed on the front of a Plymouth. Our childhood was preserved among the big fire at the Catholic church, a Greyhound bus accident on Fort Henry Road, and a tornado twirling up Martha Whitmore's bean field. We all sat watching the movies and eating buttered popcorn made in the black-and-white-speckled pan that was always greasy, no matter how many times you scrubbed it. The disasters took up more reels than we did, and Dad narrated them like a pro.

So why was Dad skimping on the details about this dead girl? Maybe it wasn't bloody enough for him.

I couldn't get that school picture out of my head. I needed to know what had happened to that girl. If she was dead, something had killed her, and I wanted a heads up just in case whatever it was might be lurking nearby.

That night I casually swiped the newspaper off the cluttered coffee table and headed down the hallway to find my brother, Jamie. Nothing scared him.

He was sitting on his bedroom floor putting together a plastic model of a '69 Shelby Cobra Mustang.

"Can you read this out loud?" I held up the paper.

"Why can't you read it?" he asked, looking up from his project. He had most of the chassis put together.

"I *can* read it, but I want you to." He stared at me. I held up a Milky Way left over from my Easter stash.

I couldn't tell Jamie I didn't want to read the details of that girl's death by myself, especially with her staring out at me from the front page. I didn't want him thinking I was chicken.

"It has to be right now?" he asked.

"Mom says I have to go to bed in a minute," I said.

He twisted the lid back onto the blue-and-white tube of Testor's glue and wiped his hands on the filthy dishrag he kept in his supplies shoe box.

"Let's go," he said. I followed him to the dark landing of our musty basement, where the four of us kids congregated for secret business.

"Here," I said, handing him the paper and the candy. I was glad Jamie wasn't too curious. He hardly ever asked questions about anything.

We sat crouched on the landing. I held the silver flashlight with the words "Black and Decker" printed down the side. Dad owned a hardware store in downtown Elk Grove and earned the flashlight selling ten hammers in two months, but he tossed it to me when the lens cracked. Jamie and I sat facing each other cross-legged with our foreheads touching, staring down at the white circle of light. He began to read: "'Driver Faces Charges in Bike Rider Death'—"

"Bike rider? She was killed on her bike?" I craned my neck to see the paper right side up.

"Do you want me to read this or not?" Jamie tore open the candy bar wrapper.

"Go ahead," I said, thinking of my own bike, a gold Schwinn with a leopard-skin banana seat. I'd spent hours running it up the wooden ramp Jamie had built beside the alley behind our house. Cars ripped through there without ever slowing down.

Jamie took a bite and began reading again: "'Mason County's fourth traffic fatality of the year occurred Tuesday afternoon with the death of Sarah Rebecca Keeler, eight-year-old daughter of Mr. and Mrs. Herbert Keeler.'"

Eight years old? I was eight. I grabbed the paper to take another look. She was my age, but I didn't recognize her from school. I felt a pang of disappointment as I handed back the paper.

Jamie continued, "'Sarah Keeler was a member of St. Mary

Catholic Church and was a third-grade pupil at St. Mary School.'"

That's why I didn't know her; she was Catholic. Catholics were considered the equivalent of snake handlers in our small Ohio town. I didn't know much about them except that they made Methodists like my parents nervous. This made Sarah more mysterious. Anyone who unnerved my parents was interesting to me.

"'Sarah was en route on North Highway 26 when struck by a car driven by Nowell Linsley, sixty-one. The report states death was apparently instantaneous, due to a basal skull fracture and a broken neck.'"

"What's a 'basal skull fracture'?" I asked.

"I guess her head broke open," Jamie said. He knew death. He'd buried dozens of small animals he'd found dead in the field behind our house, or cats and squirrels squashed by cars speeding through town on Highway 64.

I contemplated how hard I'd have to be hit by a car to have my head crack open like an egg. My oldest sister, JoAnn, had her head split open on the corner of the coffee table when we were little. Dad deliberately stuck his foot out and tripped her. He thought it was hilarious until bright red blood began trickling down her face.

I was trying to picture someone's *whole* head laid open, hair and brains and blood on the asphalt, when I began feeling woozy and sweaty.

"Hold the flashlight still," Jamie said. I shook my head and steadied the light. "'A Breathalyzer test was taken on Linsley, and he was charged by the sheriff's department for driving under the influence of alcohol.'"

"The guy was drunk," Jamie said, handing me the paper. I thought of Uncle Ernie, the only person I'd ever seen drunk. He'd come to our front door one night after running down the street from the dilapidated Galesburg Tavern, where another drunk had been hitting him over the head with a pool cue. Dad wasn't home.

Ernie's forehead was bleeding and Mom looked pale and nervous, especially when he asked to use one of her good bath towels. The next morning I heard Mom call him a "sweet drunk," so he'd probably never kill anyone on a bicycle. Even so, I'd be on the lookout for his white pickup.

That night I lay in my small wooden bed and relished the attention Sarah Keeler must have received. I fantasized that it had been me on that bike and I'd been struck from behind. I hoisted my arms above my head on the pillow and pretended to be lying on the road. In my fantasy my dad drove by and stopped, not because he recognized my bike (my dad had no idea what color my bike was); he stopped because it was potentially gory. He jumped out of the truck with his movie camera but realized it was me lying there—bleeding and dying. *Double jackpot*, he thought: one less mouth to feed *and* he'd get all the attention. People would feel so bad for him.

Dad resisted the urge to film the scene, opting instead to bend over my limp body, pretending to be struck with grief. He was surprised when he could actually squeeze out tears. Everyone closed in around him . . . and that's when I canceled that fantasy.

If Dad shoved me out of the limelight even in my death scene, if he couldn't even love me while I was lying on the asphalt, there was no hope.

Maybe others would have been sad to see me dead in the street. I thought of Mom curled up in the nubby orange chair reading *Rich Man, Poor Man*. Surely she'd have been devastated. But Mom was a human cork; she floated to the top of any awful situation. My mom, who'd told me the earth was flat, always created her own reality. She would have been fine.

I was beginning to wonder if dying was such a good idea.

It wasn't as if I wanted to be dead; it was just that I was miserable and felt in the way most of the time. There was something wrong with me. I always knocked over my milk, I got sick every time we drove long distances in the car, and I wet my bed every night, even though I was in third grade. But when Dad started in on us, knocking Jamie across the kitchen and then kicking him in the side, or jerking my pants down in front of strangers, that's when death seemed possible, even preferable.

If God could make me normal like everyone else in my class, or pull me out from under the rage of my own father, I might be happy instead of nervous and ashamed all the time.

I remembered the funeral details Jamie had read:

Friends may call on Saturday at Kilner and Sons Mortuary between 4:00 and 8:00 p.m. On Sunday there will be Mass at St. Mary's, with burial following at Maple Creek Cemetery.

Until Sunday, when Sarah Keeler was sunk in a deep, lonely hole and the world forgot and moved on, I could pretend I knew her. I could wallow in the glow of her spectacular departure. Sunday was years away.

I woke up the next morning to sunshine and bushy green trees rustling outside my bedroom window. I rolled over and felt under my pillow for the newspaper. Still there.

I crawled out of bed to change my wet sheets and pajamas. Bed-wetting kept Mom from buying me a spiffy twin bed like the ones my older sisters, Becky and JoAnn, had.

Their fancy twins were on either side of mine, decorated exactly alike with smoky blue comforters trimmed in fluffy white ball-fringe. Their white wrought-iron headboards twisted into elaborate curlicues that mirrored each other.

My bed was narrow with white wooden rails that went halfway up on either side. The mattress was slick, quilted, and smelled of urine. It was a bed to be embarrassed by. A baby's bed. A peed-in bed. I'd slept in it my whole life.

I walked into the bathroom and threw my pajamas and sheets into the tub.

I thought of Sarah Keeler as I looked in the mirror and imagined my own face on the front page of the *Elk Grove Courier*. More than anything else, I wanted to see her on Saturday between four and eight p.m. lying in her pink (I imagined my favorite color) coffin, her freshly washed hands folded over her lap, shoes double-tied for oblivion. I had to find a way to go to that viewing. And I knew the person to take me there was Granda.

Granda was my mother's mother, but the opposite of my mom in every way. Granda was a realist, and that's how she needed to be approached. She could be very sentimental and loving, but she'd also killed her own cat. He bothered her. She had a bad hip and she'd gotten tired of getting up and down out of her chair to let him in and out of the aluminum door of her trailer. So she'd locked him in her freestanding garage that the pole barn company had built for her right beside her trailer; she'd lured him in with a raw hot dog, closed the door, and left the Buick running for three hours.

I felt she could be persuaded to attend a funeral.

After breakfast I walked across Whitmore's back field to Granda's green-and-white double-wide. Granda was sitting at the kitchen table peeling new potatoes. I needed to be convincing but not too eager. I sat down across from her.

"A girl I knew died," I said.

"Oh, honey, who was it?" Granda stopped peeling.

"It was in the paper yesterday."

"That little girl on the bicycle?" she asked.

I nodded. I was glad I didn't have to say her name as if I really had known her. "Mom doesn't think I should go to the funeral home." Granda started peeling again. "I feel like I should."

"If your mom says you can't, then you can't." Granda pointed the silver potato peeler in my direction for emphasis.

"Yeah, I guess so. The whole town's going."

Granda salted a piece of raw potato and handed it to me. I ate it slowly, the salt stinging my chapped lips.

"I was hoping maybe you could take me over there." I looked at the table as my face flushed red.

"Honey, you don't want to see that. It's a terrible thing, very upsetting."

"Well, I might go with Suzanne Beckner's family, but I'd rather go with you. Mrs. Beckner said the entire county's going." I rested my hands on the table and put my chin on top. Granda was scrutinizing me.

"Didn't that girl go to the Catholic school?"

"I guess so."

"And you knew her?"

"Not very well," I lied, "but enough to feel like I should go. Suzanne does too." I ended with the one line I knew would really get her. "Mom can't understand." Granda prided herself on wholly understanding me.

She said she'd think about it, which was a good sign. When Granda had to think about something, it usually meant yes sirree. Besides, Granda rarely passed on any kind of local drama. It ran in the family.

Saturday night Granda and I made the eight-mile trip to Elk Grove in her cat-killing Buick.

The line of mourners outside Kilner and Sons Mortuary snaked down Main Street, past the Liberty Movie Theatre, and ended in front of old man Conroy's pharmacy. Mrs. Beckner had been right; the entire county was there.

No one said a word. If someone caught someone else's eye, it was just a somber shaking of the head as if to say, *It can't be. It just can't be.* I shook my head too.

Granda and I took our place at the end of the line. I felt a kind of personal satisfaction with the huge turnout, as if I'd had something to do with it. I was sure that Sarah could see all of it and was secretly smiling and enjoying the attention. My tights itched the back of my leg right behind the knee, but I tried to ignore it. This was a dignified occasion and I would refrain from scratching.

We waited as the line snailed closer to the front doors with the initials K & S etched in script on the frosted glass.

As we pushed through the fancy doors and climbed the plush purple steps, my breath was coming in short spurts. Granda saw my pale face and gave me one last chance to leave before we turned the corner and entered the main room. There was no way I was leaving. I craned my neck and saw the flower arrangements stacked floor to ceiling and heard the soothing Muzak dragging above the voices.

Where's the coffin? I wondered as my stomach fluttered with fear and excitement. I shifted my weight.

Suddenly we turned a corner, and there she was. I could only see the top of her head because the casket was resting on a high platform with a maroon pleated skirt. It was pine with (and I'd called this) a pink interior. I looked at Granda with pleading eyes. "Could you please pick me up just for a second?" She was uncomfortable. She lifted me quickly and then—boom, back down on the carpet. I saw Sarah Keeler for one second. It was all the time I needed.

Her hair was cut exactly like in the picture in the newspaper, but her features didn't look the same. As often as I'd studied that picture, I wouldn't have recognized her. She was wearing a softball uniform, which threw me. I had imagined something tastefully frilly. She must have liked sports—another stabbing disappointment. I hated sports and was myself dressed in something tastefully frilly. We were not the same.

My gut clenched. I looked around and recognized no one. I looked back at the coffin. Sarah Keeler was going to be wearing that softball uniform forever, and she was not coming back, because there was no way back from wherever she was.

Granda was handing out condolences as I waited in the back of the room near an enormous gurgling coffee pot. She was right, there was no mistaking death when you saw it face-to-face, and Sarah's face kept flashing in front of me, her skin thick and powdery. Jamie told me later that it was makeup used to hide the bruises, which gave me the creeps. Her eyelids had been glued shut with what looked like rubber cement, and her lips had been smudged with light pink lip gloss that didn't even stay in the lines. I wasn't allowed to wear lipstick. Her hands were small like mine.

My mother was right; I shouldn't have seen this. And now I couldn't even tell her I had. I stared at Sarah's coffin, and I knew I could not choose death, because nothing, not even Dad, could be more frightening than ending up in a coffin with your lips sewn shut.

Even with Dad the way he was, always hitting and humiliating us, and even if Mom never noticed, I didn't want to die—not really. And besides, there was always Granda. Granda still took the best care of me and loved me more than anyone. She walked up beside me, and I grabbed her hand for reassurance.

On the way to the car we stopped to chat with Etta Mae Shaw. I waited, looking at my feet. It wasn't until then that I realized that somewhere between the coffin and Mrs. Shaw, I'd peed in my shoes. My socks were yellow and wet on the inside of my ankles, and the familiar stickiness of my soaked panties confirmed it. Granda kept an old brown furniture blanket in her trunk for just such occasions. I sat on it all the way home.

The next morning I woke up around five a.m.

I got up and peeled off my wet pajama bottoms. *Don't throw those wet pants on my hardwood floors,* Mom harped in my brain. I tossed them on the wet sheets and rolled the whole thing up into a ball. The house was silent. I tiptoed to the bathroom and threw the whole mess into the bathtub. On the way back to bed I peeked in Jamie's room.

With his hands resting on top of his blue-and-red-striped sheets, eyes shut, and breath barely noticeable, Jamie looked dead. I panicked. "Jamie!" I screamed. "Jamie!" He jumped out of bed, grabbed my arms, and jerked me into the dining room in one move.

"What? What is it? What's going on?"

"I thought you were dead," I mustered.

"I almost died when you screamed," he shushed me. I was shaking like crazy as we listened to hear if the fuss had woken up Mom or Dad. No one. "Shit, Monica, you freaked me out. I think that dead girl tweaked your brain. Come on."

Jamie tiptoed me back to my room, where JoAnn and Becky were peacefully sleeping. I pulled on another pair of pajama bottoms and he helped me with my early morning ritual, putting a beach towel over the pee spot and a dry sheet on top of that. With luck, it wouldn't soak through.

I climbed into bed in my mismatched pajamas: pink hearts on top, blue rocket hand-me-downs on bottom. I longed for a time when I would eat breakfast in matching top and bottom pajamas. No one else seemed to notice. My clean pajamas and sheets just regularly showed up, no comment. I managed in silence along with everyone else. That morning I wanted order in my world. More than anything else, I wanted my pajamas to match.

Jamie started out the bedroom door. "That girl gets buried today; they'll be digging the hole this morning," I said. He turned and looked at me. "Yep, today's hole day," he said. I shot him my *Please don't leave me* look. He came over and sat down on the floor beside my bed, leaning his head against the wooden side railing. The top of his hair was bristly from the buzz cut Dad had given him earlier that week. I patted it in thanks. "Go to sleep, Monica." I curled up in a ball.

Odds were, with Jamie there, I could sleep. If the planets aligned, I also might stay dry until I woke up. Just as I was settling in, my stomach tightened. Out my window the sun was coming up, but not for everyone. Some of us were dead.

CHAPTER TWO

The morning of Sarah Keeler's burial, I sat in the Galesburg Methodist Church between JoAnn and my father, whose heavy arm rested on the back of the pew right above my head. My legs were too short to touch the floor, but if I pressed my toes down, I could almost reach it. I was growing.

The church sat kitty-corner across the street from our house, but we were late every Sunday. The service started at nine a.m., and at nine ten my family would be running across the street in uncomfortable dress shoes, Dad calling us "idiots" as the opening hymn, "Love Lifted Me," wafted out the church windows.

The service that morning, led by the small and dreary Reverend Morse, was a dull drone, and I found myself staring at the large stained glass window on the left side of the church. I loved how the sun moved across that window every Sunday and how by the end of the service it was centered right in the middle of Jesus's face. This depended on where you were sitting, but we always sat in the exact same pew, so as long as it wasn't cloudy, the sun ended on Jesus.

I wasn't attached to Jesus, exactly, but I had heard about him since birth and held a kind of respect for all he'd been through. The hymn "Low in the Grave He Lay" pretty much told it all: He'd had a difficult life and a pretty rotten death. So I gave him the inner thumbs-up as I watched the sun and prayed for it to cross his left cheek, which would mean I was almost out of there.

Church was the only place where I sat close to my father. He felt less prickly there, and as much as I hated him, I wanted him to love me. In the silence of church I tried to steal closeness.

He seemed almost friendly in church because of his expression while singing hymns he knew by heart. His head would tilt to the right, eyes closed, forehead lifted. He looked so relaxed. When he took a breath, his head would dip with each inhale. His voice was beautiful. How could he sing so well and be so mean? The voice didn't fit the man, but it gave me hope.

The ending prayer finally came and I wiggled off the pew. Free—sort of. We still had to go to Sunday lunch at my grandparents' house.

After walking home and changing out of our church clothes, my family piled into our white station wagon and drove three blocks to Mammaw and Papaw's house. We could never just walk down there because there were too many hot covered dishes that had to be hauled along. I spent many Sundays sitting in the backseat holding a kitchen towel around warm baked beans with bacon sizzling on top, or a rectangular metal pan filled with cream cheese and lemon Jell-O mix meant to pass as a cheesecake.

Sundays with the Petersons, my dad's side of the family, were a recurring nightmare. Every weekend Mammaw and Papaw's six sons (my dad being the oldest) came with their large families in tow. My uncle Carl rarely came, but his family, Aunt Evelyn and the three boys, did.

Carl drove a Greyhound bus, so we hardly ever saw him. When we did, his eyelids were sleepy and droopy from driving strangers all over the country. Uncle Carl was the only one of us who traveled, and his sons, Ben, Tim, and Paul (who also had droopy eyelids), were the only cousins we liked.

The other cousins, whom I knew only because we shared the same pathetic gene pool, poured out of station wagons with scowls on their faces. Uncle Bill's son Troy talked like he had a sock stuck in the back of his throat, and my cousin Karen looked sad, even when she was laughing. All of my cousins were scared of my dad.

Dad took special pleasure in humiliating children; all of us had been the butt of it at one family event or another. Today it would be my turn again.

Uncle Ernie got out of his truck. The night before he'd been drunk again and someone had tossed him through the front window of the Galesburg Tavern. He was covered in cuts and bruises. I watched everyone talk to him as if his nose were still firmly attached.

Mammaw, oblivious to Ernie's injuries and our sour faces, loved a crowd and was always glad to see us. If we came right after church, she still had her teeth in, but if it was later in the day, she was all gums, and her shoes were long forgotten.

Mammaw rarely bathed, which bothered my overly bathed mother, but if you spent the night there, you didn't have to bathe either. And forget having to brush your teeth.

Mammaw embarrassed me with her red SOS-pad hair and her yellowed toenails. I was ashamed to feel that way because she loved all of us—fiercely. Mammaw never forgot a birthday even though there were more than thirty of us grandkids.

I felt sorry for Mammaw. I suspected she'd seen her share of tragedies. One Saturday afternoon we were standing on her back porch when the front tire of my gold bike exploded from the heat of the sun. It made a loud boom and Mammaw thought someone had fired a shotgun. She dropped to the kitchen linoleum and lay down flat, her thick arms protecting her head. The speed at which she hit the floor told me she'd been shot at before. It didn't surprise me.

Dad told us that when he was little, Papaw would drink whiskey and then sit down at the dinner table and say, "I can't stare at you bunch of lazy asses anymore. I'm gonna blow my goddamn head off." He'd scoot his chair back, grab his shotgun, and head out to the barn. Mammaw and the six boys would sit silently at the table waiting for the gun to go off. It never did.

Today for the Sunday get-together, I saw Papaw setting up card tables in the garage and on the lawn. Extra chairs were borrowed from the Galesburg Volunteer Fire Department across the alley. There was always a table heaped with food and a big orange plastic container with a white screw-on lid filled to the brim with iced tea laced with plenty of liquid saccharine.

Mammaw and Papaw lived in town now, but they used to manage a farm out on the county line. My dad grew up on that farm, killing chickens right before he cooked them, and butchering hogs in the barnyard. They'd been desperately poor, but Mammaw and Papaw, uneducated and fertile, kept having sons one right after the other. Those boys slaved away on that farm under the eye of my ferocious papaw. He was thin as a rail and bent over by the time I knew him, but I saw pictures and heard stories of what a big man he used to be and how he used to beat his kids, and Mammaw, too.

At these family get-togethers I usually stayed outside the house to avoid my father. I also considered my personal safety at risk whenever Mammaw cooked.

Her kitchen was an exotic and dangerous place, the main culprit being a pressure cooker that sputtered and splashed on the stove. If I had to be in the kitchen while she was cooking, I was always ready to duck if that thing exploded. It actually happened once, and my uncle Bill was scalded all the way down the left side of his body. No one but me seemed to be worried about a second occurrence.

Mammaw was a creative cook, concocting meals of squirrel, brains (any animal), pig's ears (which were actually the pig's scrotum), and greens pulled right out of her yard. She pickled anything standing still and jellied anything on a vine. Her egg noodles were thick, creamy, and delicious. I enjoyed them as best I could, considering I didn't know what was in them.

She stored all kinds of vegetables and relishes she'd canned herself in a dirt root cellar that Papaw built for her below the kitchen. The only way into the root cellar was a wooden door stuck right in the floor of the pantry. Sitting at Mammaw's kitchen table, I'd sometimes hear a jar explode down there. After the *CRACK*-and-*SPLAT* sound, Mammaw would look toward the pantry and say, "Fermented," and continue chopping carrots. When she finally pulled open the door in the floor, the stench would be unbearable. I assumed "fermented" meant "explodes and stinks like hell."

But this Sunday, as Sarah Keeler was being lowered into the ground, I walked into Mammaw's backyard. I was trying to figure out the best place to disappear to, when I saw my dad staring out the window at me. I felt that familiar jerk in my stomach. He was mad at me for something, and I had no idea what it was. I turned and walked in the other direction, feeling his eyes on me the whole way.

The world wasn't safe today. The truth was, this world was never safe.

I walked around the back of the garage where Dash, Mammaw's dalmatian, sat chained to his house. Dash had one blue eye and one brown eye and wasn't overly friendly—due to the chain. He sat there staring at me with those crazy eyes. Feeling crazy myself, I decided to take a load off.

I pretended to pet Dash, who never wanted to be petted, in case someone saw me sitting out there alone, though no one would. He smelled like shit. The nub of his tail was dabbed purple with some kind of cure-all that Mammaw had used on the farm to castrate pigs.

Mammaw invented her own medicines. She created a salve for drawing out splinters that was made up of three different poisons. It would have killed you if you ate it, but slap a dab on a splinter, and your worries were over. JoAnn joked that if you used too much, it might actually pull up an organ.

I sat down next to Dash and looked up at the sun. Sarah was

probably under dirt by now. I thought of her eyes, nose, and hands in the airless pitch-black grave. I looked at Dash and the mud-splattered doghouse and wasn't sure which was worse—a shitty life or a shitty death.

Plucking up blades of grass, I wondered if I'd be able to see Sarah's grave when my school bus rolled by the cemetery tomorrow. Maybe . . . unless she was buried in the back somewhere. I started to feel better, thinking I might be able to sneak a moment with Sarah on school days. Maybe I could even get Granda to take me over there some weekend to see her grave up close.

I was used to seeing graves because there was a cemetery right behind our house. It wasn't as big as Maple Creek, but it was big enough. A stone cement bench sat up there, perfect for playing rummy or jacks on, and an enormous beige hornets' nest dangled from one of the elm trees. The spookiest feature was a sunken grave that dipped six inches lower than the ground. I imagined a bony finger poking up through the soil and slowly but steadily digging itself out. I hated that grave, but I never went up there without looking at it.

Dad started yelling for me to get my ass into the house. They were saying the prayer and filling plates. I jumped up and ran for it. If Dad had to call you twice, you got spanked.

Inside, I grabbed a plastic orange-and-white-flecked plate, a fork, knife, and spoon, and a white paper napkin, and bowed my head for the prayer Papaw was about to recite. My nose started itching, and when I went to scratch it, Dad slapped the back of my head, causing my plate and silverware to clatter to the floor. "Clumsy ass," he hissed. Everyone looked over for a second and then bowed their heads again. One of us kids being slapped was no reason to stare. My uncle Larry and aunt Betty smiled at me.

Larry, the youngest of the Peterson boys, was always sweet to his small son, Steve, holding his hand, sitting next to him while he ate.

Papaw continued the prayer, but the cousins got tired of waiting and started lining up for food. "Respect the goddamn Lord," Papaw bellowed. Everyone stopped in their tracks until he finished with a soft "Amen."

If there is a Lord, I thought, my chin starting to quiver, *he sure created a bunch of losers when he pooped out this clan.*

After the food, Dad decided he wanted a picture of his four kids. We lined up according to height just as he ordered us to, facing directly into the sun. The scowling cousins were watching.

It was four o'clock and the sun was directly over my dad's head and right in my eyes. I tried to smile in his direction as my dad clicked off four pictures on his new Polaroid camera, but the sun was too bright. Each time Dad clicked the shutter, I accidentally covered my eyes with my hands at the last minute. For the sixty seconds it took for each of those Polaroids to develop, I had plenty of time to imagine what punishment was in store for me for ruining Dad's "perfect family" pictures.

"You're a goddamn idiot," he yelled at me. "Can't you stand still for one minute? If you blur one more picture, I'm going to blister your ass."

My face was bright red. He'd spanked me many times, not caring where we were or who was looking, and usually he jerked my pants down right there in front of everyone to do it.

I tried to explain that it was because my eyes were light blue that I couldn't look directly at the sun, but he interjected, "I'm not wasting any more film on you. Get the hell outta here." He dragged me out of the line by the front of my shirt.

What was so confusing was that everyone looked at me as if I had caused the whole mess. I had somehow ruined everything.

The minute Dad turned his back, I ran for the station wagon, where I lay down on the backseat with tears and spit rolling off the gray vinyl. I cried so long, I forgot why I was crying and fell asleep.

When I woke up, it was dark. The family get-together was still going strong, so I climbed out of the car and walked home. The lights were on; Jamie was already there. I opened the screen door and headed to my room. I was hungry again, but it wasn't worth the effort to scare something up.

I lay on my bed, searching under my covers for my Casper the Ghost doll. Pulling him up by his arm, I could feel a hole torn in his fur and some fluff poking out. Granda would have to sew it for me. I pounded down his stomach, making a dip to lay my head in.

Hearing the station wagon pull up, I wondered if Mom would look in on me. She didn't. Becky came in, tossed a sweater onto her bed, and threw me a disgusted look. I had ruined their day again, by making a scene, by causing Dad to get mad, by so many things I didn't understand. I was ashamed and angry.

When I heard Dad open the tailgate of the station wagon, I got up and looked out the window. He pulled his Bell + Howell Super Eight movie projector and his fold-up home-movie screen out of the back. Dad must have shown movies at Mammaw's. I wondered what I'd missed.

I lay back down.

I closed my eyes, but just as I was drifting off, images from Dad's collection flickered through my head: a tornado demolishing Willard Bank's outhouse; a train explosion in Dunreath; my uncle Ernie in black rubber fire boots up to his hips wading through a flood near Pattonville, waving at the camera.

I sat straight up.

Maybe Dad had filmed Sarah Keeler's accident. Hers was *huge* compared to a cow being hit by a Plymouth.

Dad could hear an ambulance, police siren, or fire truck from a dozen blocks away, and when he heard one, he followed it. Lucky for him, he didn't have to strain his ears because the police *and* fire

department were within one block of his store. He never missed anything.

I bet he was there, and if he was there, I bet he filmed it. My
heart was racing as I wondered how I could find out.

I heard the screen door slam shut. I jerked my pink quilt up over
my shoulders and tried to quiet my breathing. If he was still mad at
me, I didn't want him knowing I was awake.

The next morning I walked into our yellow-and-white kitchen in
a plaid skirt and bare feet. Mom was in a good mood. "It's about
time you got in here," she said, dumping a spoonful of white sugar
across the top of my oatmeal. She was pretending I hadn't spent
yesterday sobbing in the back of the car. She was good at pretending.

I walked into the bathroom, tossed my pee-soaked sheets and
pajamas into the bathtub, and headed back to the kitchen.

Dad was reading the *Elk Grove Courier* and slurping Maxwell
House instant coffee he'd made by adding warm tap water to the
coffee crystals in his mug and whipping it up with a metal spoon.
I'd seen him do it a hundred times, his thick fingers choking the
mug.

I sat down at the table and stared at Dad, who continued reading the paper. I wondered where he stashed his home movies. Dad
titled and dated each one by writing on the rim of the plastic reel
with a Magic Marker. If he'd filmed Sarah Keeler, the reel probably
had her name on it or at least the date.

Dad dropped one corner of the paper and snapped, "What are
you gawking at?"

I looked down at my oatmeal. I heard Dad flip the paper back
up in front of his mean face. He hated me.

I thought about Dad standing by the side of the road filming her
crumpled bike, her body lying on the asphalt. I imagined that he'd

filmed her shoes, blown clear off her feet from the impact, lying in two different places.

I looked at Dad cutting through sausage patties with a butter knife. I was surprised he hadn't run over any kids himself, considering how fast we had to scramble out of his way when he sped through the alley behind our house, the wheels of his blue pickup spewing gravel in all directions.

If he ever did, the police would arrive with sirens blaring and I'd watch as they hauled Dad away in handcuffs, hauled him away forever to Cincinnati or Cleveland or even farther. Someplace he could never come home from, a place where he could never yank my pants down again with everyone staring. Someplace he deserved.

"Eat it, don't play with it," Mom said, jerking my head back slightly as she ran a brush through the back of my hair. I looked up to see Dad staring straight at me.

He probably knew what I was thinking.

CHAPTER THREE

I hadn't always wanted Dad to die or go to jail. There was a time when I felt sorry for him when bad things happened.

I was five. We were living in the little house down on Greenleaf Street.

It was a cool day in November, and Mrs. Beckner was driving Suzanne and me home from kindergarten. We couldn't ride the bus because kindergarten was only a half day.

As we were driving down County Line Road, I saw swirling black smoke mushrooming up on the flat horizon. "That's probably my dad's store," I said, knowing perfectly well it wasn't. My dad's hardware store was at least eight miles from where we were.

"Whatever it is, it's big," said Mrs. Beckner.

"Huge," I said, my heart pounding with excitement. Something enormous was burning down.

When we pulled up in front of my house, Mom was standing on the front porch with her brown wicker purse slung over her arm, and Granda was leaning against her white Pontiac. Something was up.

As Mrs. Beckner put her car in park, I popped the door handle and jumped onto the grass near the sidewalk.

"Thanks, Mrs. Beckner," I said.

"See you tomorrow," she said, waving.

I ran over to Granda's car.

"Hey, cutie," Granda said, brushing my bangs across my forehead.

"What's going on?" I asked.

"You're coming home with Granda," she said.

I turned to Mom, who was walking toward our station wagon. "Where're you going?"

"Your dad's store's on fire. I've gotta see if I can help." She walked back, kissed my forehead, and headed for the car.

"Dad's store—" I was ready to ask a million questions, when Mom interrupted.

"Stay with Granda," she said over her shoulder. "And don't play with the hose. You already have a stuffy nose." She got in and pulled away.

Who said anything about the hose? I was always being warned about things I wasn't going to do, until I was told not to. But today nothing could take my attention from the fire.

I shot Granda a devious look. "I saw the smoke," I told her. "You can see it driving down County Line Road."

"Oh, it's a big fire. I think it's an entire block," Granda said, her right hand patting her chest.

"I guess we'd better not go over there," I said, hoping she'd disagree.

Granda smiled. "You bet we're not going over there. Your mother told me to keep you at my place. Besides, we have to be here when the other kids get home."

"When's that?" I asked.

"Three o'clock," she said.

"How long's that?"

"Three hours," she said.

"Don't you want to see the smoke?" I asked. "Just a little drive down the county line and back?"

"It's lunchtime for you. Aren't you ready for a sandwich? I have some fresh turkey over there and some deviled eggs."

"I'm tellin' you there's a black cloud swirling clear up in the sky.

You won't believe it." She smiled at me. "It's *huge*," I reiterated.

"You're going to get me in trouble," she said.

"We won't be in town. Mom won't care if we take a little ride," I said.

"Do you have to pee?" she asked.

"No."

"Go pee." She pointed toward the door. "And wash your hands," she yelled after me.

I ran into the house. Our collie, Buddy, was there to greet me. I leaned down. "There's a big fire, girl. Granda and I have to take off." Buddy followed me to the bathroom.

Granda and I stopped by her trailer so she could make us a couple of sandwiches. Granda would never take a chance on my being hungry. She made turkey sandwiches on white bread with butter and wrapped them in aluminum foil. Soon we were heading up the county line.

I sat in the front seat with my bare feet resting on the console and craned my neck to the west. When we got around the *S* curve, I saw the swirling smoke cloud. Earlier the cloud had been fascinating; now it was so gigantic, it was freakish.

"Oh my word," Granda said, impressed.

"Can we *please* see the fire up close, Granda?" I pleaded. "I've never seen a fire like that."

I wanted to see the fire, but mostly I wanted to see Dad fighting the fire and Mom right beside him. I wanted to see firemen hooking up their hoses. I imagined a small explosion and me running into the flames barefoot and dragging first Mom and then Dad to safety.

"I'm not taking you over there. Now stop asking," Granda said.

"Can we at least drive toward town so we can get a closer look at the smoke?" I asked.

"We'll drive a little closer," she said, "but don't get any ideas."

The next thing I knew, we could see Elk Grove's enormous limestone courthouse in the distance, which meant we were almost to town. Granda told me to duck down a little so if by chance Mom or Dad saw us, they might not think I was with her. This made no sense because of course I was with her, but I did it anyway. Hiding only heightened the excitement of being undercover.

When we drove into Elk Grove, we saw flashing red lights and thick white hoses stretched across Orchard Street and Highway 64. Granda had been right, the entire block was on fire, and heavy black smoke was rolling into the sky, causing my eyes to burn. I pulled my turtleneck up over my nose and mouth like Mort from the *Bazooka Joe* comics to keep the fumes out. There were ambulances standing by.

We saw Dad running out the front door of his store tossing wheelbarrows, saws, drills, and even a lawn mower into the street. Other men were trying to help him salvage whatever inventory he could before the roof caved in. It took only about ten minutes from the time Granda and I arrived. When that roof dropped into the building, Dad ran backward looking up with his hands in the air as if he could stop it from happening. His glasses were smudged and his face was smeared with black soot.

"We should do something," I said.

Granda's eyebrows flew up. "We aren't here, remember?"

"I know," I said defensively. Seeing Dad's head and face all wet from the spray of fire hoses and watching him cough up black mucus and spit onto the pavement made me want to help.

"He's not getting sympathy from me." Granda stared right at him, her jaw set just so. She had seen Dad at his meanest, especially the night he beat three-year-old Jamie so bad that Mom snatched up Jamie and JoAnn, who was only a year old, and drove them to Granda's house for the night. In the morning Dad arrived, sorry and humbled, to take them back home.

"That son of a bitch deserves whatever he gets," Granda said. "I just feel bad for your mother and you kids."

"That son of a bitch isn't gettin' sympathy from me, either," I agreed. Granda burst out laughing.

"Is there anything you won't repeat, Monica? You can't be using curse words. It'll make Jesus mad." She shook her head.

I wondered if Jesus was at the fire.

Dad walked over to the back of his pickup, opened the tailgate, and sat down. He poured water from a silver thermos over his head and neck.

All of a sudden we heard windows popping and cracking and realized they were from cars parked clear across the street from the blaze.

By the looks of things, Jesus was not at the fire—and neither was Mom. She'd probably opted for a quiet lunch at Bullard's Drive-In instead. Less stressful.

That night Dad was on the evening news. Several reporters from television stations in Cincinnati drove down and interviewed Dad in front of his burnt store. Dad, Mom, JoAnn, Becky, Jamie, Mammaw, Pappaw, and I sat in the living room and watched in disbelief. No one from Galesburg had ever been on TV. Dad wore an Elk Grove Fire Department helmet and a black-and-white reflective firefighter jacket, which made him look important. Mustering all of his skill from narrating our home movies, he reenacted the fire:

"We lost at least half the block. Four businesses, including mine, were lost, maybe more," Dad said into the silver microphone.

"Were there any injuries or loss of life?" the female reporter asked.

"None whatsoever. There were fire departments here from all over the area, and we couldn't be more pleased with the way this was handled. It's tough to think of rebuilding the hardware store from scratch, but at least no one was hurt."

"Thank you for talking with us." The reporter turned toward the camera and said, "Glen Peterson owned Peterson's Hardware. We're in Elk Grove, some fifty miles east of Cincinnati, where a massive fire has destroyed a city block." We all clapped for Dad. He was instantly a local hero.

I was definitely going to get attention at kindergarten the next day.

I ran out to the screened-in porch to find Buddy. Dad's filthy clothes were heaped on the floor, smelling of stale smoke. His faded brown boots sat by the door with the soles melted from running in and out of the hot building. I ran one palm over the drippy, bubbled surface of those boots and the other over Buddy's fuzzy head.

That night Dad seemed happy to be with us, and I was glad he hadn't burned up with all those wrenches and caulking guns.

A month later, when I wasn't even thinking about Dad's store anymore, I dreamt our house was burning. I ran into Greenleaf Street in my pajamas and saw JoAnn, Jamie, and Mom, but not Becky. Dad was across the street at the volunteer fire department, where he switched on the huge siren that summoned the volunteers, and then tried to get the big fire doors open so he could get a truck out. Everyone stood watching the blaze and I kept asking, "Where's Becky?" No one said anything until we heard screams.

In my dream her escalating, high-pitched shrieks confirmed that Becky's blue-and-white flowered nightgown had been ignited, followed by all that blond hair and freckled skin and white bones. Dad struggled to run back into the house, but the fire forced him back. He was wailing and trying to climb up the side of the house. It took ten minutes for Becky to stop screaming.

I woke up terrified and sweaty. I tiptoed over to Becky's bed, where she was sleeping with her hand flung back against the pillow. Her Mrs. Beasley doll was under the covers with the top of her scrubby blond head sticking out. I wanted to snuggle in beside them, but I knew I'd wet her bed.

Panicked and convinced we'd all burn to death someday, I crawled over shoes and boots through the dark closet that connected our room to Mom and Dad's. As I got closer, I could hear Dad snoring.

Once in their room, I walked softly over to the bed. Mom was sleeping on her side facing the doorway.

I looked down at Dad. His eyes opened, and I jumped. "What's going on?" he whispered.

"Becky died in a fire," I explained quickly.

"Where?"

"A dream," I said. He sat up, stuck his hands in my armpits, and deposited me in between the two of them.

"Go to sleep," he said, rolling back over. I lay there in shock. What had I been thinking, coming into Dad's room? And now that I was squished in the middle, how would I get out?

I waited until Dad's snoring settled into a reliable snort-and-blow pattern and then carefully scrambled over the top of him, crawling back through the closet on my hands and knees. Even if he was skilled at helping in disasters, it wasn't worth the risk of being too close to his hands.

Once in my bed, I hugged Snoopy and thought about Jamie and me lighting matches behind the garage. I wouldn't do that again.

Fire came fast, and the Petersons were not fast runners.

At church that Sunday I snuck glances at Becky and prayed for her safety.

I prayed all the time. I prayed for the robin that flew into our sunporch window and knocked himself out; for Hazel, the drunk who swayed down our street every morning, half-dressed, on her way back from the Galesburg Tavern. I prayed for Mr. Davis, who lived on our corner and had no legs. He'd opened a paint shop in his garage and spent all day lying on a little homemade cart, rolling around on his stomach to mix the paint, dragging the heavy cans around behind him.

I prayed for all of us kids whenever Dad's pickup squealed into the driveway.

It was odd to keep doing something that never seemed to help, but just in case Reverend Morse was right, I prayed.

CHAPTER FOUR

The Monday after Sarah Keeler's burial, I stood at the bus stop and hoped that I'd see her freshly packed grave as the bus passed Maple Creek Cemetery.

I knew Maple Creek because every school lesson in Ohio history ended with a field trip to Wendell Willkie's grave. Wendell had been a Democrat, like Mom, but became a Republican, like Dad, and ran for president against Franklin D. Roosevelt. Wendell had lived in Akron after fighting in World War I. Sarah Keeler shared a cemetery with a famous man.

I wasn't dead. I wasn't famous. I wasn't anything. So I told lies.

I looked at JoAnn, who was sitting on top of her backpack. Jamie was throwing rocks across the highway, trying to hit the Griswold's mailbox, and Becky was talking to our neighbor Sally Whitmore. I turned to Kyle, Sally's brother, who was kneeling on the ground, stuffing a sweatshirt into his backpack.

"Buddy has cancer," I told him. "Our dog's dying." Buddy was in perfect health.

I expected a huge show of sympathy from Kyle, but he looked at me nonchalantly, sniffing in clear snot that was dripping just below his nostrils. Clearly, I would have to elaborate.

"Mom doesn't think she'll live till Friday." Kyle pointed across the street, where Buddy was swiftly chasing a brown squirrel across Dottie Griswold's yard. I was irritated.

I decided Kyle was just too green to understand the seriousness of cancer or to be aware that children could be killed for no reason at all. People in Galesburg didn't know what mattered and what didn't. Real life, exciting life, happened in Elk Grove, not out here in Hick Town, where there was only one blinker light and no courthouse.

Bus number sixty pulled up and we climbed up the tall steps, single file. Our driver, Walter Coons, welcomed us wearing faded blue overalls with a crisp red hanky tucked into his pocket. Most bus drivers in our county were farmers who were awake at dawn anyway, feeding hogs and cleaning out horse stalls. They earned extra money driving us around, which probably wasn't that different from driving livestock.

I climbed into the third seat from the front with my *H. R. Pufnstuf* spiral notebook and sat on the side of the bus that would face Maple Creek Cemetery.

Looking over my shoulder, I saw JoAnn take two fingers and swoosh a "77" in the condensation that had formed on the windows, the year she would graduate and move away from Crap Town. Mine was "81"—a million years from now.

The next stop was Sam Lunsford's house. I always made a point of watching him climb down the three wooden steps of his front porch and slump toward the bus. Sam was only ten, but he'd already killed a man.

He owned a rifle, just as all of us owned rifles, only mine sat leaning up against the wall behind the door in Mom and Dad's bedroom. I didn't care about guns. I cared about recreating *The Sound of Music* in our backyard.

When Sam killed that man, he'd been shooting tin cans off the wooden fence behind the old grain elevator. He'd barely noticed when the three o'clock freight train came rolling down the tracks. The train was about thirty feet away when one of Sam's bullets missed the can, grazed a telephone pole, and ricocheted into the cab of the moving train, killing the engineer instantly. The engineer's head flopped onto the windowsill as the train continued on down the track. It took several farmers and the entire Mason County police force (eight men and six volunteers) to jump the train and finally get it stopped.

The Whitmores and all of us were playing touch football in the grass next to the cemetery when we saw local farmers Ray Henderson, Hoover Griffin, and Jim Tracy running through the fields with rifles in their hands.

We heard Ray yell, "You kids get inside now. Go on home and stay in the house. Someone's gone and shot the train conductor." My heart dropped and all of us took off running. We looked out our back window at the policemen searching the fields for the shooter.

The next thing I heard, they'd taken Sam Lunsford, who was sweet-tempered and shy, into custody. They kept him a couple of hours for questioning and sent him home with his mom and dad.

After that, Sam didn't talk at all. He climbed onto the bus, collapsed into the front seat, and slept the whole way to school. I felt sorry for him, but he knew what it was like to kill a man, so I watched him.

After the bus left Sam's house, the ride was uninteresting. I just wanted to get to Elk Grove so I could spot Sarah's grave, but we still had ten stops to make, including Wanda Henderson's house, and Wanda always made us late.

When the bus pulled up to her mailbox, she would just be starting her walk down the lengthy lane that led from her farmhouse to Highway 64, where the bus (and all of us) sat waiting. Soon Mr. Coons would toot the horn and Wanda would start running.

As her beefy red face came closer, I knew what was going to happen—we all did. She'd heave herself onto the bus with this queasy look on her face, take in a quick gulp of air, and throw up bacon and eggs onto the gray-and-white-speckled floor.

Mr. Coons would turn around and throw kitty litter (which he'd learned to carry with him) down the aisle, and we'd be on our way.

I watched her do this every single morning and was mad at her for not figuring out how to get down the lane *before* the bus pulled up, so she wouldn't have to run. How hard could it be? We would *never* get to Maple Creek Cemetery at this rate.

The next stop was Liddy Ingle's saggy house. This was where, almost every day, Dad's truck would appear behind the bus. Without fail, he'd speed up, and despite the stop sign sticking out from the left side of the bus and the alternating flashing red lights, he'd pass us on the two-lane road. And here he came again.

Dad was gunning for someone, maybe even Liddy, who couldn't afford socks and wore the same skirt almost every day. I was convinced he was going to kill someone, either a kid crossing the road to get on the bus or a person in the car waiting for the bus to move on. He was homicidal—especially in his truck.

The way I saw it, Dad was just mad. He drove mad, he ate mad, and if anything turned him happy, he ruined it immediately.

When we finally got to Elk Grove, Mr. Coons decided to step on the gas for the first time all morning and we rattled past Maple Creek as if we were suddenly competing in the Indianapolis 500. I couldn't tell one fresh grave from another. Was it possible to have worse luck than mine? Now I'd have to wait until the afternoon to see Sarah.

As we rounded the corner at Orchard Street to head up to school, I saw Dad climbing out of his pickup beside his store. He'd only saved a few minutes by passing us.

What a shitty morning, and it was only Monday.

The following Saturday, Dad hollered for us to get into the station wagon. We were going someplace as "a family."

I didn't want to go anywhere as a family, but Mom told us to hurry and get dressed.

Becky, JoAnn, and I wore matching pant sets that Mom had laid out on our beds that morning: stretchy navy slacks and white button-down cardigan sweaters with white sneakers.

JoAnn was furious. She didn't want to be associated with Becky or me; we were the babies and she couldn't even believe she had to wear the same outfit as us. JoAnn preferred faded brown corduroys, her jean jacket with its many pockets for smuggled cigarettes, and a tan leather belt with acorns stamped all the way around the waist.

"Why does Jamie get to wear whatever he wants?" she complained bitterly.

"He's a boy," Mom snapped, as if that made any sense.

Mom supervised everything we wore, day and night. She'd just started making the three of us wear nightgowns with no panties underneath so we could "air ourselves out" while we slept. JoAnn had protested, crying and holding up pajama pants, but Mom wouldn't let her wear them. I'd told JoAnn to sneak them on during the night, but she wouldn't have gone against Mom.

JoAnn sat in the car wearing that pant set, head turned toward the window, biting the inside of her cheek. Becky and I were in the way back, singing:

Going down the highway,
Going sixty-four,
Jamie cut a stinker,
and blew us out the door.

We laughed so hard, tears were streaming down our faces. Jamie was plucking dried mud out of the soles of his sneakers with the tip of his hunting knife, trying to ignore us.

Finally (and we knew it was coming) Dad yelled, "Knock it off or I'm taking off my belt!"

We quit singing but couldn't quit laughing. We ducked down in the way back and tried to stifle the giggling, but guttural noises kept spurting out of us.

As we pulled into the Rotary Club's gravel parking lot, we saw that a barbecue was in full swing. There were huge charcoal grills covered with unshucked corn on the cob, steaks, and heavy metal pots filled with barbecued baked beans. This might be fun.

Dad wheeled into a dirt parking space, and we all piled out before the dust settled.

I looked around for someone I knew.

JoAnn disappeared into the crowd with our cousin Ben, who looked exactly like her. With their reddish brown hair and freckles, people often mistook them for twin brothers, not realizing JoAnn was a girl. When I saw them later, they were sharing a cigarette behind the wooden grandstand, JoAnn wearing Ben's blue jean jacket pulled clear down over her stretchy slacks.

Becky ran off with Donna Frazee, who looked exactly like Becky. The two of them looked like every girl in Mason County: blond ponytails, perfect complexions, and a few freckles sprinkled across their noses.

I was a brunette with my hair cut hopelessly short. The only person I resembled was lying over in Maple Creek Cemetery.

Donna and Becky didn't invite me to tag along, so I pretended not to care. Becky was only eighteen months older than I was, but we were two years apart in school. When we were alone, she was happy to build blanket-forts or play Mousetrap, but when her friends were around, I was invisible.

Jamie headed down to the dirt track to look at the tractors that were competing in the tractor pull. I was sure Papaw was down there, and since he was capable of turning on you at a moment's notice, I stayed where I was, climbing up to sit on the hood of the car.

Dad wouldn't notice me on the station wagon because he was

doing a solo stampede toward the grills, where most of the men were hanging out.

Dad cracked some hilarious joke as he arrived and everyone started laughing. "Glen, you always liven things up." I watched Dad grab a red-and-white-checked paper apron, tie it in the back, and pick up a spatula. Flipping steaks was the only way to be the center of attention at a barbecue, and in Elk Grove, Dad was a popular guy.

He was kind to everyone but us, happy to help his neighbors change a tire or to lift a heavy bag of groceries for a senior citizen at Kroger Supermarket. At home he didn't bother to step around me if I was playing Barbies on the floor, choosing instead to kick them across the room. I watched his friends enjoying his company and wondered why Dad hated us so much.

Dad was president of the Rotary Club and chairman of the sesquicentennial the previous spring, reigning over all the special events and local attractions that helped celebrate Elk Grove's 150th anniversary. In May he rode a flying horse attached to a small plat-form in a giant parade with twenty marching bands from all over the state, and floats like the one from the *Elk Grove Courier* "Depicting 132 Years of News." Diana Reynolds's majorettes twirled and threw their batons in unison, and even Dwight Lovejoy's four-horse hitch-and-beer wagon rolled by. Mr. Kenworthy, the mayor, rode in an old-fashioned convertible, covered in red-white-and-blue bunting.

Coming down Main Street, Dad and the spectacular mechanical horse led the parade. Dad was a superstar in his red-and-white-striped barbershop quartet jacket, waving his straw hat to the crowd, the horse bucking up and down. The crowd cheered and waved back.

I stood on the curb and saw Dad turn in my direction. My hand automatically flew up to wave, but I quickly realized he wasn't wav-ing to me.

In Elk Grove, Dad was a great guy.

At the Rotary Club barbecue, Mom drifted over to where Martha

Whitmore (Kyle's mom) was holding court. I watched her pad over in her brown leather loafers, burnt-orange-and-brown-plaid pants, and a beige sweater. Her hair, which had just been frosted, was pulled back off her face and swooped up into a French twist on the back of her head. She always looked clean and sophisticated, even at a dusty barbecue.

I looked back at Dad, who was now wearing a paper chef's hat and gesturing with the spatula. I couldn't watch him another minute. I slid off the hood of the car, slammed into a man who was walking by, and ended up on my butt in the dirt.

"Oh my gosh," I said, jumping up and wiping dust off my pants. "I'm sorry."

"Don't worry about it." He smiled. "Are you a Peterson?"

I had to admit I was.

"I saw you pull up with your mom and dad," he said. "Which one are you?"

"Monica," I said, checking my elbows for bloody scrapes.

"I'm Dave Kilner, a friend of your dad's," he said, and held out his hand.

I forgot the scrapes and looked up. I was staring at "Kilner" from Kilner and Sons Mortuary. I shook Dave's hand and wondered if it had touched Sarah Keeler.

He was saying something about the barbecue, but I was staring at his face.

I'd imagined "Kilner" to be short, pale, and creepy with greasy dark hair and maybe a black cape, but this man was downright gorgeous. He was blond, with a Barbie-and-Ken-type smile, and he wore a bright blue sweater with khaki shorts.

I was instantly in love with Dave Kilner and his tan legs.

He pointed toward a picnic table. "Those girls over there are mine. Would you like to meet them?"

"Okay," I said, wondering where the "sons" from "Kilner and Sons" were.

I followed him over to the three girls. I was surprised that an undertaker would have a normal, non-zombie family, and disappointed that my dad sold hand tools instead of funerals.

"This is Julie, Liz, and Amanda," Dave said.

"Hi," I offered.

"This is Monica. Her dad's a friend of mine." I wished he'd quit saying that. Dave turned to me. "Julie's on a softball team in town." Julie smiled with her mouth closed. She had wavy black hair down to her shoulders, a small turned-up nose, and beautiful green eyes surrounded by thick black lashes.

I wasn't allowed to play softball in Elk Grove because it was too far for Mom to drive me to practices and games.

Julie and I stared at each other.

"Well, I'm going to leave you kids to your fun," Dave said, patting my shoulder and walking away.

I turned to Julie. She looked at me. I looked at Liz and Amanda, who were a lot younger than we were. Liz looked just like a boy. I couldn't even imagine that she was, in fact, a girl. Julie was picking a scab on her knee.

"So, your dad owns the mortuary?" I asked. Julie looked up, surprised. "I was there once," I added for clarity.

"What does your dad own?" Julie asked.

"Buzz saws," I answered. "But I own a collie."

"I have a beagle," Julie said. "His name is Sparky."

"My dog is Buddy, but she has cancer."

"Sparky has allergies," she countered. Damn, that sounded worse than cancer.

"Terrible," I said.

Julie smiled with her teeth showing. "Let's eat," she said, and we ran toward the food line. Liz and Amanda stayed at the picnic table.

Julie and I spent the day climbing tall Black Walnut trees that surrounded the Rotary Club. The walnuts were lime green and filled with brown juice that squished out, staining my hands and sweater. Julie and I picked them off branches and hurled them at predetermined targets: a trash can, a gray rock, a rotting tree stump. Each time we hurled one, barely missing a parked car or a squirrel, we howled with laughter. Mom was going to kill me for acting like a "heathen" in public, but I didn't care. Julie climbed higher than I did, even though I was a good climber. I gathered the courage to follow her, and way above the barbecue, we spied on people we knew.

"Your dad is hilarious," she said, indicating the laughter coming from the barbecue pit.

"Yeah, he's funny," I said.

"You're lucky," she said. "My dad's *so* boring."

"He seems okay," I countered.

"He's not like your dad," she said. I looked at Dad. He did look okay. In fact, he looked almost handsome, like someone I'd want to know but didn't.

"That's my sister Becky," I said, pointing to the swings. "Her hair's so long, she can sit on it. If she doesn't hold it up, it gets in the toilet." Julie's eyebrows flew up, impressed.

The tractors were huffing and puffing over at the tractor pull, and from up in the walnut tree, we could see black smoke coiling up in the air and my Papaw sitting in the black metal seat of his red Farmall tractor. He was turned around backward, watching the pile of gray cinder blocks that had been loaded onto the pallet he was pulling. The front two wheels of his tractor weren't even touching the ground as he kept gunning the engine.

"I think my papaw's going to do a backward roll on his tractor," I said, pointing toward the action.

Each time a tractor made it past the finish line, the crowd cheered and clapped as another weight was added. The last tractor still moving at the end would be the winner.

Papaw had four trophies with tiny gold tractors on top sitting above his television already, and it looked like he was headed for his fifth.

Jamie and my cousin Paul were perched on a white wooden fence, watching the competition.

"That's my brother, Jamie, over there," I said, pointing.

"He's cute," Julie said. I was startled by this, so I didn't say anything. Finally, Julie asked, "Where do you live?"

"Galesburg," I said.

"You live really far from me," she said. "I live in Elk Grove."

I felt my face flush. I wanted to live in Elk Grove too—especially in the funeral home.

"Let's go on a hayride," I suggested, changing the subject.

We climbed down and ran toward the hay wagon, sawdust blowing around our bony ankles. It was a perfect day.

After the trophies were awarded (Papaw got second place) and the homemade ice cream was served and eaten, it was time to get into the station wagon and head home.

Dave Kilner patted my back. "You'll have to come to the house one of these days," he said. I was giddy with excitement, picturing myself playing Twister in the mortuary.

"I would love to," I told him.

"Well, see ya," Julie said, shrugging her shoulders.

"See ya," I said as I climbed into our station wagon next to Becky. There was no way I was getting a window seat.

As we drove off, Dad gave a "great guy" wave to his friends. We'd barely pulled onto Highway 64 when he growled, "Quit kicking my goddamn seat." I wasn't kicking his seat, but I smiled anyway. I'd just met the undertaker-father of my dreams, and his family.

Dad wasn't going to ruin my day.

CHAPTER FIVE

The night before I started fourth grade, I couldn't sleep because I was worried about my new classroom. Fourth grade was in a bigger building with a pink steel tube snaking out of the second floor and slithering to an end on the asphalt playground. If there was a blaze, I worried that teachers would toss us headfirst into that dark, winding fire escape and we'd zip to the bottom, landing in a huge pile of skinned knees and chipped teeth on the blacktop.

In fourth grade I'd have to change classrooms for the first time in my life. I was supposed to stay in Mrs. Eaton's room all day until two p.m., and then I had to walk next door to Mr. Nash's class for science. After that, it was back to Mrs. Eaton for homeroom. I would never remember it all.

I was so worked up during breakfast, Jamie offered to walk me up there.

"I won't hold your hand, though," he said.

"Don't hold mine either," I snapped over my shoulder as I got up to get dressed.

That morning I didn't even watch Sam Lunsford get on the bus. I leaned my forehead against the window and worried.

After Wanda had thrown up and Dad had passed us at Liddy's house, Jamie escorted me to fourth grade. As we clomped up the stairs, Jamie said, "I don't know why you're gettin' all worked up. I'm the one who has to take algebra."

"Because I'm the one who has to be in a new place," I said.

"I'm the one who has to take shop with Mr. Smythe, the dictator," Jamie continued.

"I'm the one who barely survived Mrs. Baker's class last year," I said, "since she *hated* me."

"She liked you, but you wouldn't stop talking," he said. I rolled my eyes.

We rounded the corner on the top floor and I saw her—my salvation—my chance at a new family, a family that lived in a mortuary, where the dead side of me would be welcomed. Julie Kilner was standing right beside the doorway to room 214, Mrs. Eaton's room.

She was wearing a bright red cotton jumper with a blue-and-white-striped turtleneck and wire-rimmed glasses shaped like two octagons. I ran to Julie.

"Are you going to be in my class?" I asked.

"I guess so," she said.

"I'm Monica. Remember me?" She looked vague. "We rode in the hay wagon."

Julie nodded.

Waving off Jamie, I turned to her. "This'll be a piece of cake. Let's go in."

Jamie walked back downstairs and I put my arm around Julie's waist, as if she were one of the senior citizens down at Marigold Manor nursing home, and guided her into the classroom.

"Well, hello, girls," a sweet voice called out. I turned and saw something I had only seen about three times in my entire life: a black woman. Mrs. Eaton, my new fourth-grade teacher, was *black*. Her hair was the same length all over and curled under just below her ears. She wore her navy sweater around her shoulders like an elegant cape that was clasped just below her neck with a stylish red stickpin. She was beautiful.

"I'm Monica and this is Julie Kilner," I said. "She's new."

"Are you from Bloomfield School?" Mrs. Eaton asked.

"There's not school there anymore," Julie said.

Mason County was closing many of the smaller county schools and consolidating them into one. It turned out there were three new kids from Bloomfield School in my class.

Mrs. Eaton showed us to our seats. Julie sat in the third row because her last name started with a *K*, but I was back and toward the middle because of the *P* in Peterson.

Two weeks later Mrs. Jenkins, the music teacher, told our class we'd be dancing to "Meet Me in St. Louis" for the fall music festival. There weren't enough boys to partner all the girls, so Mrs. Jenkins pointed to me and said, "You're a boy."

I was furious as I stood there in my pleated skirt and white knee socks. *Do I look like a boy?* I wanted to know. It had to be my crappy short haircut that doomed me.

My partner turned out to be Julie Kilner because I was tall and she was short. We spent our time at rehearsal talking and laughing instead of dancing.

Julie was becoming my very best friend.

At the open house that fall Dad actually showed up. But when Mrs. Eaton came over to talk to him, he started stammering instead of speaking. That's when I remembered Dad hated black people. I had forgotten that Mrs. Eaton *was* black.

As we were walking back toward the car, I heard Dad say, "I didn't know the coons were going to be there." He laughed.

"Don't start, Glen," Mom said.

"What did I say?" he asked, grinning. I wasn't even sure.

"Let it go," Mom said.

"What, the nigger in there? I just didn't know I was paying taxes for a nigger to teach my kid, that's all." Mom shook her head and glanced at me. My mouth flopped open in shock, and a wave of fury swept over me.

I never wanted him near Mrs. Eaton again. I worried she knew Dad hated her. I worried she would think I was the same.

One Saturday afternoon Mom took Granda to JC Penney's to buy a new nightgown.

At around five o'clock our local radio station reported a tornado had been spotted on the ground. As soon as Dad heard the news and checked the falling barometer on the dining room wall, he shoved our reluctant hind ends into the station wagon and drove seventy miles an hour toward Flora Meyer's farm.

"That's where they're brewin'," Dad said excitedly to no one in particular.

"Great," I said, making Jamie laugh.

"You're gonna love this," Dad said, flipping on his movie camera as he drove. He glanced at our pale faces in the rearview mirror and smiled. He knew we were petrified, which made him positively giddy.

I couldn't figure out which was more worrisome, seeing a real tornado or Dad losing control of the station wagon, hitting a phone pole, and ejecting us out into Curly Tillison's cornfield.

In the backseat Jamie was sitting by the window, then me, then Becky, and JoAnn by the other window.

The four of us figured it was only a matter of time before we met death by car or by weather. Maybe today it would be both. If there were such a thing as death by humiliation, we would have been dead already.

Jamie looked over at us and mouthed, "Holy shit," but he was smiling.

"We're dead," I mouthed back, making a slashing gesture across my throat. I was only half-kidding.

Becky elbowed me. I pointed to her and rolled my eyes at Jamie. JoAnn faced the window, silent.

As if it weren't harrowing enough, Dad rolled down his window and stuck his head out, preparing to film as we sped down the narrow country road.

"I see one. Look right over there," he crowed. "I knew it. I *knew* it!" He pointed with the hand that was supposed to be guiding the steering wheel. We swerved, but he managed to maneuver the car back onto the road.

I craned my neck to see what he was pointing to, and there in the western sky were four tornados dipping up and down. They were skinny and black, winding against the sunset. I grabbed Becky's and JoAnn's knees. "I see them," I said, holding my breath.

"Four at once!" Dad yelled back to us. "We hit the jackpot!" He whipped the car into a tight U-turn and came to a stop facing the other direction.

"You gotta get out and see this," he said. "You might never have another chance." He bolted out of the car.

Our stomachs were still getting over the U-turn as we opened our doors and grudgingly stepped out. I was starting to get mad now. We were at the mercy of a crazy man.

Dad's face looked completely different: open, hopeful. Here was a chance for us to be a part of his life, to have him include us, yet none of us could even speak. We stood by a barbed wire fence, watching the tornados heading straight for us.

"Oh shit! It flattened something. Did you see the debris?" Dad said, one eye squeezed shut, the other pressed against the viewfinder of the camera.

When he didn't hear a response, he looked over at our stunned, angry faces. "You bunch of cowards," he said. "You don't think this is exciting?" he asked.

No one answered. Dad shook his head and looked back toward

the west. His face didn't look open or hopeful anymore. He swung around. "Get in the car. Hurry. Get in the car. It's changed directions."

All five of us climbed over one another trying to scramble back into the station wagon. When Dad made it into the driver's seat, he turned the key and stepped on the gas without making sure we were all inside. Jamie's door wasn't even closed yet.

On the way back he drove just as fast, the movie camera, which was now turned off, bouncing across the passenger seat.

We skidded into our driveway and the four of us kids bailed out, running toward the basement stairs. Dad stayed in the car. As we made it down into the basement, I heard him hit the gas and squeal away.

We all reacted differently to our volatile home life. Jamie played sports, JoAnn dreamed of "77," Becky pretended everything was fine, and I continued to tell lies.

Wearing my red-white-and-blue poncho with the white fringe around the edges, I sat cross-legged on the playground at school, playing jacks. My mom had permed my hair over the weekend and it bounced in shrunken ringlets around my face while I dropped the ball, swooped up jacks, and talked in a low, secretive voice. The other fourth-grade girls were huddled around listening. Leslie Hathaway, the only fourth grader with red hair, asked questions.

"How do you know she wants to kill you?"

"Because she gives me clues while she's directing the choir." I bounced the ball and grabbed the last two jacks.

"Like what?"

"Like Tuesday when we were practicing in the auditorium for the concert, she pointed at me and mouthed, 'You're next.'"

"No way. Mrs. Jenkins?"

"Wait and see." I shook the jacks in my closed palms and watched them scatter.

"When?"

"In the middle of the winter concert, when no one can hear the shot or know where it's coming from."

"She's going to shoot you?"

"Yes." I rolled my eyes and scooped up more jacks.

"That's crazy. Why would Mrs. Jenkins want to shoot you?"

"I don't know. She's been interested in me for a long time." I bounced the ball.

"Do you know which part of the concert?"

"While we're singing 'Embraceable You.'"

"That's a spooky song."

"Exactly."

The bell rang, signaling the end of recess.

The winter concert came and went without a single shot fired. I was annoyed that no one was surprised. Wasn't anyone taking me seriously?

One Wednesday night in early spring, the phone rang and it was Julie's mom, Joan Kilner. I heard my mom say, "Yes, that would be fine. I'll pick Monica up on Saturday." Julie's mom had invited me to spend the night.

It would be my first overnight and it would be at Julie Kilner's mortuary/house. Would there be beds or coffins? Would there be wilted flowers in their house left over from funerals? Would someone die in the night, causing all of us to wake up and get busy?

I was bouncing off the walls. I would need a sleeping bag, I figured, and some new pajamas. Mom figured I didn't need either.

Friday I climbed onto the bus with Mom's square green suitcase packed with my yellow pajamas, my toothbrush, a pair of panties, socks, jeans, a long-sleeved shirt, a brush, and my macramé belt. Kyle Whitmore was curious.

"Are you running away from home?" he asked in his dry voice.

"No, I'm spending the night at Julie Kilner's," I informed him. I was *so* much older than him now, even though he was a whole year older than I was. "I'm going home with her right after school, so I won't be on the bus tonight." Kyle looked at me blankly. I flipped my nonexistent ponytail and hopped up the stairs of the bus. I couldn't wait to get to Julie's house. This day was going to last forever.

When school finally ended, I walked beside Julie and was surprised when we climbed onto a school bus. The mortuary was within walking distance of school.

As we rolled past St. Mary church, Julie said, "I have two friends that go there."

My head jerked up; maybe she'd known Sarah Keeler. I would remember to ask her later.

I looked out the window. The bus rolled right past Kilner and Sons Mortuary and headed out of town.

"Don't you live in Elk Grove?" I asked in a panic. After all, the mortuary looked just like a house.

"Yeah, but out by the bowling alley." She was brushing her hair. Julie carried a brush, Dr Pepper–flavored ChapStick, and pencils with her name on them in a plastic navy purse. No store ever had things with *my* name on them. Monica was a weird name, a goofy name. I didn't even know where Mom got it.

All I wanted to be was normal—like a "Jill" or a "Laura" or, and this was the best, a "Julie."

When we turned down Julie's road, I noticed she lived in the wealthy part of town. I fiddled with my backpack.

The outside of Julie's house was beautiful: a modern one-story with beige stone on the outside. The entryway was large and trimmed in black, and when we walked in, there was an elegant living room with fancy couches and glass end tables. To the right was a kitchen that opened up into a large family room with a stone fireplace. I realized my family didn't have as much as other families. I started feeling less confident.

Julie said I could put my suitcase in her room, so we headed downstairs to the basement, which was fully remodeled.

There was a large pool table and a sauna, which I had never heard of. It smelled like Granda's cedar chest. Julie explained, "You sit in there with your clothes off and sweat." I hoped we wouldn't be doing that.

Julie took me into her room, which had been built especially for her and was separated from the rest of the basement by a brown paneled wall and a beige louvered door.

When we walked in, the first thing I noticed was a toilet sitting right by her dresser. It had a green fuzzy toilet seat cover, which matched her green bedspread and the "This Is Horse Country" rug lying on the floor beside it. There was a tall wooden bunk bed against the wall, and I hoped Julie would let me sleep on top.

I put my suitcase down by her bed, and that's when it hit me— I was a bed wetter. Why hadn't I thought of it before? I wet the bed *every single night*.

I hadn't put this into the equation when Julie had asked me to spend the night, and Mom hadn't mentioned it at all. I panicked, until I thought of the only solution; I would stay up all night and I would even sit on that toilet, out in the open, if I needed to. Now I would have to sleep on the bottom bunk so I could get up and pee.

Julie nudged my arm. "Let's grab a snack."

Her mom offered us a taco pizza she had ordered from the local Pizza Palace. I rarely had pizza from a restaurant, and who'd ever heard of a taco pizza? It turned out to be a regular pizza except instead of sauce it was covered in refried beans, chicken, cheese, lettuce, tomato, and tortilla chips. We sat down at the kitchen table and Joan opened bottles of Cokes for us. We didn't have Cokes at my house.

Dave came in the back door and joined us. He was wearing tan pants, a white oxford cloth shirt, and a dark brown sweater vest. He looked like the dad from *Dennis the Menace*.

"You've grown a little since the barbecue," he said, reaching for a piece of pizza. "You're going to be tall like your dad," he said. My dad wasn't tall, and I didn't want Dad in the conversation.

"I look like my great-aunt Lillian," I countered, even though I'd never met her. But that's what Mom always said.

We ate pizza and laughed about school. Dave asked questions about my family.

"How's your grandma Mildred?" he asked. That was Granda's formal name.

"She's pretty good," I said, "but she has to have surgery at the Allensburg Clinic for piles." I didn't know what piles were, but Dave nodded.

"And your mom?" he asked.

"My mom?" I wondered. Why would Dave care about my mom?

"We went to high school together," Dave said.

"WHAT?" I said, louder than I meant to. It occurred to me quickly that Mom had made the biggest mistake of my life by not marrying Dave Kilner. I could have had a toilet in my bedroom. I could have owned a mortuary.

"Your mom and I were in school together," he repeated.

"I didn't know that," I said. Now I was flustered. Even though she bought clothes and furniture at fancy stores in Cincinnati and drove a black Oldsmobile Cutlass, it was clear to me now that my mom had no taste whatsoever.

At that exact moment I knocked over my Coke and flooded my own plate with soda. I sat completely still, waiting for Dave to erupt in fury. Instead, he said, "Whoa, looks like you need another plate." He stood up and walked it to the counter.

I was ashamed and worried. "I'm sorry. I wasn't paying attention," I said, tears stinging my eyes. Now they would never ask me back.

"This happens around here at least once a day," Dave said. Tears fell anyway.

Joan leaned over, smiling, her hand patting the center of my back. "Monica, don't worry about it. It's no big deal."

It was a big deal at my house. I once saw Dad knock Jamie off a stool with the back of his hand when he accidentally spilled milk on the table.

Dave placed a clean plate in front of me and walked to the family room to pick up the newspaper. I resisted the urge to wipe my runny nose on the cloth napkin in my lap. I hadn't even wiped my mouth on it for fear of staining it.

"Are you okay?" Joan asked.

"Yes, definitely," I said, sniffing, and Joan got up to join Dave in the family room. As soon as she walked away, I took a swipe at my nose with the napkin. I had to. Snot was really starting to drip.

Julie and I were finishing our pizza when I looked at her and quietly said, "We could have been sisters, you know. My mom almost married your dad."

"What?" she said between bites.

"My mom and your dad went to school together. We could have been sisters," I reiterated. Julie looked at me blankly. Clearly she hadn't been paying attention.

Later that night we were in the basement playing The Dating Game when Dave came downstairs. I couldn't imagine what he was still doing home.

"Are you having fun?" he asked.

"Sure," I said.

"I'm making popcorn if you girls want to come up in a minute."

"Okay," Julie answered.

Why was Dave hanging around?

We went upstairs for popcorn in our pajamas and then sat on the couch for a movie. Dave sat down too. I had a crush on him, but he was starting to get on my nerves.

Finally, Julie and I went downstairs to brush our teeth for bed. There was a deep white plastic sink down there beside a shower that sat right out in the open with just a thin blue curtain around it. That's when I finally got the courage to ask about Sarah Keeler.

"Did you know that girl, Sarah, who was killed on her bike?" I asked. "She was at your dad's funeral home."

"Sure," she said, toothpaste foaming around her mouth. "She died right out there," Julie said, casually pointing her toothbrush toward the front of her house.

"What? Are you kidding me? She was killed by your house?"

"Yeah." Julie tapped her toothbrush on the sink. "We used to play together. She lived right over there." She pointed in the same direction. "Lowell, who lives above the mortuary, pronounced her dead. But Dad embalmed her."

I couldn't think of which questions to ask first. I started with, "Did you see it happen?"

"No." Julie offered me a green terry cloth towel. I took it and wiped my mouth off.

"So you guys were friends?" I asked.

"I told you, she lived in the neighborhood." Julie began combing her hair.

"Did she spend the night here?"

"No."

"Did my dad film the accident?" I asked.

"What?"

"My dad takes home movies of accidents," I explained. Julie gave a pretend shiver. I felt embarrassed to have a dad like that, but I needed facts.

"Why do you want to know about Sarah Keeler?" she wondered. No one had ever asked me that, because my obsession with Sarah Keeler was a secret. I thought up a lie.

"I met her once at a church picnic," I said quickly. "Then I saw her picture in the paper and wondered what happened."

"At St. Mary's?" she asked.

"What?"

"The picnic, was it at St. Mary's?" she asked again.

I nodded. Julie shrugged.

"Do you want to make bracelets?" she asked, grabbing a shoe box from under her bed.

I wanted to say, *No, I don't want to make bracelets. I want to go out to the road, in the dark, and lie in the place where Sarah died. I want every detail. I want your dad to tell me what she looked like when he saw her. Did she look sad or scared or just dead? Were her eyes open or closed?*

"Sure, let's make bracelets," I said, pulling out some colored yarn from the box. My stomach was flip-flopping all over the place.

I couldn't sleep that night even though I was exhausted—because if I did, I'd wet the bed.

While Julie slept on the top bunk, I sat crouched on the bottom, humming to keep myself awake. I thought about exploring the basement, but it was too dark to do anything but stay where I was.

Besides, I started hearing scary creaking sounds coming from the Kilner's basement stairs. I was afraid it might be Sarah's ghost coming back to kick my ass for pretending to know her.

I imagined all the ghosts of all the people Dave had buried traipsing through the house, and prayed that Julie's louvered door was strong enough to keep them out.

There weren't windows in the basement, so I couldn't tell when the sun was rising, allowing me to pee one last time and still get a little sleep.

The next morning Mom picked me up in her black Oldsmobile Cutlass wearing large Jackie O sunglasses. Dave and Joan came out to the car to chat with her. Julie and I stayed inside until Mom yelled that it was time to go.

Driving away from their house, Mom asked how it went.

"Really fun," I said, "but Dave's kind of weird. He hung around the whole time. He didn't leave once. And he kept asking us questions," I said, rolling my eyes.

"That's the way it should be," Mom said. "That's the way dads are supposed to act. They stay home." She turned onto Highway 64 leading to our house. "They like having families and want to spend time with them."

My chest hurt. I looked at the cornfields barreling by.

We were the weird ones.

Part II

FATHER OF THE YEAR

CHAPTER SIX

The following Saturday the phone rang and the woman on the other end told Mom she was dating my dad. Mom called Casanova at work.

"Get your butt home," she barked into the phone.

"What?" he asked.

"I just got a call from your 'girlfriend.'" Mom slammed down the receiver.

JoAnn, sensing things were about to blow, grabbed her single-shot twenty-two rifle out of the coat closet and headed out across the field to find Cousin Ben. When things got tense, they hiked back to the creek and shot cans off fences and chain-smoked Lucky Strikes.

Jamie wasn't home; he was at practice. He was fourteen years old and a freshman track star. After practice he'd tie his long pole to the top of Mom's Cutlass and bring it home so he could pole-vault over everything. I'd look out the kitchen window at Jamie vaulting over the back fence or an old tree lying out in the field. He catapulted his skinny body over anything higher than four feet. Girls were calling him all the time now.

Becky and I had spent the day building a rambling Barbie village under the baby grand piano, complete with beauty parlor and roads made out of masking tape. We somehow missed the urgency to clear out.

It took Dad under four minutes to make the eight-mile trip from Elk Grove to Galesburg. He was pronounced guilty by the speed at which he drove home to deny the "girlfriend."

When Dad skidded into the driveway and we heard Mom yell, "That son of a bitch!" Becky and I jumped up and ran to the back-yard, leaving Barbie and Skipper to fend for themselves.

We sat on the metal swing set listening to them fight. We didn't swing or go down the slide or even look at each other. Buddy sat tucked under my grass-stained feet.

The fight escalated into Mom slamming out the door, jumping into her Cutlass, and squealing out of the driveway. Becky started crying.

Dad came out a few minutes later in just a pair of shorts and tennis shoes. He walked to his truck, grabbed a sledgehammer out of the back of it, and began attacking the neglected one-car garage that Mom had been harping on him to tear down. I guessed today was the day.

Boards and nails started flying, so Becky, Buddy, and I moved to the back fence. Obviously, he wanted to kill something, and we'd rather it be the garage than us. We sat in the grass watching that building collapse around Dad. Becky and I were picturing Mom's car crashed up against a tree by now, or her deciding to drive away forever.

"She should have married Dave Kilner," I told Becky.

"What are you talking about?" she snapped.

"Mom had a chance to marry Dave Kilner, but she married *that*." With my hand I indicated the maniac on the lumber pile. "Thanks a lot, Patricia," I said to Mom, who wasn't even there.

"You're a weirdo," Becky snapped, and tears started running down her face again. "Mom can't help the way *he* is."

"Maybe she shouldn't have bothered with him in the first place," I said.

"Maybe she shouldn't have bothered with YOU in the first place," she said.

"She would have done me a HUGE favor," I countered. "I

could've missed all of this." I made another huge sweeping gesture with my hand.

"And she would have done me a huge favor too, because I wouldn't have to put up with YOU," she cried.

"Why are you attacking me?" I asked.

"Why are you attacking Mom?"

"You're just mad because she left without you," I snapped.

Becky pounced on me with all her ten-year-old strength. She thumped me in the chest with her fist and I yanked her ponytail. She knocked me onto the grass and I kicked her legs. She smacked my arm as I was trying to get up so I hit her as hard as I could in the back. She stopped, looked right at me, and yelled, "I HATE YOU!" She yelled it over and over again as she ran toward the house.

I started crying because it shocked me to hear her say she hated me, but I hated her too.

I hated all of us.

A half hour later Dad was standing on top of a pile of broken lumber, sweaty and panting, covered in dirt and sawdust. His thumb had been ripped on something and he kept flicking the blood off it.

He screamed my name. Oh shit. I ran to where he was hulking over the lumber pile.

"Grab those boards and carry them out to the field," he hollered.

I stared at that lumber in disbelief. It would take me weeks to haul it to the back field, but I was in no position to argue. I started dragging boards, heavy and filled with splinters and nails, out to the field, where he was going to set "the whole damn thing on fire." A weenie roast was probably out of the question.

In between trips I hustled Buddy into the house. I was afraid she'd get a splinter in her paw if she kept following me around, or that Dad might kick her in the side if she accidentally got in his way. He'd kicked her before.

I picked up a board, and a nail went clear through to the other side of my hand. I pulled out the nail, which was probably a mistake, because then it really started bleeding. I held it up to show the monster.

"What the hell's wrong with you?" he asked. I stood there, staring him down. I was really pissed off now. In fact, I felt like knocking down a building myself, preferably with him inside.

Finally, realizing I wasn't going to walk away, he took a used white hanky, crusty and wrinkled, out of his back pocket and tied it around my hand. It stopped the bleeding.

Then it was Becky's turn.

Dad found a huge rat's nest in the back of that garage. He filled a tall white plastic bucket with water, scooped up the nest—babies and all—with an enormous snow shovel and threw it into the bucket. He gave Becky a wooden yardstick and made her stand there and stir until they were all dead. She did it, tears pouring down her face, stirring and stirring. I could see shadows of all the little bodies swirling against the side of the plastic bucket.

Becky could not look at me the rest of the day. Mom didn't come back until after dark.

The next morning we all ate bacon and eggs as if the garage were still standing.

Three days later, when the four of us kids got home from school, Fielding Brothers Home Furnishings had delivered a brand-new living room set, the one Mom had been coveting for more than two years.

There was peace (and new furniture) in Galesburg.

Summer came, and that meant long, warm nights where we could stay out and away from home as long as we wanted.

One night the Whitmores invited us to play a new game up at the cemetery. It was called Dark Side of the Moon, after Pink Floyd's album.

During the game, we walked cautiously up the gravel path

toward the pitch-black cemetery, and when we least expected it, Jamie or an older Whitmore would rise up behind a headstone with an old flowered bed sheet over his head and howl. We'd turn and run as fast as we could, but if you were too slow, and I always was, a sheet dropped over your head and you were captured. Prisoners lay flat out on top of someone's grave until everyone was declared dead.

JoAnn refused to play because, as she put it, "I don't like to be stalked." Becky loved to play but insisted on bringing Mrs. Beasley. I played, but got so terrified every time I was captured that Jamie let me sit cross-legged behind the tombstone he was haunting instead of lying parallel to a buried person.

The only problem with playing in the graveyard was Alton Cotterman. His property butted up against the cemetery, and he used to sit in his green-and-white metal glider with a shotgun across his khaki-covered knees, ready to shoot any animal that dared step foot in his yard. During the day, shots could be heard on and off all summer long. All of us kids kept a close eye on Buddy.

He mostly shot cats, but we were positive he'd shoot a kid one of these days. I always picked out brightly colored T-shirts to wear so as not to be mistaken for a fur-bearing creature, thus improving my chances of survival. With Alton nearby, Dark Side of the Moon was a life or death situation.

One Saturday afternoon JoAnn saw Alton Cotterman walking up the lane, holding a yellow cat by its tail. It was still wiggling, but there was blood all over its side. When he got to the cemetery, he swung the cat over his head and banged it against a headstone until it was a mush of blood and fur. Then he tossed it over the fence and into the field. JoAnn ran and got Becky and me so that poor animal would have a decent funeral.

We were all in tears looking down at that cat, bones busted and skin split. Bullies chose the smallest and most silent. We were all at risk.

JoAnn brought over a shovel and we gingerly scooped the goopy, bloody mess with the torn ear into an old striped pillowcase and buried it under a locust tree. We cut peonies out of Etta Mae Shaw's yard, and the Whitmore kids came, out of respect.

It wasn't a classy Kilner and Sons funeral, but I did make small remembrance cards out of white envelopes cut in half. I drew a cat on the front and wrote the date he died on the back.

As we lowered the pillowcase into the ground, JoAnn recited a poem from our old nursery rhyme book that Granda had read to us many times. It seemed appropriate.

> *Dear Father, hear and bless*
> *The beasts and singing birds,*
> *And guard with special tenderness*
> *Small things that have no words.*

One day, while I was sitting on Mammaw's front porch shelling peas from her garden, I heard this coming from the Zenith clock radio sitting in the window behind the screen: "WMCR is holding its annual Father of the Year contest. Write an essay about why your father is the number-one Father of the Year, mail it to our studio here at 120 South Orchard, Elk Grove, and the winner will be announced July twenty-fifth at three p.m."

I knew where the radio station was; it was right next to Dad's store. I decided to write an essay.

I wrote about how Dad tried to save his store from the fire, how he cooked steaks for us on Saturday nights and always provided money. When I was at Dad's store the following week, I walked the essay over to the radio station and handed it to Eugene Fox, who was sitting behind the front desk.

It was my attempt to enter Dad's fan club. If he were chosen, people would see that I thought he was a great guy too. It would also convince Dad that I saw what other people saw in him, and maybe things would change.

I knew from church that he had a soft side, and I knew from the Rotary Club barbecue that he liked to have fun, so it was possible he might include us someday.

Dad was not chosen on July twenty-fifth at three p.m. I figured whoever was choosing the winner either didn't buy my story or my letter lacked the passion necessary to win a title as impressive as "Father of the Year." Whatever the reason, I received a note thanking me for my submission, and life went on as before.

CHAPTER SEVEN

Despite the lack of invitations coming from me, Julie continued to have me sleep over at her house. I managed to stay up and never wet her bed. Each time I stayed awake, the night seemed longer and spookier, but I would rather have been at the Kilners' than at home.

One Saturday morning Julie and I were riding around town in Dave's white station wagon when he said seven magic words: "I have to stop by the mortuary." I couldn't believe it. I'd waited so long to get back there.

Julie said, "Can we stay in the car?" but I immediately countered with "I have to go to the bathroom." No parent would take the chance of letting a bathroom request go unfulfilled. I was definitely in.

The place was quieter without the line of mourners, but I could still imagine all the funerals of all the women and men and children. Julie headed upstairs to the office for a soda, but I stood in the entry-way, mesmerized and sweaty from my proximity to death. Where were the bodies, and what were they doing to them?

This was my first time in Kilner and Sons since Sarah Keeler's funeral, and even though I hadn't been there in over a year, I felt like a regular.

Dave pointed to the bathrooms, which were near the front doors. I managed to force a little bit of pee out, flushed, and, of course, washed my hands. If Dave Kilner were listening at the door, and I imagined he was, I wanted him to know I took personal hygiene seriously.

As I came out of the bathroom, immediately to my left I saw maroon carpeted steps leading down into darkness. I stood on the first step and leaned over at the waist to see if I could get a look at anything down there, but it was too dark. I walked down two more steps, and then I saw something: two large wooden doors slightly ajar so that fluorescent light was spilling out of the crack between them and onto the carpet. I heard water running and eerie suctioning sounds. The hair on the back of my neck stood up.

Suddenly a tall man with a rectangular-shaped head and black glasses swung open one of the doors and growled, "Who's there?"

I turned—in midair—and bounded up those steps, slapped my palms on the glass doors, and pushed my way into the bright parking lot, where a black hearse was parked. I was frantically looking for a place to hide when the rectangular-headed man opened the glass doors behind me.

"I didn't mean to scare you." He laughed. "I thought you were Julie. I'm Max Cooper," he said, holding out a gloved hand that until a moment before had probably been working on the body behind the door. I stared at his hand and he laughed and pulled off the glove.

"Okay," I said, still unable to shake that hand. "Okay." My chest was heaving up and down.

Julie and I began frequenting the mortuary.

There were parks and grassy backyards in Elk Grove, but I preferred the spiffy casket showroom in the basement of the mortuary. It was down the hall from the dreaded embalming room but was cheery with light yellow paint and it showcased all types of wooden caskets with silk interiors in various colors.

At first I was petrified of the coffins, imagining a corpse rotting in each one. But it was peaceful down there, and here was a chance to lie in a box where someone would spend eternity. If I looked at it that way, it was almost an honor. In the showroom, I could be dead without dying.

Julie and I took turns lying in our favorite coffins. Mine always had a pink interior (like Sarah Keeler's) encased by a light-colored wood, usually maple. Julie, being somewhat introspective, chose walnut, always with a blue interior.

When I kicked off my tennis shoes the first time and crawled in, I was surprised that it wasn't comfortable. Lying in a coffin was like lying on a barn door. How was I supposed to make it through eternity laid out like that? Where was the fluffy mattress? Of all the times I needed to be comfortable, "dead forever" was at the top of the list.

It was cold inside a coffin, especially where my feet were. I'd remember to tell Dave to put tube socks on me if I ended up in a casket—which, of course, someday I would. Regardless of my pink fancy dress, I needed thick socks on my feet.

Inside my maple coffin, I placed my head on the small silk pillow so the top of my hair was showing, like Sarah Keeler's. When I peeked out, I could see Julie in her casket. She was relaxed with one hand behind her head and chewing the thumbnail of her other one. I wondered what she was thinking.

I looked up at the ceiling and imagined faces walking by, peering down at me. Who would come to my funeral? Granda would be there, and Mom would make JoAnn and Becky come, and Jamie wouldn't miss it. Dad would be there for sure. I felt gooseflesh on my arms thinking of Dad looking down at me. If he decided to haul off and slap me, I wouldn't be able to move my hands to defend myself, not that I ever *did* defend myself. Still, laid out powerless in front of Dad was a lethal place to be, even as a corpse.

I lifted my head and looked over at Julie. Her eyes were closed and she was humming something I couldn't hear very well. I lay back down. There was nothing to be scared of, no one to hurt me, but I was panic-stricken. I shouldn't have pictured Dad staring down at me.

When I sat up to orient myself, an eerie feeling came over me. I was sure that something was about to snatch me out of the world, but

I couldn't see or hear it. Everything looked normal and safe, but it wasn't.

"Are you okay?" Julie asked.

"Sometimes I feel creepy in here," I said.

"No kidding."

I heard Max slam the doors to the embalming room. I didn't want Max to embalm me, because I worried he might be a little rough. I'd seen him roll a body onto a gurney only to have it roll off the other side.

But if Dave embalmed me, he'd see me naked, which was mortifying. I wasn't like Kathy Brooks's mom, Evelyn, who'd told us she couldn't wait to die just to have "Dave Kilner's hands all over my naked body."

"Hey, Monica, close my lid," Julie said, sitting up in her coffin and looking at me.

"What? Are you kidding? I'm not closing you in there," I said.

She was serious. "Close the lid; I can lift it back up myself."

"What if it locks and you can't breathe?" I asked.

"There's no way. It only locks with a key." She lay back down. "Just close it for a quick second." Julie gestured for me to come over there. Her hand waving me over was all I could see sticking up out of the box.

I climbed out of my coffin. "Closing it gives me the willies," I said, padding over in my socks. We never wore shoes inside the coffins. We weren't even supposed to be in the coffins.

I looked in at Julie. She was wearing navy shorts with a yellow-and-white-striped tank top and her gold wire-rimmed glasses.

I put my hand on the lid. Only the top part of the coffin was open. In the showroom the coffin lids were closed at the bottom and opened at the top, just like it would be at a viewing.

"I don't want to do this," I said.

"If you're worried, just close it for a second, leave your hand there, and open it back up," she said.

I pulled down the lid and kept my hand under it so it wouldn't make contact with the bottom. "Are you okay?" I asked.

"Okeydokey," she said. I waited.

"Are you ready to come out?" I asked.

"Not yet."

I looked around the showroom. On the white shelf over by the door sat three miniature vaults. One was silver, one was bronze, and the other one was a dull gray. These were small versions of what the coffin sat in once it was lowered into the grave. I loved picking them up and holding them at eye level. I liked miniature things.

"Open the lid," Julie said, so I raised it up.

"What was it like?" I asked.

"Not bad," she said.

"Don't ever do that to me," I told her. "I don't like to be shut in."

"Okay," she said, climbing out. It was harder for Julie to get out because she was still shorter than I was, so I helped by entwining my fingers and letting her step into my hands and then onto the floor.

We both rearranged and smoothed out the silk interiors of our coffins so they'd look good as new, put on our shoes, and ran upstairs for a snack. There were mounds of cookies stacked in tins in the office, all flavors, waiting for someone's funeral reception. The Kilners must have felt that sad people needed snacks, because at every funeral they laid out a nice spread in the back of the viewing room.

The next week at the mortuary I was heading downstairs with a Ding Dong in my hand when I came across Donald Macy's grandmother lying on a gurney in the hallway with her hair in rollers. I thought, *What is Mrs. Macy doing here by the pantry?* And it occurred to me, *She's dead!* And then it occurred to me to scream, which I did. I had just seen Mrs. Macy, days earlier, decorating her mailbox for Halloween.

My scream made Dave think maybe we were hanging around the mortuary too much. He said he wanted us to "go bowling or bike riding or shopping. Stop hanging around this old depressing place." He even offered us spending money.

We ignored Dave's suggestion because by then we'd met Jeannette.

Jeannette was filling in for Virginia, who normally did hair and makeup at the mortuary. Virginia and her husband, Lowell, who lived in the apartment over the mortuary, were on vacation.

Jeannette owned her own salon called Shear Attitude and was stylish for Elk Grove. She sported platinum blond hair that was cut to her shoulders with one side shorter than the other. That was the style in *Cosmo*, she assured us.

Jeannette was a big woman—tall, but buxom as well. She took care of her nails. I had never seen fingernails as long as Jeannette's, or as pampered. She kept a nail kit with her at all times and was constantly gluing one of her tips back on and repainting it.

I wasn't allowed to wear nail polish or makeup, but Jeannette put it on me at the mortuary, and we'd take it off before my dad picked me up to go home.

I sat on a tall metal stool on the opposite side of the gurney while Jeannette applied makeup to the face and hands of some "poor soul," as she put it. The whole time she was working, she sang hymns.

> *Why should I feel discouraged?*
> *Why should the shadows come?*
> *Why should my heart be lonely,*
> *Longing for heaven and home?*
> *Jesus is my potion,*
> *My constant friend is He.*
> *His eye is on the sparrow,*
> *And I know He watches me.*

We sang those hymns at church, but she didn't invite me to sing along, so I listened and watched.

Fresh dead bodies were scary enough, but when Jeannette worked her magic (with a little eye shadow and peach blush), the dead looked alive, and that's when I expected them to sit up and ask for a cup of coffee or a ride home.

But they didn't sit up. They lay there until Dave or Max came down and lifted them into their coffins.

I prayed for their souls whether I knew them or not. I wanted them to rest in peace and not stalk me at night.

I wanted to get past my obsession with death. I wanted, more than anything else, to be happier.

CHAPTER EIGHT

Emily Atkins had a roller-skating party for her tenth birthday. I was excited because when I skated, I went really fast, passing everyone, just like Dad passed the bus. I wasn't a fast runner or a fast biker, but I was a fast skater. Even so, it always took at least five or six complete circles around the oblong rink before I got the hang of being on skates again; skating parties were a rare (and intoxicating) event.

Mom always went with us because she loved to roller-skate—not down the sidewalk like Becky and me, but gliding across the smooth wooden floor of the Elk Grove Roller Rink. I'd never seen Dad skate.

At the rink there were white roller skates for rent with the number six on the heel, a snack stand with bottled Cokes and candy bars, and a popcorn machine by the front door. The whole place smelled like sweat, leather, and popcorn butter.

Nothing was more exhilarating than hurling around the rink while the sound system blasted Three Dog Night's "Joy to the World."

The only problem was just when I got used to skating in one direction, the lights flashed and Sherry, who owned the rink and who had a distinctive masculine quality about her, would turn on the loudspeaker and say, "TURNABOUT." Simple enough word, but everyone had to turn around and skate in the opposite direction, triggering all kinds of collisions.

Some of us could stop, but some of us didn't know how yet. One kid would stop in front of another kid, and those two would go down, triggering the kid behind them to fall. I never understood why switching directions was necessary. Maybe Sherry, who was young but wore an old-lady-type dress, was trying to spice things up.

At Emily's party Sherry tried something new, announcing we'd be skating in a line. Was she out of her mind? Maybe she wanted one of us to break a bone so she could close the rink early, go home, and smoke Camels on the wooden deck of her green-and-white trailer behind the Dairy Queen.

We all managed to get in a long line. We started out pretty slow, but once we rounded the second turn, Susan, who was last in line, involuntarily spun off the back from centrifugal force. We picked up speed. One by one, girls were hurled off the back until someone in front finally fell and we all ended up piled on one another's backs with our skates sticking out behind us.

When everyone rolled off, I noticed my hip was hurting, and not the kind of hurt a Band-Aid could soothe. It hurt so bad I had trouble getting up on my skates. Julie helped me over to the thickly painted gray wooden benches against the wall. By the time we got there, my hip had sort of clicked back into place. Mom skated over and pulled down the side of my stretch pants to check for injury. There was no horrible bruise or blood, just my regular skin.

I continued skating.

The next morning, Saturday, I was supposed to ride my bike three miles with the Girl Scouts. I told Mom I didn't think my hip felt good enough to go, but she said, "I think you'll survive." She was right, too, because my hip looked normal. I kept checking it myself.

I pedaled with everyone else to the Girl Scout cabin without any trouble. We parked our bikes outside and started a big fire inside. We sang my favorite song sitting around the fireplace:

> *It only takes a spark to get a fire going*
> *And then all those around can warm up to its glowing.*
> *That's how it is with God's love, once you've experienced it*
> *It's fresh like spring, you'll want to sing, you'll want to pass it on.*

I liked the words to the song, but mostly I liked the way I sounded singing it. Most Girl Scout songs were written for sopranos, but I was an alto. If I could sing low, I sang great. If I had to sing anything above a B-flat, I was screwed.

The fire was warm, our faces *were* glowing, and I was worried about peeing in my sleeping bag. It turned out I didn't have to worry about that; I spent the whole night awake with a throbbing hip.

The next morning I biked the three miles home, but my hip was really hurting. When I got home, I couldn't put weight on it. If I tried to stand up, I ended up on my butt. This frightened Mom, who decided I needed to see a doctor. We *never* went to doctors between our annual checkups at Dr. Landaw's office, which we never missed.

On Monday, Mom and I drove to Cincinnati to see Dr. Goldman, a pediatric orthopedist, at St. Vincent Children's Hospital. Granda found him through her arthritis doctor.

Dr. Goldman was soft-spoken with dark brown hair and thin lips. He took X-rays and had me lie on my back while he moved my leg up in the air and around and around in circles. Painful.

"We'll need to keep her tonight," he told Mom, still holding my leg up. Mom and I both did a double take.

"Tonight?" Mom asked.

"We need to get this leg into traction. When the skate hit her, it must have knocked the hip out of the socket, draining fluid that allows the bone to move freely," he explained. "We're going to slowly pull the leg back with weights and let that socket fill up with fluid again, and then gently ease the hip back into place. After a few weeks on crutches, she should be fine."

Crutches? All right! Every kid I knew wanted crutches. What could be cooler than walking around on crutches with everyone staring? I was liking this, but Mom did not look happy.

"Can I take her home tonight and bring her back in the morning? That way we could get her pajamas and underpants," she said.

Underpants? I was humiliated. I didn't want her to say "underpants." I was concentrating on that, when I noticed Mom was getting very upset. I was so *happy*. Mom showing such deep concern for me was like eating a whole frozen pizza without sharing it with anyone—only better. Between the promise of crutches and Mom's worry, I neglected to be bothered by the idea of being in a hospital full of strangers an hour away from home.

We drove the fifty miles back to Galesburg in silence, with Mom holding my hand the whole way. I would be in the hospital for at least a week. We were in shock, and at the same time, I felt close to Mom. She loved me, I knew she loved me, but she hardly ever showed it physically. It wasn't much, her hand on top of mine, but it was a big show of affection for her.

When Dad got home that night, he was worried. He hadn't expected a hospital stay and his "us against them" mentality kicked in. Dad hurt us, but no one else could.

He walked into our bedroom. My heart jumped as I pretended to sleep. He stood at the door and looked at me for a few minutes and then walked out. I heard him say to Mom, "Let's just take care of this and get her home."

It was the kindest thing Dad had ever said.

The next morning the other kids got on the bus, Wanda threw up without me, and I lay on the couch while Mom packed the green suitcase. My hands shook as I dressed Casper the Ghost in pale green doll pajamas and white socks. The day before, it had been fun to be injured, but today it was terrible.

Mom and Granda drove me to Cincinnati. I sat in the back with my leg stretched across the seat. Granda kept looking at me and winking, which prompted tears from me.

"Why can't somebody stay with me?" I cried.

"Grown-ups can't stay at a children's hospital," Mom reasoned.

"Can I go to the hospital in Elk Grove?" I asked.

"You need to be in Cincinnati with specialists," Mom said.

"We'll come see you every day, honey," Granda assured me. "You've got to get better."

I hugged Casper and stared out the back window, as Galesburg got farther and farther away. I wished I hadn't gone skating. I wished I hadn't wished for crutches.

When we got to the hospital, Mom pulled up in front. She and Granda got out and a man in soft blue pants and a white shirt pushed a wheelchair toward the car. My stomach flipped over. After the man lifted me into the chair, he put my suitcase under the seat and rolled me into the lobby. Sitting in that chair was the first time I realized that something had happened to my body that was serious, and that I wasn't in control. I was on the verge of a full-on panic attack—hyperventilating, a sweaty forehead—but we just kept rolling.

Granda walked beside me while Mom parked the car. The nurses and administrators were pleasant, but I was nauseous. Casper was on my lap.

Once Mom came, and I was checked in, we all went upstairs to my room. The elevator doors opened to a long beige hallway painted with giant green monkeys, purple elephants, and giraffes with spots in all the primary colors. Any moron knew that monkeys were brown. What the hell kind of place was this?

A brunette nurse with a smock covered in characters from *Bambi* showed us to my room. *Bambi* was the saddest movie I'd ever seen. This was not looking good. When we got to my room, I saw there were five other beds in there. I could see a girl in a pink nightgown sleeping on her side with her thumb shoved into her mouth; two girls had their families with them, and one was watching TV. The bed next to mine was empty.

I changed into a blue-and-green-checked nightgown and climbed into bed, which felt like a strange thing to do in the middle of the day when I didn't have a fever or anything. I didn't need a nightgown for a sore hip.

Suddenly a big-boned nurse with thick white-framed glasses wheeled a gurney into the room. She didn't have Disney characters on her smock.

"I'm taking her for X-rays," she said to Mom and Granda.

Holy shit. "Can they come too?" I asked, alarmed to be carted off like that.

"It won't take long," she assured me.

"Granda and I can grab some lunch," Mom said casually. She was going to leave me with this woman? How could she eat knowing I was being taken away by a stranger?

Once I was on the gurney, the nurse covered me in a single white sheet and wheeled me out into the hallway and onto the elevator.

I started to panic. The elevator went all the way down to the basement, and when the doors squeaked open, there was nobody down there. It was so quiet that the wheels of my gurney sounded like the rumble of a semi as we rolled down several gloomy hallways.

We finally came to beige swinging doors that the nurse pushed open with her butt, pulling me in behind her. She told me to slip off my panties because they were going to X-ray my pelvis and hip area. I was horrified and imagined she wanted to touch me and that's why she wanted my panties off. She wasn't going to X-ray me, she was evil, and I wasn't even supposed to be in the basement. Where were all the people? Didn't Mom tell me to keep my panties on during the day? Something was horribly wrong.

I thought about pushing myself along the hallway on the gurney to get the hell out of there, but Nurse Panties-Off would probably be too fast for me.

I was thinking of another exit plan when a blond man pushed through the doors and said, "I was at lunch. Sorry." Was everyone at lunch but me? "Who do we have here?" he asked.

"Monica Peterson. Dr. Goldman ordered X-rays," the nurse said, handing me off to the man. I was happy to hear Dr. Goldman's name. If these two worked for Dr. Goldman, then I was supposed to be there.

The man smiled and I managed to smile back even though I was still under one thin sheet without panties. He took X-rays without lifting the sheet, instead placing the machine directly over me and shining a small square of light over the area he was photographing. He also laid a thick heavy gray blanket over my chest and another one over my "reproductive organs" to protect those body parts from radiation. The nurse with the white glasses sat in a metal chair and flipped through *Reader's Digest*.

When I was back in my bed, Dr. Goldman came in with two nurses. They clamped a large metal vise on the foot of my bed and then placed a white foam cast on my leg all the way to my knee. They fitted a metal piece around the cast and wrapped that with a wide ACE bandage. Weights hung off the end of my bed and they attached these to a metal piece on each side of my foot. My leg was being pulled down, but it was so gradual, I couldn't feel the pulling, only the ache that had been there before. There were two long pillows placed on each side of my leg so I couldn't move it. I was not getting out of bed for a long time.

The only good news was I wouldn't have to worry about wetting the bed because a nurse would wake me up twice a night so I could pee in a bedpan. I was embarrassed by the bedpan, but I'd have been more embarrassed if I wet the bed.

When they left the room, I fell asleep. I woke up to Mom and Granda talking softly beside my bed. Mom was rubbing my arm and Granda was patting my good leg. Just then a gurney came through the door with another little girl on it. She wore a yellow nightgown with capped sleeves and her hair was as long as Becky's, only dark brown. She didn't look hurt as she climbed off the gurney and scrambled into bed. Her mom, who was short with curly black hair, stood beside her.

"This is Annie," her mom said. "What happened to your leg?" she asked, pointing to my crazy traction device.

I thought if you had traction, your leg was supposed to be in the air like Jethro's was in that one episode of *The Beverly Hillbillies*, but mine was flat on the bed. I couldn't even get traction right.

Mom and Annie's mom started talking, and Granda walked over to the side of Annie's bed. She was going to help break the ice.

"Monica's in fifth grade," Granda reported. Wherever we went, Granda introduced me to other children, including at Marsh Grocery Store or Art's Cafeteria, where she often took me for lunch.

"Me, too," Annie said.

"Monica hurt her hip roller-skating," Granda said.

"Oh." Annie didn't say where she was hurt.

When it was dark outside and time for Mom and Granda to leave, I started to cry. Annie got out of her bed and crawled into mine, careful not to knock into my leg.

"Let's watch TV so you won't think about them leaving," she said.

As Mom and Granda disappeared around the corner, Annie showed me a remote control, which I had never seen before. We sat in bed and changed channels without getting up.

I looked at Annie. She didn't cry when her mom left, and I wondered why. How could she be so calm?

The week was long, but it picked up when Mom and Dad arrived with a large cardboard box that had STANLEY TOOLS printed on the side; it was filled with all kinds of presents. I had never seen so many wrapped gifts.

"These are from everyone at Galesburg Methodist. They figured you could use some cheering up," Mom said. Dad looked out the window of my room (probably checking the weather) and came over to the bed.

"You really bummed up your leg," he said.

"Yeah," I said.

"Are they treating you okay?" he asked. I couldn't believe it. Dad had asked me a question.

"Pretty good," I said, but as I was starting to tell him about the remote on the television, he walked out into the hallway.

Annie helped me open all those gifts: Monopoly, Barbie dolls, *Ramona the Pest* books, Magic Markers, a Scooby Doo puzzle, thick pads of drawing paper, and a Thumbelina doll. We were excited, but by the time we got everything unwrapped, Annie was too tired to play. She climbed into her bed and fell asleep.

Granda and Mom kept their word and came every single day. On some days Martha Whitmore came too.

Uncle Larry and Aunt Betty drove up even though my cousins Steve and Ellen were too little to come. They brought me the most beautiful gift of all, a huge cardboard castle with colorful cutouts of all my favorite fairy tale characters.

Two nights later Dad drove JoAnn, Becky, and Jamie up to see me. They weren't allowed in my room, so I had to be wheeled down the hallway to the waiting area on a gurney. It was awkward because it felt so formal. None of us knew what to say.

I told Becky the church had sent tons of presents. I thought she'd be happy about all the new toys (especially the games), but she didn't seem to care.

JoAnn was wearing a multicolored patchwork halter top she'd made in home economics. She had recently begun wearing high platform shoes, pooka bead necklaces, and striped pants with what she called "elephant legs." She finally dressed like a girl, only in the coolest way.

I had the impression JoAnn didn't like me very much. She was never mean, but she didn't talk to me either. I was really loud and she needed quiet—all the time. When I tried to be quiet, it never worked. But in the hospital waiting room, she walked over to the gurney and put her hand on the side of it. I looked at her and shrugged my shoulders, not knowing what to say.

"You'll be home soon," she told me.

"I know," I said defensively.

"You can play my *Jesus Christ Superstar* album until you're allowed to go back to school."

I stared at her in disbelief. No one touched her albums, especially me, who (as she often pointed out) always had marshmallow fluff or dirt on my hands.

"Thanks," I managed. Dad wheeled me backward down the hallway in the opposite direction of everyone. I looked at Jamie, who gave me the peace sign.

A week later it was time to go home and Annie started to cry.

I told her, "You're going home really soon and we can visit each other."

She nodded but kept crying. I used my crutches to get over to her bed. "And we can write letters. I've never mailed a letter to anyone." Annie nodded. I felt sorry for her, but I was happy to be getting out. I hugged her tightly and promised her a letter soon.

When we arrived downstairs, I welcomed the fresh Ohio breeze. I was never indoors, even in winter, and I hadn't been outside in over seven days.

Granda and Mom were in the front seat, and the car was stuffed with all the toys from church, my nightgowns, socks, and Casper. I fell asleep as soon as we started out of Cincinnati, but I woke up later to hear Granda say, "Did she say how bad it was?"

"This is her fifth hospitalization," Mom said. "Her lungs were full again." I didn't know whom they were talking about.

"What did her mom say it was?" Granda asked.

"Leukemia," Mom said. "Absolutely terrifying."

Granda shook her head. "She's such a pretty little girl. Breaks my heart."

"She'll go home for a little while. Her mom thought in two weeks—maybe," Mom said, and I realized they were discussing Annie. It sounded like she was seriously ill, but I'd never heard of leukemia.

When I finally wrote to Annie, six months had gone by. Her mother wrote to my mom saying Annie had died.

I frantically searched for the Polaroid picture Mom had taken of us in my hospital bed. I looked in boxes under my bed, I rifled through all our photos from the past year. The longer it took to find that picture, the more agitated I became.

Finally I dumped out a manila envelope that held the get-well cards from my hospital stay—and there, among the smiling animals and good wishes, was the Polaroid. We were lying side by side in my bed, and she was wearing that yellow nightgown with the capped sleeves and I was wearing my blue-and-green-checkered nightgown. It must have been taken the first night I was there.

I studied her face for clues of impending death: dark rings around her eyes or a haunted expression. She looked normal, which was worse.

Another one of us gone.

CHAPTER NINE

On Easter Sunday, Dad was up at dawn for sunrise service at church. He was in charge of making breakfast for the congregation: sausage gravy and biscuits, scrambled eggs, hot coffee, and orange juice.

Mom allowed us to attend church in jeans or sweatpants for the sunrise service, but after we ate breakfast in the church basement, we all went home and changed into fancy dresses and suits. Christ had been resurrected by then, so we dressed accordingly.

The night before, I thought my mother might have to be resurrected. She and Dad got into such a horrendous fight that he tried to choke her. All of us ran toward the kitchen when the screaming stopped, because it was so jarringly quiet, and we saw Dad's thick fingers around Mom's neck and Mom just staring at him unable to breathe or make a sound. Jamie hit Dad in the back as hard as he could and Dad let go of her. Dad stormed out of the room, knocking over a kitchen chair and screaming, "You're all crazy. You're a bunch of lunatics. I don't know why I put up with any of you." A few minutes later I heard his truck back out of the driveway.

JoAnn poured Mom a glass of water and Jamie was staring out the kitchen window toward the field. I could tell by the way his jaw was clenched that he was fighting tears. Becky and I sat down at the kitchen table. Dad could have killed her. No one said a word.

Finally Mom got up and put two huge pots of water on the stove to boil Easter eggs. The next day was the church egg hunt at Vivian Bank's farm.

Easter morning Mom told us that Dad hadn't been trying to choke her. We let it go for the sake of the holiday.

After the sunrise service and breakfast prepared by Dad, who was in "great guy" mode, after fancy dresses and suits, Mom insisted on hiding our Easter baskets in the backyard. Jamie was fifteen, JoAnn was thirteen, Becky was eleven, and I was ten, so no one wanted to hunt Easter baskets anymore. I decided to take Buddy and find the baskets myself.

I was walking up the steps clutching them all to my chest when Uncle Dale, Mom's only sibling, pulled into our driveway in his squad car. He was a state policeman and always looked exceptionally handsome and important in his starched blue uniform and gold badge. He walked in the side door, and I ran to see what was up. I set the baskets on the living room floor near Jamie and gave Uncle Dale a hug. I could tell by his face that something was wrong. He leaned down and said, "Is your dad here?"

"Yes," I said, and ran to the kitchen to get him. I figured Dad was going to jail for "not choking" Mom.

Dale followed and told me to run and get Mom, too. I called for Mom and she walked in and nodded her head for me to get lost. Dale was talking in a serious whisper.

I ran back to the living room and tried to distract myself by separating the black jelly beans from all the others that had collected in the bottom of my Easter basket. I handed Jamie a coconut egg. He hated coconut and threw it at my head. "Kiss my ass," I whispered to him, and he cracked up. I'd been cussing for a while now, but if Mom heard me, I got smacked.

"Bare it and we'll share it," Jamie said, and we died laughing. I was so nervous I would have laughed at anything.

Dale was there only a few minutes and waved to us as he left without Dad. Mom and Dad went into their bedroom and slammed the door. They weren't speaking to each other after what had happened the night before, so now all four of us were worried. We tried to figure out what had happened.

"Granda died," I offered. (Granda was only sixty-four, but seemed ancient. Every time there was some kind of bad news, I was sure Granda had died.)

"Shut up," Becky snapped.

"Someone broke into Dad's store," Jamie said. "That's why the state police were called."

"Maybe Dad's girlfriend came back," I said.

"Maybe Sam Lunsford shot Granda as she was driving by his house," JoAnn said dryly.

"Nobody shot anyone," Jamie assured us.

"Maybe Dad's going to jail," I told them.

They just stared at me.

"Why, for being a fucker?" Jamie said. My eyebrows flew up. We had never used the *f* word before.

Just then, Dad came out of the bedroom, slammed out the side door, and took off running down the sidewalk toward Mammaw's house. I jumped up and looked out the living room windows. I'd never seen him run so fast.

Mom turned off the record player, which had been playing nonstop Frank Sinatra albums, and yelled, "You kids come in here."

We slowly filed into the kitchen.

"Your uncle Carl passed away this morning. Your dad's very upset. So, give me a minute and let me make some phone calls and figure some of this out. Your dad went down to tell Mammaw and Papaw."

Uncle Carl wouldn't be driving that Greyhound bus anymore. I wondered what had happened.

"Did Sam Lunsford shoot him?" I asked.

"No one shot him," Mom replied. "He died in his car."

"A damn car accident," I said, smacking the counter. I was always waiting to die in a car wreck. Part of it was the calamities I'd seen on our home movies and part of it was the daredevil way Dad drove when we were with him. Carl's accident confirmed it for me. We would all die in cars.

"Quit cussing. I already told you." Mom smacked the side of my head. "And it wasn't a car accident," she said. "It was something else."

We all stared at her, confused. Carl was only thirty-nine years old, not sixty-four like Granda—what could have killed him?

"Stop asking questions," she snapped, and went into the bathroom to put on lipstick. Clearly, we would be having company.

JoAnn started crying and Jamie had his hand over his mouth in shock. They were both close to Uncle Carl and Aunt Evelyn, spending many afternoons at their house across the field, playing with Paul and Ben. They'd played together all their lives.

It turned out that Uncle Carl was found dead in the parking lot of a restaurant in Cincinnati. He was sitting upright in his blue Mercury with the engine running. Carbon monoxide poisoning. Being suddenly dead was trouble enough, but a young lady was dead too. She was found in Uncle Carl's passenger seat, and she wasn't Aunt Evelyn.

All the radio channels were airing the story and saying, "Foul play has not been ruled out." It would probably be on the eleven o'clock news as well. Dad knew that Mammaw and Papaw always had their police scanner on, so he had to get down there quick before they heard it on there. And someone still had to tell Carl's family.

Mom picked up the phone and called Dave Kilner to make sure he had gotten the call to retrieve the body from the morgue in Cincinnati. Dave told Mom he would send his brother Hugh instead, so he would be at the funeral home when Dad came over to make the funeral arrangements.

Mom called the rest of Dad's brothers: Clarence, Bill, Larry, and Ernie, who all headed over to Mammaw's house and then down to Carl's to tell Evelyn and the kids.

Aunt Evelyn took the news of her husband's death badly, but she took the news of the twenty-nine-year-old girlfriend with a heavy sedative.

It was all so dramatic—having to be sedated over Uncle Carl. Who knew he had it in him to have a girlfriend, just like Dad? And now he was dead.

When Dad came back to the house to change clothes, his eyes were swollen and red. I could not believe it, he was actually crying. I didn't know how to react. He hated me so much, I wouldn't have tried to hug him or go within two feet of him, but he needed something from someone.

Dad changed his clothes without saying a word to any of us and headed to Elk Grove to go over funeral details with Dave.

Mom took a chicken casserole over to Carl's house but didn't stay long. Mom was happy to pour Campbell's cream of chicken soup over some noodles or make phone calls, but she wasn't good at tears and hysteria.

The *Elk Grove Courier* carried the story on the front page the next day with the headline:

GALESBURG MAN FOUND DEAD IN CAR IN CINCINNATI

The family was already devastated and now they were publicly humiliated, as the article laid out where Carl was found and the name and age of the woman found in the car with him. The story continued on the second page, listing those who survived him, and there was Dad's name right after Evelyn and the boys.

Ironically, right below his own brother's obituary there was a picture of Dad in his Shriner's fez celebrating the "newly formed Elk Grove Shrine Club" at the "gaily decorated" Elks Club.

At the mortuary that week Dave let me arrange flowers for Carl's funeral, which I did by color: yellows to the far right, then pinks, whites, and reds. All greenery was on the left along with the larger sprays. Carnations were placed in the far back. I hated carnations.

Uncle Carl was downstairs with Max Cooper getting ready for the viewing, but Dave didn't let me go down there. I wouldn't have wanted to see Carl like that, laid out on the white porcelain table with the two drains in it. It was not comforting to think of a family member being embalmed by Max and made up by Virginia, who had been back from vacation for a while now.

The night of Uncle Carl's visitation, the Peterson family began arriving at four thirty p.m. I felt a prick of resentment as they invaded my mortuary. It was the one place where none of them could get to me, but here they were, walking through the front door. Dad was the first one through.

I stood by the guest book and greeted everyone along with Dave and Max. I was as much a part of the mortuary staff as I was Carl's niece, and if I thought of myself as staff, I wouldn't have to be a part of "them."

My father stood beside the coffin all night. He wouldn't leave Carl's side and kept swiping his nose with a white hanky that had his own initials embroidered on it in navy stitching. He shook people's hands and, for once, he wasn't doing it for attention. He wanted to be there, next to his brother, whom he had taught to ride a bicycle and who had worn Dad's shoes and pants long after Dad had outgrown them.

Then I saw Mammaw and Papaw. They came in through the back and were in terrible shape. As mean as Papaw was, he didn't deserve this. Mammaw looked red-eyed and confused. They had lost a child. She couldn't invent a salve for this kind of hurt.

When Dad saw his parents, he hurried over and set up chairs for each of them. He asked Mom to get them coffee. I was watching someone I didn't know.

Even odder than seeing Dad as a loving brother and caring son was the image that hit me as I walked into the formal room (what I called the "body" room) of the mortuary. I was older now and didn't need to be lifted up to see inside the casket. I glanced at Uncle Carl lying there, and from that angle, me standing at the foot of the coffin (a Batesville solid maple with beige crepe interior), Carl looked exactly like my dad. I hurried to find Jamie and made him stand in the exact same spot.

"He looks like Dad," he said.

"*Exactly* like him."

I gave myself a few minutes to fantasize that it *was* Dad and felt surprisingly unhappy, even sad. Dad was violent, but I didn't want him in a casket. I didn't know what Jamie was hoping, but both his fists were clenched.

My big brother was too cool for me to hug, so I wrapped my sweaty fingers around his narrow wrist. We stood there a long time.

The next day we followed Kilner and Son's black hearse through Elk Grove and onto Highway 64 for the slow ride through Galesburg and then up County Line Road to tiny Clover Hill Cemetery, where all the Petersons were buried. Seeing the hearse in front of us and all the cars pulling to the side of the road as we passed overwhelmed me with grief—for Carl and Aunt Evelyn, for Tim, Ben, and Paul, and for everything that constantly went wrong. I cried for the first time that year. I was afraid I might never stop.

CHAPTER TEN

During the first week of summer break between fifth and sixth grades, all the kids in Galesburg were out on their ten-speed bikes or playing softball behind the community building over by Granda's.

The Whitmore kids and I were playing army. We had a stash of plastic weapons (no real guns allowed) hidden under the pine bushes and snacks concealed in a dead log out in the field behind our house. There were two teams, five kids each, hiding from one another, trying to steal snacks and weapons.

If you were shot or captured, you were marched, blindfolded with a red bandana tied around your head, to the Whitmores' white wooden shed, where you sat on a plastic milk crate until you got so bored and hot you just walked out and started playing like you hadn't even been captured in the first place.

Kyle and I were rounding the corner of Mrs. Shaw's house when we spied Jamie and his friends playing basketball. Jamie had just gotten a brand-new Wilson basketball hoop and backboard that Uncle Dale had nailed up on the telephone pole that stood beside our driveway. Jamie was too old to play army. He played basketball instead. For the past year the only time I saw him without a ball or a pole-vaulting pole in his hand, he was either eating or in church.

Kyle and I decided to engage in a surprise attack. He would shoot off an impressive amount of popgun bangs from his silver pistols while I ran onto the court and streaked off with the ball. This shit made Jamie so mad, but I couldn't help myself.

Kyle and I were poised for attack when Dad's pickup unexpectedly squealed into the driveway. Kyle took off running toward his own yard. We all knew there was no messing around when Dad was home.

I didn't know why Dad was there, but it couldn't be good. He never came home in the middle of a weekday.

I went into the house to pee, and when I came out of the bathroom, Dad was standing in the kitchen staring out the window at Jamie and his friends, who had resumed their game. They were laughing out there and calling to each other: "Throw it to me." "Over here, man, I'm clear." Dad was grinding his teeth, his jaw moving slightly back and forth. He was thinking something mean.

When Dad was little, he didn't play; he worked. On the farm, he was up before dawn doing chores, walked to school in shoes that were too small, and came home to more work. His family was so poor that at Christmastime Dad pulled a wagon into the field and filled it with old corncobs, which could be used in fireplaces for fuel. He sold them in town to get money so his five brothers could have a present for Christmas.

I think those memories filled him with hate when he saw us kids having a carefree summer day or unwrapping a Christmas box and discovering exactly what we'd circled in the Sears catalog.

Dad slammed down the glass of iced tea he'd been holding and raced for the side door. I moved to the kitchen window, knowing that Jamie was in for it. I didn't want to watch, but I stood there anyway.

"Goddamn it, Jamie, you stupid idiot. You can't track mud all over the damn driveway," Dad's voice thundered out the door. The boys scattered, and Jamie's face was scarlet. The sides of his eyes turned down and his jaw was tight to keep tears from coming. There wasn't any mud on the driveway.

Jamie tried to say "I didn't know there was mud there," but Dad interrupted with "Shut up, you sissy," which was the worst thing you could be called in front of Wayne Brooks and Duane Nelson.

Dad grabbed the sledgehammer that was lying against the side of the house and beat that basketball hoop to the ground. He pounded it until the metal rim was twisted beyond recognition and the backboard lay in splinters. Then he threw the sledgehammer on top of the mess and said, "That's the end of that." *The end of what?* I wondered. *The end of the basketball game? The end of the world?* It was definitely the end of something.

Jamie's friends grabbed the basketball and headed over to the church to shoot hoops. Jamie stood there with tears of humiliation and rage rolling down his cheeks.

Dad turned on him. "That's right. Cry like a girl. I should make you wear dresses." It made no sense, and that was what worried me most.

Jamie took off on JoAnn's bike that was parked on the back patio, his white T-shirt still tucked into the back pocket of his jeans. I watched him pedal down the sidewalk as fast as he could and out of sight.

Dad opened the back of his truck and took out pallets of bright orange marigolds and purple pansies, a hoe, and a shovel.

He had come home to plant flowers.

I watched from the living room window as Dad roughed up the dirt along the driveway, dug a series of holes, and delicately pulled the plants from their small plastic crates, placing them gently in holes, carefully covering their roots with dirt.

When he finished, the driveway looked warm and welcoming.

The next morning at breakfast Jamie was mean to me. I tried to scoot behind his chair to get to my place at the breakfast table and he shoved his chair back and pinned me against the wall. It knocked the wind out of me. When he finally let me go, I was holding my chest, not so much in pain as in shock. Jamie was changing.

One Saturday morning Julie and I decided to clean the mortuary. We needed to earn money to buy the new Carpenters album *A Song for You*.

At Kilner and Sons we took the body elevator down to the basement to pick up cleaning materials. The doors of the elevator were outside the mortuary so a dead person could be rolled in from the parking lot. We stood inside as it slowly rattled to the basement—the one place I knew for sure Sarah Keeler and I had both been.

The supply room, which was cold and damp, freaked us out, so we picked up Endust, Windex, and paper towels as fast as we could. The door to the embalming room was closed. We yelled "Hello" to Max as we ran by and he began clinking his tools to scare us.

"Very funny," Julie yelled, but it unnerved me.

We rattled back up in the body elevator.

While we were cleaning, we heard the elevator clattering its way down to the basement. I looked over at Julie.

"Somebody corked," I said. Julie shrugged. "Who do you think it is?" I asked.

"I don't know," Julie said.

"Aren't you curious?" I asked.

"Not really." She squirted the window with Windex.

I walked to the top of the stairway and leaned down. I saw Hugh Kilner, Dave's brother, pull a gurney out of the elevator. It was a person covered in a black velvet drape with red trim. Hugh rolled it into the embalming room.

I turned to Julie. "It's a body, all right."

She started laughing. "Monica, there are bodies here every day."

I walked away from the staircase and sprayed Endust on the wooden podium that held the guest book. I had just finished dusting it when I heard the elevator going back up.

"It's going back up," I said.

"Hugh's putting the gurney back in the van," she said.

It didn't matter how many times I heard the elevator or saw a family walking into the office to make arrangements, I wanted to know who had died and how. Was the person young, old, or in between? Had they left children behind?

I sat down on the third step from the top and listened to noises coming from the embalming room. I couldn't imagine what all the clinking sounds were. The week before, Julie had offered to take me in there while Max was working, but I wasn't ready for that.

Later in the afternoon Joan drove us to Lewisburg to buy *A Song for You*. We listened to it in Julie's bedroom as we lay on her green shag carpet, our bare feet propped up on her bed. We read the lyrics off the inside of the album cover and sang "Top of the World" together.

On slow days at the mortuary Max took Julie and me for rides in the back of the hearse, where the casket usually sat. People always pulled to the side of the road when they saw us coming, even though there was no casket back there. One time Mr. Bartlett jumped off his riding lawn mower, took off his green John Deere hat, and saluted us. Julie and I peered out the long, skinny back windows: a dead person's perspective.

We made intricate plans regarding who would drive us to our graves and which route we would take. I, of course, chose Dave to drive, with one complete trip down Main Street, through Bob's Burgers drive-through, and on to Maple Creek Cemetery to be buried next to Sarah Keeler. Julie, who was more sophisticated than I was, chose Mick Jagger to drive and just a quick trip through the Dew Drop Inn liquor store drive-through window. She figured it wouldn't matter that she was underage if she were the one in the box.

Aside from rides in the hearse, I also took rides with my mom in her car—not rides to the grocery store or the pharmacy—scenic rides.

There was no better afternoon for Mom than a Henry Mancini cassette drowning out the crickets while we coasted along Ohio back roads, her foot off the gas, watching for bright red cardinals and spotted deer.

Mom and I were noodling along with the windows open one summer afternoon when I asked about my birth. I knew the story, but I hadn't heard it since I was little.

She smiled. "Well, you came early, for one thing. You weren't supposed to come for a few days, and it was the night before Uncle Larry and Aunt Betty's wedding. I was excited because I thought I was going to make it to the wedding, but around four in the morning, here you came. I got your dad up and we headed to the hospital."

"Were you excited?" I asked.

"Becky was only eighteen months old, so we had our hands full. We'd only planned on having three children but, suddenly, there you were." Mom pulled the car over to watch a hawk circle overhead. I hadn't known that part of the story.

I looked at her, confused. "What?"

"We were planning on three children, but I guess you wanted to come too." She stuck her head out of the window, trying to track that bird.

"I wasn't planned?" I asked.

"We didn't know it was *you*. When I found out I was pregnant, Becky wasn't even walking yet." She laid the back of her head on the windowsill and looked straight up. "We were finished with babies."

I was trying to figure out how to process this information, when Mom pulled her head in, found a comb in her purse, and smoothed down the top of her hair.

"When I realized I was pregnant again, I cried for six weeks straight. I waited as long as possible to put on maternity clothes, but when I finally *had* to, I saw Genevieve Linsley at the post office and she said, 'Oh, Patricia, I'm so sorry.' I could have died from humiliation. But what was I supposed to do? I was stuck. I felt like white trash, having one kid right on top of the other."

She looked over and saw my eyebrows pressed together. "We didn't know it was *you*," she repeated, pulling the car back onto the road and leaving the hawk behind. "We didn't call you Monica until you were two years old. We just kept saying 'Get Baby' or 'Baby needs a bottle.'" I was startled, so she clarified. "Babies aren't really people until they're at least two years old."

"What are they, giraffes?" I asked.

"You know what I mean," she said. I didn't.

"Becky was supposed to be the baby of the family," she said, "but it doesn't matter now."

I wasn't sure what had shifted, but something had. My chin started to quiver, but I couldn't figure out why I was so upset. It wasn't such a bad story.

We drove along in silence until Mom popped in a 1950s gospel cassette. I hated gospel. The music started:

Operator?
Information.
Give me Jesus on the line.

If I got Jesus on the line, I'd sure as hell ask why he sent me to Galesburg. My family didn't even want anybody else. Surely there were people somewhere in the world who were hoping for a baby girl. Why squeeze me in here?

I put my arm on the windowsill and rested my chin on top. The hot Ohio breeze was making my forehead sweaty. I tried to think of happy things, like playing Checkers with Jamie or riding my bike around the firehouse parking lot, but the tears came anyway.

CHAPTER ELEVEN

For most of my friends, summer vacation was something they wished would never end. For me, it couldn't end soon enough.

One of those summers, Mom found a key to Dad's truck and secretly made a copy at Ben Franklin's Five-and-Dime. Dad didn't think the government needed to know how much money he made, so he kept large amounts of cash in bank bags stashed under the driver's seat of his pickup. Mom knew because she'd helped Dad with his bookkeeping when we were little.

Mom needed to burgle Dad's truck because if he was mad at her or us, he cut off her grocery money. She'd pace the house wringing her hands, wondering how she was going to pay for everything, until Dad relented and gave her some money.

In similar fashion, every week Mom made the four of us go into the bedroom and wake Dad so he could give us lunch money. This made him irate. Every Monday at breakfast I couldn't eat, knowing we'd have to wake him.

At the last possible minute before the bus came, we'd walk into the bedroom and stare at him.

He'd open his eyes and snarl, "What do you want now?"

"Lunch money," one of us would blurt out.

"Goddamn moochers," he'd yell, throwing off the covers and swinging his legs off the side of the bed. Dad slept in boxer shorts and a white T-shirt, so I worried about the gap in the front of those shorts as he bent down to grab his wire-rimmed aviator glasses off the side table. Then he'd walk over to his crumpled jeans and search around in the pockets for money.

"It never stops," he'd complain. "'I need money for this, I need money for that.' All you do is stand around with your hands out."

By then we were waiting outside the bedroom because the bus was going to be there any minute. Finally he'd toss our lunch money, coins and dollar bills scattering, on top of the stereo. I'd grab my two dollars and fifty cents, feeling like I'd just robbed someone, because that's exactly how Dad felt—robbed.

By copying that key, Mom was stealing a little financial security.

The heists took place during the week when Dad came home from work just long enough to change out of his jeans and into polyester stretch pants and a nice dress shirt so he could get back to Elk Grove for a Rotary Club meeting.

He drove Mom's Cutlass at night, leaving his locked pickup in the driveway. No one locked cars in Mason County. They threw keys under the front seat and went about their business. But Dad couldn't take any chances.

After Dad pulled out, Mom asked me to stand at the end of our driveway as a lookout. Out by the road, I'd anxiously scan the horizon in case Dad forgot his tie clip or wallet and turned around to get it. Then I'd eyeball Mom, who'd be poking around under his seat. I didn't know why they had such big problems, but I knew I shouldn't have been standing there.

One night I looked over and saw Mom's car heading back up the street.

"He's coming back," I screamed. "Mom, get out of there. He's coming." If he caught her, he'd probably beat her to death. I ran up the driveway as Mom slammed the door of the pickup. We both raced around the house to the back door. I hustled into my bedroom as Mom opened the refrigerator and looked inside.

Out my bedroom window, I watched Dad climb out of the Cutlass and walk over to the truck. *He knew. He had to know.* He tried the driver's door, found it locked, and walked back to the Cutlass. To my surprise, Mom stepped outside.

"Why'd you come back?" she asked.

"No reason," he said.

"Did you leave something?"

"I thought I forgot to lock the truck," he said, climbing into the car.

Mom came back inside the house. I met her in the dining room as he was pulling back out.

"That was close," I said.

"Too close. He thought the truck was unlocked," she said. "I think I was the one who locked it when I slammed the door. Let's forget it for now."

On another night a little while later, Dad hadn't come back—yet. I stood at the end of the dark driveway, hopping up and down, saying, "Hurry, hurry," under my breath. Once Mom was inside the truck, it wasn't a quick transaction. She couldn't take the money out of one bag, or Dad would figure something was up. She had to steal a little from each. Also, the bags had to be returned to their exact original position because he was wily and suspicious.

Mom helped herself to twenties, tens, and fives, swiping an extra twenty for me.

It was unnerving stealing from my father, because I always had the feeling he was watching me.

I put my dirty money in my flowered jewelry box with the plastic ballerina, who twirled in front of a diamond-shaped mirror and collapsed flat when I closed the lid.

The extra money helped Mom relax about the future. She wouldn't go without as long as he didn't trade in that pickup.

✦ ✦ ✦

In the beginning of that summer a tornado came through around five o'clock in the morning, waking everyone up and sending us hurrying to the basement. On the way down, I stopped in the hallway and called Granda. It took her a while to get to the phone because I was waking her out of a deep sleep and her bad hip always slowed her down.

"This had better be good," she said when she picked up the phone, breathing hard.

"Granda, there's a tornado warning. You need to get over here and get in the basement," I urged.

"Honey, there's not a tornado strong enough to blow my fat ass out of this trailer. Don't worry about your granda."

"Please come over," I pleaded.

"You get yourself in the basement. I'll be just fine. Now go on, honey, I don't want you talking on the phone when there's lightning around. It could come through the phone and kill both of us." I reluctantly hung up, grabbed Buddy by the collar, and headed to the basement.

The storm blew in quickly and was so violent that all eight of the Whitmores (who had no basement of their own) came running over in their pajamas to join us in our basement. If it was too dangerous for Dad to grab his movie camera and speed away, it was the real deal. The entire town could blow away.

I sat on the filthy cement floor in my nightgown, with Buddy situated between my knees. I held on to her brown leather collar with both hands. Our neighbor's dog, Buttons, ran away during a storm and was never seen again. I imagined that crazy-eyed black-and-white mutt tumbling and swirling around inside a giant black tornado and landing somewhere in Pennsylvania.

The idea of Buddy being lost and wandering the countryside looking for us was the saddest, most heart-wrenching scenario I could imagine. I held on tight.

The worst of the storm blew through with a sudden dip in temperature, and the pressure dropped so fast, my ears popped. Sheets of rain pelted the windows, and hail pinged off the roof and the top of our car. I was so keyed up, I had diarrhea, but I couldn't leave the basement to go to the toilet.

Dad was running up and down the basement stairs, reporting the blow-by-blow with a transistor radio pressed against his ear. First he was standing at the top of the stairs looking out the back door.

Then he hurried back down and said, "There's a tornado southwest of Elk Grove. A house was hit." He raced back up.

Soon he'd holler back down, "They think it's heading this way."

I wished he'd shut the hell up. His commentary was making a tense situation a hundred times worse. I was petrified, worried, and freezing all at the same time. I hugged Buddy and quietly sang the prayer from church:

> *Praise God, from whom all blessings flow;*
> *Praise Him, all creatures here below;*
> *Praise Him above, ye heavenly host;*
> *Praise Father, Son, and Holy Ghost.*
> *Amen.*

I didn't want to meet the Father, the Son, or the Holy Ghost that day, so I praised them and hoped for a reprieve.

When the lights went out, my terror level shot up and I braced for the big hit. I pictured the wooden ceiling above us splintering into tiny toothpicks and all of us being sucked up into the furious tornado that Dad had reported was just outside of Galesburg. Mom turned on the one flashlight we had and threw blankets over our heads. Buddy was sweating from the end of her tongue, saliva dripping onto my leg.

The wind became stronger, and suddenly we felt a thud that

bounced me about three inches off the floor. My heart was racing and Buddy was whining and struggling to get away. I held her tighter.

"Something fell," Martha said.

"Something's definitely down," Dad confirmed, bolting back up the basement steps.

I looked up and saw the house still over our heads, so that was good.

"Two houses destroyed in Elk Grove," Dad yelled down the stairs. "But they're not saying anything about what happened here." We weren't going to see the sun come up, I was sure of it. We'd be dead, buried under debris that would include our shitty oven that never worked and all of Mom's fancy furniture.

Five or ten minutes later the wind died down and, miraculously, the rain stopped.

"Looks like it's headed over to Harrisburg," Dad reported, setting down the radio. All I knew about Harrisburg was that I'd seen an enormous billboard that read JESUS IS LORD OVER HARRISBURG right outside of town. If that were true, they'd probably be okay.

We climbed up the basement stairs. Buddy was jumpy but had settled down enough that I could let go of her.

Dad ran outside to see what had fallen. I was dreading the moment when I'd discover what the wind had destroyed.

The sun was just coming up and the clouds were creating a spectacular sunrise, complete with thick rays of light shooting up in the east. Through the sunrise, I saw the back of the storm, black angry clouds swirling toward Harrisburg.

The backyard was littered with leaves and branches. But when we walked around to the side of the house, we saw our maple tree, one hundred feet tall and fifteen feet around, lying on its side. It gave me gooseflesh to see its heavy, wet branches crunched onto the highway and its scraggly long roots sticking seven feet up in the air. Nothing that big should be on its side.

The Whitmores and the Griswolds were looking at the damage and saying, "You were lucky, Glen. If that tree had fallen the other way, it would have crushed the house."

That caught my attention. Smashed to smithereens was not the way I wanted to go. I loved trees, but I looked at the remaining two maples with absolute dread.

That night I heard Dad say, "I'm gonna take those other two trees down tomorrow while we have the city out there hauling away all those branches."

"You aren't touching those trees. We'll have no shade at all," Mom said.

"Would you rather have them come down on the house?" he asked.

"Don't be so dramatic," Mom answered.

"You'll think 'dramatic' when they do come down and we're hauling dead kids outta here," he said.

"You aren't touching those trees," Mom said. I heard a door slam.

I didn't like my father, but I trusted him when it came to disasters. After all, he was an expert.

The first night after the tree fell, I stayed up as long as I could, straining to hear creaking that would indicate the trees were falling, giving me time to get the girls up and out of the house. From that night on I imagined those two trees hovering like death's hand, ready to swoop us up in the night; scoop us up while we were sleeping, only to be deposited on Max Cooper's embalming table.

In the fall I was turning eleven and starting sixth grade and, most important, JoAnn, Becky, and I were going to get our own rooms. Dad hired a contractor, Mr. Thorton, to turn the attic into three bedrooms.

It was just in time because I had finally, and for no reason I could explain, quit wetting the bed. One morning I woke up dry and was never wet again. I'd pictured that day arriving with a marching band or an expensive gift from Sears, but it snuck in like any other day. I was finally liberated from the moldy pee bed.

Mr. Thorton worked up there all summer, and when he was done, I was surprised to see the ceilings were triangular-shaped, just like the roof.

In an uncharacteristic move, Mom allowed each of us to pick out furniture, colors, and carpets for our own rooms.

JoAnn chose black walls and psychedelic black-and-white swirly curtains. The curtains and her door were always closed. Becky chose light yellow with Mom's help and guidance. I went against Mom's advice, ordering pink shag carpet and outrageous wallpaper covered in bright orange and pink flowers. I also wanted my new twin bed built into the wall. The ceilings were so low that building a bed into the wall was a mistake, but we did it anyway. If I woke suddenly—and I often did—I banged my forehead when I sat up.

All three of us girls spent hours in the luxury and privacy of our own rooms. I could finally have friends stay overnight.

Toward the end of that summer, Mom wanted to go on a vacation. I didn't know why she was pushing it, since Dad had just paid for the new upstairs. Besides, he hated vacations, which is why we didn't take them. According to Dad, vacations were silly: a waste of time, and too expensive.

JoAnn had left on a European trip with her beloved French teacher, Mrs. Cleary, and her French class to have a wonderfully cultured time. She wouldn't be joining us.

Jamie would stay home so he wouldn't miss track practice. Mom told him to watch the house, but I doubted there'd be much watching between the smoking and drinking he had begun enjoying.

On Saturday, Dad, Mom, Becky, and I took off around seven in the morning in our old green station wagon and made it to a Holiday Inn near Gatlinburg, Tennessee, that night. Our vacation would be driving Mom all around the Smoky Mountains.

Mom was passionate about the Smokies. She'd spent years making the annual trek to Tennessee with Martha Whitmore, where they crept along mountain back roads oohing and aahing at the same breathtaking yet oddly monotonous scenery.

Mom was excited and wanted to ride along with her head sticking out the passenger window and her hair blowing—sniffing in the mountain air and admiring the rolling, forested panorama. It was beautiful. But I was eleven and I didn't care about riding up and down curvy roads searching for waterfalls. I was carsick most of the time, which made the trip excruciating. From their blank looks, it seemed Dad and Becky didn't care about mountains either, but there we were, zooming along Highway 641 straight through the Great Smoky Mountains National Park.

Mom was mad because Dad was driving like a maniac. When she stuck her head out the passenger window to admire a favorite mountain pass, there was so much wind from the speed of the car, she couldn't even open her eyes. She looked like Buddy hanging out the window on her way to Dr. Dobbs's office for her shots.

Mom turned to Dad, her hair sticking up on one side. "I don't suppose you could slow down."

"Why?" he asked.

"So I can see the mountains." Her teeth were clenched. Dad was driving between sixty and seventy miles an hour, while the speed limit was posted at forty. He smiled.

"I can see fine," he said, not slowing down. Tears rolled down Mom's cheeks.

I couldn't remember ever seeing Mom cry or Dad so happy.

Becky and I were in the backseat bored out of our minds and

trying not to piss anyone off. If we had to pee or eat, we still wouldn't say anything. We wished we were invisible. Only we weren't—we were trapped in the car between the hatred my parents felt for each other, and probably for us. We couldn't do anything but ride it out.

Problem was, it was hard to ride it out when your ride just turned off the highway and directly into oncoming traffic.

In the next instant a small Honda plowed into my door, throwing all of us to the right and showering us with glass. The impact was so loud, I couldn't hear anything afterward.

Dad jumped out and ran to the lady in the Honda, not bothering to look back to see if Becky and I were okay. I was right when I decided in fourth grade that Dad wouldn't love me at my death scene. It was actually worse: He wouldn't even notice.

Mom leaned over the front seat, grabbing us to check for injuries. Luckily, Becky had been reading *Little House in the Big Woods* by Laura Ingalls Wilder and had had the book in front of her face. The glass hadn't cut her, but there were tiny bits of it covering her hair. Oddly enough, she sparkled.

At the exact moment of impact, I had leaned forward to tell Mom I'd seen a Holiday Inn sign, so I wasn't injured by my door, which was now a jagged *V* crunched into the spot where I'd been sitting. I'd missed being killed by inches, but Dad was still busy checking on the other driver.

We looked outside and saw him squatting beside the open door of the smashed Honda, talking to the attractive young redhead sitting dazed in the driver's seat, the front of her car still fused with my door. She had a large purplish bump on her forehead, but I didn't see any blood. When we climbed out of the station wagon, we saw that the entire right side of it was demolished and the windows on my side were blown out.

The next morning Dad insisted we drive the car back to Ohio. We looked at him in disbelief, but when he climbed into the driver's seat, we climbed in too, wiping broken glass off the seats with Becky's yellow sweatshirt and laying a beach towel on the glass-strewn floor. Dad wanted to get home to cook steaks for the Rotary Club the next night. Mom's dream vacation, and I could have predicted this, was a catastrophe.

We clanked and clattered along at considerably less speed. Mom finally saw her beloved mountains, and there wasn't any glass to obscure her view. The wind blew our hair, and my door was shoved in so far that I was forced to sit right next to Becky, which pissed her off because every once in a while I'd accidentally touch her with my arm or leg. "Don't touch me," she'd growl.

We assumed the worst had already happened, and I was relieved in some weird way that the accident had actually occurred. It was a physical manifestation of what had already been going on inside the car. The outside now matched the inside—damaged beyond repair.

We drove without stopping until dusk. Dad picked a different route to get home, one that avoided the highway so we wouldn't be pulled over for driving an unsafe vehicle. Problem was, he didn't know where we were. He'd taken a wrong turn somewhere and our crippled car was suddenly headed straight up a steep mountain road.

Becky broke the silence. "Where are we going?"

"A shortcut," Dad said with a grin.

Our back wheels were spinning, trying to get traction on the gravel, so Dad gunned it and we fishtailed up that road. As we swerved to and fro, I could hear pieces of shattered glass rolling back and forth in the frame of my smashed door.

Becky and I clutched the bottom of our seat. It was getting dark and we were starving, but Dad kept flooring the car up that twisty dirt road. Any dumb-ass could see there wasn't anything up there, but we didn't say a word, especially when all it would have taken to shut us up for good was a turn of the steering wheel.

It was getting even darker on that mountain, where there were no streetlights or stores, but I could still make out the crappiest houses I'd ever seen in my life. I'd never seen such poverty—shacks with faded laundry strewn out in all directions, and startled faces coming to peer out of cracked windows that were covered in thick dust from the gravel road, just to see who was crazy enough to be driving up there. These houses scared me as much as Dad's driving. He was humming Bill Monroe's "Blue Moon of Kentucky" even though we were still in Tennessee.

More than halfway up, Dad happily announced, "We're almost out of gas. We'll have to coast down."

This sent me into an inappropriate laughing fit. I wasn't allowed to get angry, and I couldn't cry, so I laughed—a lot. Becky wanted to murder me and kept hissing, "Shut up," but I couldn't.

Minutes later, when we came to the top of the mountain, Dad killed the motor, threw the car in neutral, and let us roll down the other side.

He refused to hit the brakes as we accelerated around corners so steep that when I looked out my glassless window, I was peering straight down into an abyss. The steeper the road, the faster we went.

I stopped laughing.

Later, the three of us agreed that Dad had probably wanted us dead that night—he'd had the perfect opportunity—and yet, we made it down the mountain. I'd never hated anyone more than I hated Dad, and I swore I would scare him to death someday. I would scare him so badly, he would never recover.

Part III

IT'S MY TURN

Chapter Twelve

Dad had pulled some horrendous stunts, but when he fucked with Mom's love of the Great Smoky Mountains, he'd gone too far.

After rattling home in that demolished station wagon without so much as a stroll through Cades Cove to show for it, Mom plotted her escape.

She secretly decided to establish a career for herself and finally divorce the bastard.

When she was twenty, Mom skipped college to marry Dad. She later told us kids, "I would have died if I hadn't married Glen Peterson," which made her even more confusing to me. But now her decision to give up college left her with a marriage in shambles and no road out.

Mom's father had begged her to wait on marriage and think of her education first. But Grandpa Riley, as I'd known him, didn't hold much sway, since he'd abandoned Granda, Mom, and Dale for his young secretary some twenty-six years earlier.

Mom married Dad.

Grandpa Riley offered to pay for college if she ever wanted to go, and now, at thirty-eight years old, she was taking him up on it.

When Dad found out Mom was going back to school, he screeched, "By God, I'm not paying for it," thinking that would be the end of it. He knew she didn't have money of her own.

"My dad's paying for it," she said. "It won't cost you a dime."

"I doubt that," he said, trying to think of another roadblock to throw in front of her.

"I don't care what you think; I'm going."

"The hell you are," Dad said. I was creeping down from upstairs in case Mom needed help. It sounded like Dad wasn't going to get his way, and that's when he usually started throwing things. I sat on the bottom step.

"Our entire marriage, you've done exactly what *you* wanted to do," Mom told him. "Now it's *my* turn, and you can't stop me."

Right on cue, Dad ripped the closet door off its hinges, and threw it at their cherry wood bedroom set, leaving a permanent scar sliced across the wood.

Mom walked down the hall, snatched her keys off the counter, and said to Dad, "Tear the whole place down. You don't hold any power over me. Not anymore."

She walked out, climbed into her car, and squealed out of the driveway. I was still cowering on the step. When Dad resumed hurling things, I snuck back upstairs. I knew nothing would ever be the same after that night, and it never was. My family, which was never much of a family anyway, was starting to fall apart.

Mom signed up for classes at Wright State University in Dayton, fifty miles north of us. After being a stay-at-home mom for sixteen years, she would now be a college freshman working toward her bachelor's degree as an elementary-education major. (Her real love was American history, but she decided that teaching school would be the easiest way to support herself when she left Dad.)

Uncle Dale came by to drive Mom to her first day of classes. Becky and I walked Mom, nauseous and weepy from fright, out to her car. This was the biggest risk she'd ever taken, and she was terrified of failing.

"I'll bet they don't get past Elk Grove," Becky told me.

"They'll make it to Dayton, but she'll never make it to class." I followed Becky back inside.

Shaky and pale, Mom made it to class. Becky and I cooked her dinner that night: fried chicken and mashed potatoes.

We fell into a routine that fall, Mom driving to Dayton three days a week and either Becky in eighth grade or me, now in sixth, doing our homework with her at the kitchen table.

She wasn't scared anymore. Letting her hair fall in soft curls around her face instead of pinning it back, and wearing khaki pants, polo shirts, and cardigans, she was enjoying being a freshman.

I rode up to Dayton with Mom when I was on spring break and sat outside her class, reading, until she came out. I was proud of her, especially when I looked in her classroom and saw her taking notes among students almost seventeen years her junior.

Jamie later enrolled at Wright State too, but he wasn't there very long.

According to the dean's office, Jamie threw a party in his dorm room, where he decided to spit lighter fluid out of his mouth and then torch it with a match, just like Gene Simmons did onstage with KISS. Unlike Gene Simmons, Jamie caught the curtains and his mattress on fire. He was immediately expelled.

The next morning I was surprised to see him sitting at the breakfast table with no eyelashes or eyebrows, the front of his hair singed into a million tiny curlicues.

No one was speaking. I didn't ask.

"He'll find another school," Mom told me later that night while Jamie was smoking pot in the basement. Unlike Mom, I could smell it coming up through the registers in the floor.

Julie and I loved Jamie. If she spent the night, we stayed awake until we heard his car squeal into our driveway, then we'd run downstairs to greet him. He was always loaded.

One night we knocked on his bedroom door.

"Enter," he said.

"Jamie, how's it goin'?" I asked as we sat down on his red carpet in our pajamas.

"Young ladies, what's up?" He grinned, straining to sit up. His eyes were tiny slits.

"Your lip is busted," I noticed.

"No kidding?" He shook his head and laughed, lying back down on his pillow. "Man, I think I laid my motorcycle down too. Paul had to bring me home." (Our cousin Paul partied as much as Jamie did.)

"Holy shit, where's your bike?" I asked.

"That is a very good question," he said. "Now you girls go upstairs and let me ponder it."

"Could you drive us into town tomorrow?" I asked. "If Mom lets you borrow the car?"

"If you quit talking so loud, I'll drive you anywhere," he said.

"Okay," I whispered. "We have to be at Pizza Palace by noon to meet everybody."

Jamie waved his right hand in the air making the *Okay* sign. "Good night," I added as we ran upstairs, laughing. I was straight-laced, but Jamie looked like he was having a pretty good time.

He spent a few more months living with us, until he made the monumental mistake of taking a job at Dad's store. I stopped by one afternoon to hear Dad yelling at him in front of all the customers, "That is the stupidest goddamn thing I've ever seen." Jamie was staring at Dad, eyes brimming with tears. He was taller than Dad by at least four inches, and his arms were rippled with taut muscles from all the pole-vaulting. He could've kicked Dad's ass, but I could tell by his expression, he didn't know that.

"Only an idiot would think of doing something that stupid," Dad continued. He turned to me and said, "This dummy just rested an extension ladder on my front window." He pointed to Jamie.

"I was going to lengthen it—," Jamie started to say.

"Shut up. No one wants to hear your excuses." Dad picked up the ladder and stormed off to the back of the store. All the customers were staring.

I turned back to Jamie, but he was already outside, slamming the door of his red pickup and tearing out of the parking lot. No doubt he was heading to the liquor store.

A month later Jamie packed all his clothes, some blankets, a pillow, his albums, and his guitar and drove west. He joined a friend in Salt Lake City, where he took a job running telephone cable through the Rocky Mountains. Despite the clean mountain air, his newfound love of rock climbing, and being a safe distance from Dad, his drinking was becoming a huge problem.

One afternoon, when JoAnn was a senior, I smelled wet paint coming from her room, which was directly across from mine. She didn't like to be disturbed, but I was curious. I knocked softly on her door.

"WHAT?" she yelled.

"Can I come in?" I asked politely. She didn't say anything, but all of a sudden her door swung open and she gestured for me to enter. I looked around. She was painting "BJK" in red, white, and blue all over her walls. Each letter was a different color.

"What's BJK?" I asked, easing myself down onto her bed, hoping she'd let me stay a minute.

"Best tennis player in the world," she said, painting an exclamation point after one of the BJKs.

"Who?" I asked.

"Billie Jean King. She's paving the way." JoAnn made a circle in the air with her paintbrush. "And since you're a girl, you should know who she is. She's changing the world." This was the most JoAnn had ever said to me in one sitting. I tried prolonging our conversation.

"What's she doing?" I asked. JoAnn picked up a *Sports Illustrated* and tossed it onto my lap. On the cover was a brunette woman in aviator glasses and a short white dress tossing a ball into the air, her tennis racket blurred in the shot as she prepared to smack the ball.

I didn't recognize her, which confirmed my nerd status. JoAnn was way cooler.

"Don't tell Mom I painted my room," she said.

"There's no way I'd tell," I said, handing back the magazine. JoAnn walked out with the paint can and brushes. Our conversation was over.

The following weekend JoAnn drove to Cincinnati to see Billie Jean King play tennis, and came home talking to Mom so fast I couldn't understand what she was saying. I just stood there and smiled. I'd never seen JoAnn so animated. As I listened, I decided I was starting to really like her. She was nothing like me; she was nothing like any of us. We might not be friends, but I would watch her and try to be cool.

Tennis rackets, small bright green balls, and tennis skirts were suddenly all over the house. JoAnn took tennis lessons from Oliver Bloom, who followed her around like a puppy.

Unfortunately for Oliver, JoAnn began dating Bill Lawrence, a hopelessly gorgeous boy, six-foot-five and thin as a rail. He had curly blond hair and a Donald Sutherland-type smile. He was the cutest guy I'd ever seen. When they went to the Turnabout Dance together, JoAnn wore a short velvet dress and platform shoes. Bill wore a lime green suit and tie and hovered several feet over her. Julie and I huddled on the couch while Mom took Polaroids of them.

That same winter, Becky was changing. Her body was shapely now and her blond hair and blue eyes looked less like a farm kid and more like a stunning teenager. In the kitchen one night while Mom, Becky, and I were cooking, Mom said to her, "I want you to be careful around your dad."

Both of us looked up.

"What are you saying?" Becky asked.

Mom didn't glance up from the lettuce she was tearing. "I don't like the way he looks at you, that's all."

"How's he look at me?" she asked.

Mom shrugged. "I'm just saying, I don't trust him. I want to you stay away from him." Becky was staring at Mom, and I was looking back and forth between the two.

Becky looked at me. "What are you gawking at?"

I turned back to washing the potatoes. My heart raced. Becky was chopping carrots as fast as her knife would go.

Becky was getting prettier, and I was pretty ugly. My front teeth were now in a crooked, unattractive overbite, my hair was greasy five minutes after I washed it, I couldn't shave my knees without gouging pink oval chunks out of my own flesh, and I'd started my period on a tragic trip to Rocky Fork State Park with the entire family in the station wagon. I didn't know how to take care of my constantly changing body, and no one was explaining any of it.

As I got uglier, I got funnier. Which was lucky.

I began acting in all the school plays, and was a good singer, which gave me hope. Julie and I spent less time at the mortuary and more time in the school auditorium. Julie was a good singer too.

I joined a drama group called the White Creek Players. Every summer we put on plays in an enormous barn west of Elk Grove.

I was tall, gawky, and a terrible dancer, even though I'd been taking baton-twirling lessons from my friend Susan's mom in their two-car garage. I wanted to be poised like Susan.

I practiced baton all the time, sitting in front of the television watching *The Brady Bunch* or *F Troop*. I'd twirl the smooth silver baton through every single finger and back again. In the backyard I twirled to songs I'd sing, throwing the baton high into the air and then running in the opposite direction until it landed on the grass nearby. But that wasn't dancing.

Turned out, my lousy dancing came in handy because it was funny, and funny at White Creek was great. Mrs. Monroe, who'd created the White Creek Players, told me that I was a "character actor" and that they were the most important ones.

"Anyone can be beautiful, but very few people can do comedy," she told me. "And *you* can do comedy." She squeezed my shoulder, not realizing she'd just given me an invaluable gift: support for my pea-size self-esteem, and a career goal.

That summer I played a girl named Plain Jane, whom no one ever noticed, but she ended up becoming a huge star, just like I was planning to do. We sang "Applause, Applause," only with the words "Plain Jane, Plain Jane."

At the end of the performance there was an awards ceremony. I received the Junior White Creek Players Award for outstanding participant and the Richard Graves Award for talent and commitment. Rich was the music director at White Creek and was loved for his sense of humor and his enormous talent as a musician and actor. It was the best and most important moment of my life.

The next day my picture was finally in the *Elk Grove Courier*, and not only was I alive, I was a winner.

I began buying every Broadway album I could afford with the money Mom slipped me from Dad's truck. I listened to *Guys and Dolls* and *Gypsy*, and dreamt about life as an actress in New York City.

Wendy Johnson lived in the neighborhood right behind Maple Creek Cemetery. Although we'd been in school and the White Creek Players together, I'd never been to her house.

Wendy was glamorous, especially the way she applied her brown eyeliner and soft peach lip gloss. She walked by scuffing along on the balls of her feet, heels never touching the ground. I was fascinated by her.

Wendy had long, thick brown hair and huge brown eyes with thick dark lashes, and knew more than I did about boys, about life. She was sophisticated. I wouldn't have been surprised if she'd made cocktails or had her legs waxed before doing her homework.

One afternoon she invited me over to ride a new Tri-Rod that her dad had brought home. It was a mini-dune-buggy with three fat wheels covered in impressive squiggly tread.

Carl Johnson owned the local Ford dealership, so Wendy always had cool things to ride. Wendy's mother, Marianne, had dyed blond hair, pale skin, and bright green eyes. I had never seen hair that color. Mrs. Johnson always wore skirts and stockings with sleek leather high heels. Mr. and Mrs. Johnson were older—almost old enough to be Wendy's grandparents. Their house was stark and modern. The walls were white, the furniture was white, even the doorknobs were white.

Wendy's room had a white wrought-iron bed with a pink see-through drape hanging down from the ceiling that covered the entire bed, and a thick white shag rug on her floor.

I thought it was strange that there were no toys in the house, even though Wendy was too big to play with toys. Maybe it wasn't the lack of toys as much as the lack of anything indicating that a child lived there. I couldn't imagine Wendy as a toddler or in elementary school trying to have fun in that perfect, sterile house.

We walked out to her driveway, where she told me to sit on the Tri-Rod.

"I don't know how to drive," I said. She started laughing.

"You aren't driving it, you're riding it. It's not a car," she said, rolling her eyes. "Turn the key down there by your knee." I turned the key and the motor started. I felt cool. I had never ridden anything like that before.

"Squeeze the right-hand grip and push it back toward you," she said, which I did, before hearing the rest of her instructions.

That buggy took off so fast, I didn't know what was happening. If I'd thought about applying the brakes, I wouldn't have known where they were anyway. Next thing I knew, I was upside down against a wire fence with the Tri-Rod spinning its wheels in the air right beside me. Wendy raced down the hill.

"You killed the rabbits!" she screamed.

"What?" I was trying to figure out where I was.

"The baby rabbits. There's a rabbit's nest right here," she said, kneeling down in the middle of her yard.

I felt nauseous. I had never killed an animal before, let alone an entire family. This was the worst thing I had ever done at someone else's house.

Wendy stood up with a small white bunny cupped between her palms. She was pushing away tears with the sleeve of her shirt. I was trying to extricate the back of my blouse from the wire fence so I could stand up and help collect the smashed rabbits.

"You missed them," she said, relieved. "They're fine."

"They're fine?" I asked.

Suddenly I was mad. What the hell was a mother rabbit doing building a nest right smack in the middle of someone's backyard? Why hadn't someone rolled over them with a lawn mower? Rabbits usually burrowed underground. Not at Wendy's.

I pulled myself up, more worried about her three-wheeler now that I knew the bunnies weren't dead. I asked Wendy to help me flip it over, but she was inhaling the soft white fur of each bunny. I heaved the Tri-Rod onto its wheels. There was a big dent in the front fender.

"I dented the fender," I hollered.

"Dad won't care," she said, not even looking up.

"It's seriously twisted," I reiterated.

"I don't care," she said, still distracted.

"Do you want me to drive it back up the hill?" I asked, praying she'd say no.

"Just leave it," she said.

I turned off the key and walked over to the rabbits. I knelt down on the grass, gently pulling aside the skinny green stalks. Baby rabbits were climbing all over each other.

"Where's the mom?" I asked.

"She hopped away when she saw you coming. That's what they do to protect their babies. They run away from the nest hoping you'll follow them and not find their little ones," she explained.

I had a headache. Luckily, Mom was pulling into the driveway in her new silver Pontiac.

"I'm sorry about your Tri-Rod," I said, "but I had a great time. Thanks for having me over." I wanted to be polite, but I couldn't wait to get out of there.

"See ya later," she said, not even walking me to the car—in Elk Grove, people always walked you to your car or the front gate or the back door. That was the neighborly thing to do. When Mom and I pulled out of the driveway, Wendy was still sitting in the grass next to the nest.

I hadn't seen her parents the whole time I'd been there. I wondered if they were even home.

"How was it?" Mom asked.

"I almost killed myself on a three-wheeler her dad bought her," I said, checking my knees for bruises.

Mom laughed and asked, "What does their house look like on the inside?"

"It's hollow," I said.

"Hollow?" she asked.

"It feels empty, but there's furniture in there," I said.

"I bet Mrs. Johnson has excellent taste," Mom imagined.

"If you like the color white," I said.

I was thinking about Wendy. I'd talked to her all those years at school, but I didn't really know her. I'd admired her sophistication, but I could see it came from taking care of herself. She seemed lonely, which was something I understood.

After being at Wendy's, and spying a picture of Tom Cameron on her dresser, I was ready for a boyfriend.

Julie and I went biking through Maple Creek Cemetery. We called Tim Wright and told him to meet us at Wendell's grave. Julie was sure Tim had a crush on me.

When Julie and I rode up to Wendell's and leaned our bikes against the stone bench, I felt clumsy and nervous. What if Julie was wrong, and Tim thought I was gross?

But when he came strolling up, he looked right at me. He was clutching a life-size stop sign made out of plywood that he'd cut and painted himself in shop.

"I made this for you." He smiled, holding it out.

"Wow, thanks," I said. It was the first gift any boy had ever given me. It might as well have been a moped or a new stereo.

I carefully took it and laid it against my bike. Tim followed me. When I turned around, he gave me my first kiss. It was so quick and soft, I didn't realize at first that what I'd spent over a year waiting for had just happened.

"Well, I gotta go," Tim said. "My brother's waiting for me in his car." I looked over his shoulder and there was Ricky sitting in his Chevy Camaro. I waved and Ricky waved back.

"Okay, well, thanks again for the stop sign," I said.

"Let's meet at the Liberty sometime," Tim said. "We could see a movie."

"Okay," I said, and he left, climbing into the Camaro. We watched them wind their way out of the cemetery.

"He kissed you. I can't believe it. He really kissed you." Julie was jumping up and down in the grass. I started laughing and jumping with her.

"He asked me to the movies," I cheered.

I wondered if Sarah Keeler was watching; her grave was nearby. She would never have a first kiss or a stop sign. Now that I had both, I felt prettier and much older.

That fall JoAnn was leaving for college—"77" had finally come.

Everyone was moving away. Tim's family was moving to the Ozarks, where his father, a Baptist minister, had been transferred. We never made it to the Liberty, but we did meet at the Elks Club, where we danced to "Don't Give Up on Us" by David Soul. Wendy Johnson watched us over the shoulder of her date, Mike Harris, and cried. When I went to the restroom, she followed.

"You two are breaking my heart," she said. "It's such a love story."

I liked the idea of having a boyfriend, but Tim's leaving was more of a fact than a lost romance. Wendy's eyes were bloodshot and wet.

"I'm sure we'll see each other again," I said, offering her my lip gloss.

She waved it away. "Thanks, but I just got a new one from Lazarus." She held up a shiny gold cylinder, pulled off the lid, and twisted up bright pink lipstick. She bent toward the mirror, pursed her lips, and carefully followed the lines of her mouth. (I still wasn't allowed to wear lipstick with color.) When she finished, she walked over to the stall, grabbed a small square of toilet paper, and pressed it to her lips just like Mom did.

"That looks great," I told her.

She turned and grabbed my shoulders. "There'll be other boys, Monica. It doesn't feel that way now, but there will be."

"I know," I said.

Tim gave me a gold ID bracelet with his name on it, and I never saw him again.

Compared to Tim, JoAnn would be close by, two hours away at Ohio State University in Columbus. I was sure my chances of ever being cool were going with both of them; I now had no boyfriend and no role model.

I sat on the side steps watching JoAnn pack for college. She was stuffing Mom's Pontiac with Carole King and Seals & Crofts albums, her acoustic guitar, her chrome desk lamp, and a stereo.

The night after she moved out, I walked across the hall and gingerly pushed open her door. I flipped on the light and sat on her bed—seriously trespassing. I looked at all those BJKs painted on her walls and imagined what it would be like to be a huge success. To have everyone know who you were. To do something really important.

I walked over to the window and looked out. To my surprise, I could see right down into the Whitmores' bathroom. Had JoAnn ever seen them peeing or shaving?

There was a thick white rope hanging outside JoAnn's window. In the winter she hung a six-pack of Mountain Dew from it so she could keep them cold without going downstairs to the refrigerator. She was the only person I knew who drank Mountain Dew.

I saw her tennis racket lying against the side of her desk. She must have forgotten it, which meant Mom would be driving it up there sometime within the next week. I picked it up and swung it around a couple of times. She would have killed me if she'd known I touched it. It wasn't fun sneaking into her room without her living there—not that I ever snuck in when she was living at home.

Becky was downstairs playing the piano. I could hear her starting and stopping and then starting again as she practiced *Für Elise* for the piano lessons we both took on Saturday mornings. I never practiced.

I wandered down the hallway into her room. While JoAnn made me feel challenged and excited, with Becky I always felt comforted. It might have been our closeness in age—the fact that she was just a few steps ahead of me—but Becky felt like an extension of me.

For as long as I could remember, we had shared things (Barbies, bicycles, sandwiches), but a few years before, when Becky hit junior high, I was still in fifth grade, and I didn't understand that junior high girls want their *own* stuff. That was when all hell broke loose between us. She was in the height of puberty, and I was assuming things between us were the same as always. Then we were still sharing the same room, so borrowing from her was easy.

"I'm gonna kill her!" she yelled at Mom.

"Monica Elizabeth!" Mom hollered.

"What's wrong?" I asked, walking into the kitchen.

"Leave Becky's clothes alone," Mom said. "She doesn't want you wearing her blue sweater."

"What's the big deal?" I asked, shrugging.

Becky went crazy, flinging her arms all around. "The big deal is that you have your own clothes, and yet you always wear *mine*. LEAVE MY STUFF ALONE!" She was in tears now. "Can't I get any privacy around here?"

"What the hell is wrong with you?" I asked, sending Becky barreling toward me. I raced through the hall, hurried into the bathroom, and locked the door behind me. She pounded on it.

"Quit taking my things," she screamed.

"Quit taking *mine*," I yelled through the door.

"There's nothing in your crappy closet I want." I heard her stomp away.

✦ ✦ ✦

Now that I was thirteen and in junior high myself, I didn't want privacy. I wanted to hang out with someone. I sat upstairs on Becky's bed and listened to her practicing the piano.

Mom was gone more and more. She was taking a full class load, and had met other students who were her age, many of them divorced. These women became good friends, giving Mom hope that she could make it out of her marriage.

I was glad Mom was happier, but I was seeing less of her.

Sometimes after my basketball or volleyball practice, I'd be waiting for Mom to pick me up an hour or more after everyone else had left. When she'd finally pull up, she couldn't understand why I was so mad. She was distracted by Wright State and having trouble adjusting from life as a student to life as a mom.

"I have a crisis," I told her when she finally arrived after practice one day. Since junior high had begun, I was constantly having a crisis, so she wasn't alarmed.

"What is it?" she asked.

"There's something wrong with Miss Mattingly," I said, throwing my red duffel bag over the backseat and climbing into the front. Miss Mattingly was skinny, tall, and wore pleated khaki skorts. She taught PE.

"Is she sick?" Mom asked.

"She's perverted," I told Mom. "So I guess I'd call that sick."

"JoAnn and Becky love her," Mom said.

"What? JoAnn doesn't love her." I snapped my seat belt into the buckle. "When JoAnn's grades slipped, Miss Mattingly forced her to sit in front of the whole study hall at a special table where 'dumb people' sit, so she could watch her and make sure she was studying. But it was really about humiliating her." I was getting worked up.

"But your grades are good, aren't they?"

"It's not about grades." I rolled my eyes. "Just let me tell you and quit interrupting."

I explained to Mom that every day in gym, after we'd changed into one-piece cotton uniforms, Miss Mattingly lined all the girls along the wall and walked back and forth with her clipboard, calling out names for roll call. If you were on your period, you had to say "M" in a loud, clear voice. This was mortifying. No one wanted to announce they were on their period. I wanted to die on the spot every time this happened to me. If you said "M," Miss Mattingly marked a big red *M* by your name and you weren't expected to shower. But if you didn't have an *M* by your name, you had to take a shower. Miss Mattingly was obsessed with the crime of pubescent girls' not showering.

The perverted part took place in the shower room. Miss Mattingly sat on a low wooden chair near the showers with her clipboard and a stack of white terry cloth towels. After you showered, you had to walk up to her completely naked, say your towel number, and wait while she found your name and put a checkmark by it. Finally, she'd hand you a towel to cover yourself. Until the towel went around you, Miss Mattingly was looking you up and down. All of us were disgusted.

I was embarrassed enough by my body, without Miss Mattingly (who lived with Miss Olson) staring at me naked and keeping a record of my periods. What the hell?

Mom called Mr. Conroy, the junior high principal, who told her it was his first complaint in Miss Mattingly's tenure. Where was everyone?

My freshman year in high school, I joined the speech team as another way to work on my acting. Mr. Selman was a new teacher and speech coach, but I didn't know him very well. In October he came over to Julie's house for dinner. He was a bachelor and had just moved to town. Dave and Joan were always welcoming new members of the community.

Mr. Selman was heavyset and flat-footed with wiry black hair and thick chapped lips. When he laughed, it sounded like a foghorn going off, which made everybody laugh.

I sat down at the Kilners' kitchen table across from Mr. Selman. Dave and Mr. Selman were laughing and joking like old friends.

Selman looked over at Julie and said, "I think I saw you sitting on the Do Not Enter sign after school last week."

Julie threw a strawberry at him and his right eyeball fell into his lap. He looked down, picked up the glass eye, casually cleaned it with his napkin, and stuck it back in. I must have been gaping in horror.

"Monica, I know this looks tragic, but really, must you stare?" he said.

"I'm sorry, Mr. Selman," I said, picking up my fork.

He did the foghorn laugh. "It's okay. Seeing someone's eyeball fall out is a good reason to stare. Joan, could you please pass me the green beans?"

Julie kicked me under the table and I kicked her back. I had never met anyone like Selman, and not just because of his glass eye. He was really fun, but he looked at me in an intense way, like he couldn't wait to hear what I had to say. No adult had ever looked at me like that.

Freshman year, I had my first car date. It was with Keith Phillips, whom I met at a speech competition. I was fourteen and he was seventeen. We became inseparable from October through the spring and I was in love for the first time.

Keith and I went to high school ball games and to see *The Goodbye Girl*. We kissed and ate hamburgers at Bob's Burgers.

He invited me to his senior prom, picking me up in his mom's blue Oldsmobile, wearing a light blue tux with a ruffled blue shirt. He liked blue.

I wore a long clinging pink gown, a half bra stuffed with a

combination of rolled-up white kneesocks and bunched-up Kleenex, and Mom's uncomfortable white heels that made me taller than Keith. My bra kept slipping down until my kneesock-Kleenex boobs were jutting out of my stomach. I had to keep tugging it back into place as we danced to "Your Smiling Face" by James Taylor and "Three Times a Lady" by The Commodores. I sat right next to him in his mom's blue car as we drove home.

When we walked into the house, Mom and Dad were already asleep. Keith suggested we go up to my room. I wasn't allowed to have boys upstairs, but I didn't want to be a naïve freshman, so I said yes.

I was worried about the socks and Kleenex in my bra as we climbed the stairs. What if he tried to get to second base?

When we got to my room, Keith sat down on my bed and, instead of kissing me, told me his parents were divorcing. I wasn't surprised. I'd never even seen his dad speak to his mom. Instead he sat in his chair and grunted whenever she asked him a question.

"There's more," Keith told me. But then he began stuttering and looking at the floor.

He patted the space next to him on my bed. I kicked off Mom's uncomfortable shoes and sat down.

I was positive he was going to say he loved me, but instead he mumbled something like, "Mmm's a homosexual."

I couldn't understand him. "What?" I asked.

"Mom's a homosexual," he said quietly.

I couldn't believe it. Shirley? She had just cooked us steaks before the prom. I tried not to judge, since Keith was already upset. But that was probably causing the divorce.

"Keith, I'm sorry," I said. "I wish there was something I could do."

"You're taking this well," he said.

"I'm not going to judge it," I said, and he hugged me tight.

"I haven't seen men since we started dating," he said. "I would never have done that."

I shoved him away from me. "What?"

"I haven't seen men since we started dating," he repeated.

"*You're* a homosexual?" I asked.

"I told you I'm homosexual."

"I thought you said 'Mom's a homosexual.'" We were both confused. "Why were we talking about your parents divorcing?" I asked.

"Because I don't want that to happen to us," he said.

I stood up, not caring that, once again, my fake boobs were protruding from my stomach. If I'd been wearing a perfectly fitted Christian Dior gown with a pair of my own fabulous breasts perched high on my chest, I'd still have felt ridiculous. Everything was ruined. Couldn't he be in love with another girl? Couldn't he just think I was ugly or boring or something? Did he have to be gay? My very first boyfriend?

"I'm relieved I told you." He tried to smile.

"Well, thanks for taking me to the prom," I said, heading to the door.

"Are you okay?" he asked.

"Sure," I said, but I wasn't. I walked downstairs in my bare feet, and Keith followed.

A ticker tape of the previous six months scrolled through my brain: Keith at his classical organ concert, Keith avoiding anything but kissing, Keith getting accepted to Westchester Choir College. I wondered how many people had already figured it out, which made me feel even more ridiculous.

After he pulled out of the driveway, I sat down on the steps of the front porch in my prom dress and cried, pulling kneesocks and wadded-up Kleenex out of my bra. JoAnn had picked gorgeous, sweet Bill Lawrence, and I'd picked a homosexual.

Something was definitely wrong with me.

I stood up, wiped my nose on the wadded-up Kleenex, and headed back inside.

CHAPTER THIRTEEN

One morning the summer before my sophomore year, Mom woke Becky and me.

"Get dressed."

"What's going on?" Becky asked.

"We're taking a trip," she said.

"Where?" I asked, coming out into the hallway.

"Florida. We're getting out of here for a few days."

"It's dark out," Becky noticed.

"We're getting an early start."

Becky and I sleepily packed the suitcases Mom had left open on the floor of our rooms before she'd headed downstairs.

Mom was already showered with lipstick on, and her suitcase was packed and in the trunk of the Pontiac.

"Are we leaving home?" I asked, panicked. "Is this it?"

"We're not moving out," she said. "Your dad hasn't been home for three nights in a row. I don't know where he is or who he's with, so we're going to have a nice vacation at his expense." She waved Dad's MasterCard triumphantly.

"Right now?" I asked.

"Before he gets back," she confirmed.

"How'd you get the card?" I asked.

"Never mind." She slid it back into her purse.

I dragged my suitcase to the car. Dad was going to shit his pants when he got home.

We drove all day not knowing what to think but happy to have Mom's full attention. Mom was in a great mood. She had a jazz station on the radio, the windows down, and we were talking.

"Do you think you'll divorce Dad?" I asked from the backseat. It was Becky's turn to sit up front.

"Probably," she said.

"When?" I was fourteen years old. I still had a lot of time left at home. I couldn't imagine what we'd do for money if Dad left.

"When he least expects it," she said. I looked out my window at the mountains of southern Kentucky and saw a Stuckey's restaurant whip by.

"Won't he be mad when he sees we left?" I asked.

"I don't care. *He* left and didn't tell anyone."

"He's gonna be furious," I said, shaking my head.

"Let's just have a good time," she said. "We'll have a real vacation for once."

When we got to Florida, we stayed at Mammaw and Papaw's trailer outside of Clearwater.

"How did you get keys to the trailer?" Becky asked.

"I called and asked for them," she said.

I was glad to be at Mammaw's. That meant someone knew where we were.

The next morning we went to Walt Disney World and Mom told us to buy whatever we wanted, as she ran up Dad's credit card. I'd never seen anything more sparkling and happy than the Magic Kingdom. Every cliché and commercial I'd ever seen or heard about it was true. I walked around all day with a dopey grin on my face. After the eleven p.m. fireworks Mom bought me a fluffy pink elephant that was so enormous, I could barely carry it to the car. I slept in Mammaw's trailer with my arms around that elephant, happy and safe.

Despite the dread of Dad's inevitable wrath, I was still able to enjoy Mom's newfound sense of fun. She didn't make us pick up our clothes or shower every day. A couple of evenings she actually left dirty dishes in the sink and washed them the next morning—not asking us to help. Mom hadn't worn lipstick or curled her hair since we passed the Georgia state line.

We probably spent about a thousand dollars on Dad's card, but when we got home, he was spooky-nice to us. I couldn't believe it. Mom barely spoke to him.

Over the next few months everything snapped back to the way it had been. Mom took classes, Dad came home only to sleep, and Becky and I stayed out of everybody's way.

One evening in October, Mom put on the forty-five record of Barry Manilow singing, "Ready to Take a Chance Again" and exclaimed dreamily (a tone I'd never associated with her) that she'd met the perfect man: a man named Jim. That night she walked into the dining room and told Dad she wanted a divorce.

Amazing as it sounds, I don't think he saw it coming. I'd never seen him speechless or without the impulse to hit or destroy something, but that's what happened. He just sat there looking smaller than I'd ever seen him. I actually felt sorry for him for being sucker punched. I felt sucker punched too, even though I'd known it was coming.

"I'll stay till Christmas," he snapped, "for the sake of the kids."

"You haven't spent an entire Christmas day with us in over ten years." Mom laughed.

"I'll leave after New Year's," he grumbled, shoving his chair away from the table.

If Dad was genuinely stunned, I was genuinely panicked. I didn't want Dad around either, but where were we going to get money? Who would take care of the house? And at the top of my list was who was Jim—and what if he turned out to be worse than Dad? It wasn't as if Mom had a glowing track record for choosing gentle, caring partners.

Mom was so in love she wasn't thinking about any of those things. If she and Jim had to live in a car, it would have been fine with her.

I had to figure out what I was going to do, and in order to do that, I had to know what Mom was up to—how serious she was with Jim. Turned out all I had to do was ask. She was so giddy, she blurted out everything.

Three times a week they were rendezvousing in a park outside of Dayton. They ate in small, out-of-the-way diners and stayed in Cincinnati hotels where they wouldn't accidentally run into Dad or Jim's wife (yes, he was still married).

"It's the most exciting thing that's ever happened to me," she said, packing a small suitcase. She was meeting him at the Hyatt Regency in Cincinnati that night.

"How are we going to get by?" I asked her.

She stopped packing and turned to me. "Better than ever, that's how. With Jim, I finally have everything I ever wanted."

"What about his family?" I asked.

"He's filing for divorce too. His wife is insane—much like your father. Hey, they'd make a great pair." She cracked herself up.

I walked up to my room and put *A Chorus Line* on my stereo. I took out my jewelry box with the plastic ballerina and sat down on the carpet with my back against my bed. I flipped open the lid. The ballerina popped up and twirled to the tinny music. I pulled out the money Mom had stolen for me from Dad's truck. It didn't look like enough.

I spread it out on the carpet and counted twenty-five dollars. I had used a lot of it through the years on trips to Kings Island amusement park or to buy albums. I should have thought ahead.

I gathered it up again, stuck it back into the box, and closed the lid.

Mom was getting out. But I couldn't go anywhere.

It was freezing cold the December night Becky and I met Jim. Mom made sure to tell us that he was everything Dad wasn't. He was educated, working on his PhD, and was the head of the continuing education program for women at Wright State. He was handsome and loved good music. I didn't care about any of that. He was screwing up my already shitty life.

Mom, Becky, and I were going to see *The Nutcracker* at Wright State and then were meeting "the boyfriend" at Pizza Palace in Dayton.

Mom was happy, happy, happy. She had been in this mood since September, ignoring my inability to eat or sleep from the stress of not knowing what was going to happen.

All through *The Nutcracker*, my head was throbbing. Mom was going to be with Jim whether I liked him or not. She'd told me, "I spent my entire life taking care of kids, and now it's my turn. You can damn well deal with it." If he was an asshole, I was doomed. Becky had two years left at home, but I had three.

I couldn't concentrate on the ballet, which was a good thing, because the dancers were leaping into the air and accidentally smacking into one another.

I looked over at Becky and whispered, "What in the hell is going on up there?"

"Chaos," she whispered back. A ballerina's leotard split open down the back, buttons scattering across the stage.

"Someone's gonna trip and then it's really going to get interesting," I whispered. Mom glared a *Stop humiliating me by talking* look in our direction.

Afterward, we drove to Pizza Palace.

We got there before Jim and were sitting in a booth looking out toward Manning Road, where Mom kept pointing.

"He'll come from that direction," she said.

"You already said that," I groaned. Mom smirked.

"He has the most gorgeous long fingers," she chirped.

"You told us that, too," I said.

"Are you planning on ruining the entire evening? Can't you ever be happy for me? Oh, there he is." She leaned on the bench and waved frantically out the window. A small man in an old green Chevy Nova waved back. He parked next to Mom's Pontiac.

I watched him unfurl out of his car. He was actually quite tall, with thick whitish red hair. When he got closer, I could see his bushy red eyebrows and brown button eyes. He didn't look like an asshole. He had a sweet smile and a long straight nose. Still, I decided to hate him.

"Hello," Jim said to the table. Mom jumped up and gave him a kiss on the mouth. I'd never seen her kiss anyone, never Dad. Was she trying to make me vomit?

"Girls, this is Jim," Mom said, grinning so wide I thought her cheeks would explode. She loved him all right. She was *crazy* about this guy. I was fucked.

"Is anybody hungry?" Jim asked.

"I'm starving," Becky said. I just sat there.

"Let's order something, shall we?" Jim scooted into the booth next to Mom. He could kiss my ass.

Earlier, Mom had tried to prepare Jim for our meeting by telling him that Becky was shy and I was outgoing. But Becky and I were such nervous wrecks that she couldn't stop talking and I said nothing. Jim reversed our names throughout the entire meal. *What a loser.*

I left the restaurant hoping he would fall into a sinkhole, never to be seen again, especially when Mom left Becky and me sitting in her freezing car while she stood by Jim's Nova kissing him and laughing like a teenager. I was a teenager; I was supposed to be doing that.

I missed the old mom, the one who sat around reading books and riding down country roads looking for hawks circling overhead. At least I knew who she was.

Christmas came in a blur. Dad began moving his stuff to a yellow A-frame house he'd bought at a place called Lake Hiawatha. It was a gated community eighteen miles away with a giant wooden totem pole erected by the front gate and oversize oars hanging above the entrance. I couldn't picture Dad living in a relaxed lake community, but that's where he ended up.

On Christmas night our house was dark except for one light in the kitchen and the Christmas tree lights in the living room.

Mom was with Jim in Dayton, Becky was on a date with her big lug of a boyfriend, Paul Stanley, JoAnn was with her old high school pals, and Jamie was drinking with our cousin Paul.

I was lying on the carpet staring at the tree when I noticed a small unopened package shoved clear underneath. The tag read "Monica" in Mom's slanted elegant handwriting. I knew that inside that box was something important, since it was such a coincidence: a gift left behind just for me, to find at the exact moment I was feeling so lonely and worried.

I unwrapped it slowly, preparing myself for the monumental revelation it held. I opened the lid and pulled out a fountain pen with WRIGHT STATE printed down the side of it. I walked into the kitchen and threw it in the trash.

The next morning Dad came home to pack his clothes.

"Your mother's a slut," he told me. "She's been seeing this man for years."

"Pot calling the kettle black, Dad," I said. He threw a lamp against the wall. I jumped.

"She's a liar," he continued, "and you're just like her. The whole bunch of you are crazier than hell. Squirrelly bunch of moochers."

I turned on him. "I saw you in the car with Carol Young."

"You're full of shit."

"I saw you. She was sitting right beside you." I was starting to scream.

"You're so pathetic, all you have time to do is make up lies."

"You caused all this!" I was yelling. I couldn't control myself anymore. All the fury and hate came out at once. "You're the reason everything fell apart!"

"You'd better watch yourself. You're lucky to have a roof over your head. You don't even deserve to be living in *my* house. I could kick your ass out on the street today. You think I owe you something? I don't owe you shit." Dad laughed and turned to walk out of the room.

"I DON'T CARE WHAT HAPPENS TO ME! I DON'T CARE IF I'M OUT ON THE STREET! I DIDN'T ASK TO BE HERE!" I screamed.

Dad stopped and without turning around said, "You shouldn't be here. You were a mistake."

I clenched my hands into two tight fists, lifted them over my head, and slammed them between his shoulder blades with all the strength my arms, my fury, and my hopelessness could muster.

He swung around with his fist in the air. I closed my eyes, waiting for the impact that would have felt exactly right, but there wasn't any. When I opened my eyes, his face was about three inches from mine.

"If you EVER hit me again, you won't live one second longer. Do you understand? I will snap your neck like a toothpick," he said. "You don't believe me?" He put one hand around my neck. "Try me."

Vomit came up in my throat, but I held it in.

Dad was out by New Year's. I stayed out of his sight until all of his things were finally gone. It hadn't occurred to me, until he'd said it, that he could kick me out of the house. I wasn't going to tempt fate by exploding at him again.

Saturday morning Mom was in the kitchen putting glasses into a cardboard box.

"What are you doing?" I asked.

"I was able to rent a small apartment at Wright State in graduate student housing," she said. "I can go there between classes and study." She was now working on her master's degree and had changed her major to American history. Now that she had Jim, she wouldn't need elementary education.

"You rented an apartment?" I asked.

"To study in," she said, gathering a couple of plates.

"Are you ever going to sleep there?" I asked.

"If there's a snowstorm or something, I might have to sleep there," she said.

I watched her looking under the stove for a small skillet and saucepan. I was trying to ward off the dread that had seized me. Tears were stinging my eyes again.

"I hope you don't stay there," I said.

"Can't you be happy for me?" She turned on me, the skillet in her hand. "Why is everything about *you*? Guess what? I've done *you* my whole life. This is about *me*. Do you know how difficult it is to even get one of these apartments?"

"No," I said.

"There's a waiting list. So I'm lucky to have it." She slammed the skillet down into another box. When she turned around, I was on my way up to my room.

I told Becky that night in the bathroom as she was putting makeup on for a date with Paul, "Mom's rented an apartment in Dayton."

"So?" Becky kept brushing on mascara.

"So, do you think she's going to sleep there?" I asked.

"I have no idea," Becky said. I sat on the side of the tub. I couldn't tell if Becky was surprised about the apartment or not.

"She took some dishes and pans up there," I said.

"Who cares?" Becky zipped up her makeup bag. "Who cares what she does?" She grabbed the bag and stomped out of the bathroom. I closed the door with my foot and stayed seated on the side of the tub with my head in my hands.

On Monday, I wasn't ready when the bus pulled up, so I had to drive to school with Becky.

"I'm not driving you every day," she said.

"I know," I said, secretly happy to be sitting in the car with her.

I was a sophomore in high school and she was a junior, which meant we saw each other in the halls more often. Becky was less pleased about that than I was.

With Mom jumping ship, I signed up for every extracurricular activity I could find. Anything to be with a lot of people and take my mind off our empty house. Again, my sense of humor helped me make friends. The problem was finding a ride home after speech practice. Mr. Selman offered to drive me, but he was already standing way too close to me when he spoke. It was best to steer clear of being in a car with him. Sometimes I went home with Julie and spent the night.

Becky had her group of friends and I had mine. We didn't talk at school and we didn't socialize outside of school.

Mom and Jim began staying at their new Dayton apartment,

coming home on the weekends. I adopted Mom's attitude, deciding to be happy for her. I even began giving Jim a chance. He seemed nice enough, and apparently he wasn't going anywhere. Better to be a part of them than to fight it.

At school one morning in March I was called into the counselor's office.

"How are you?" Mrs. McCormick asked, leaning in. She looked exactly like the Charlie-in-the-box from *Rudolph, the Red-Nosed Reindeer*: round red nose, squinty eyes, and hair pulled up in a curlicue on top of her round head.

"Fine," I said, forcing a smile.

"You look awfully thin, Monica," she said. "Are you getting enough to eat?"

"Yes," I said. For once Mrs. McCormick was right; I wasn't eating much. There weren't meals at my house. I was five-foot-nine and weighed 102 pounds. What was she getting at?

"How's your mom?" she asked. She wanted to know if Mom was living in Dayton.

"Fine." I smiled. Did she think I'd admit that my family was in shambles and that I was so frightened it was difficult to get a piece of toast to stay down? Mrs. McCormick was a notorious gossip. Any information she squeezed out of students ended up all over town, and there was no way I was giving her a kernel of dirt on me.

"Is there anything you'd like to talk about in regards to your home life?" she asked.

Yes, I wanted to say, *my dad moved out and hates us, Mom moved out and doesn't care about anything except her new boyfriend, I don't have enough money to live on, and there isn't enough food in the refrigerator to put a meal together.*

I shook my head. "Not that I can think of." She stared at me. I shrugged my shoulders and got up to leave.

"I know you're going through your parents' divorce right now," she said to my back, "so if you need anything, you just come to Mrs. McCormick." I turned to see her very best smile.

She was right about one thing—I did need a caring, responsible adult around. If I could have cried on the shoulder of someone I trusted, I never would have stopped. Where were all the adults? They must not have known, and I was too embarrassed to ask for help. Mr. Selman would have been all too happy to lend me his shoulder, but that would have been a monumental mistake. I was lost.

Granda was always loving. She brought over covered dishes once in a while, but she was also fiercely protective of Mom. When JoAnn asked her why Mom was being so neglectful, Granda scolded, "You have the best mother in the world." When JoAnn chose to differ, Granda said, "I will never love you like I used to since you turned against your mom." Granda would not be on our side.

I smiled back at Mrs. McCormick and said, "I definitely will."

"By the way, is your mom's boyfriend actually living with you?" She couldn't help it; it just popped out of her.

Jim was living with us on the weekends, and I'd heard them together in the shower. It was inappropriate, but I didn't want anyone to know. I was furious that the gossip circuit had picked it up as something to snicker about. Slowly I swung back around and leaned across her desk.

"They're not really living together; they're just fucking," I said. "Anything else?"

Mrs. McCormick looked positively clobbered. Her face was pale and the sides of her mouth turned down.

"Okay, then," I said, opening the door to leave. My hands were shaking. I'd never talked to an adult like that.

I walked back toward Selman's class, but the principal, Mr. Martin, grabbed my arm before I could open the door to the classroom. Everyone inside was looking at us through the square glass window of the door.

Mr. Martin and I were good friends, but this wasn't going to be good.

"Monica, did you just curse at Mrs. McCormick?" he asked. She must have recovered enough to run to his office.

"Yes," I said, wishing he hadn't seen me in this particular light.

"She's very upset and would like an apology." He looked tired and mad.

My eyebrows flew up. "An apology? She asked me personal and insulting questions about Mom and Dad and *she* wants an apology?"

"You can't curse at faculty, Monica. I was surprised you'd do something like that."

He got me there. I was always living clean around Mr. Martin. He didn't know I'd been cussing my whole life, because I would never have cursed in front of him. I adored Mr. Martin, and he was right, I shouldn't have said "fucking" to Mrs. McCormick. I was mad at myself for losing control.

"Okay, I'll apologize after school," I said.

"Right now." He turned me back toward the counselor's office.

"She's nosy—," I said, but Mr. Martin interrupted.

"Monica, you need to be careful about the way you present yourself. You're smart and funny. You don't want to bring yourself down by behaving badly. You may be going through a tough time right now, but this is when you need to step up and be bigger than all that stuff."

"It *sounds* easy," I grumbled.

"It's more difficult to be a good person than a bad one. And you're a good person." He patted my shoulder. At least he still believed in me, and I appreciated his efforts to steer me straight. He opened the door to Mrs. McCormick's office and came in behind me. Shit.

"I'm sorry I cursed," I said quickly. I wanted to hurl her easel with the poster of a cartoon gorilla sitting on top of a skinny man with the caption "No problem is too big to solve" out the fucking window of her claustrophobic office.

"Well, I would think so," she said. "I have never been so shocked in my entire life—especially after I was trying to help you. And you used such a terrible word." Clearly, I had just added my own degrading behavior to the gossip about my family.

"I'm sorry." I stared at her. I was trying to think of a way to end the confrontation and not have her trash me. I put my hand on my forehead and I cried. It wasn't that difficult. I was already sad; I just let it come. "I wish I hadn't behaved like that. I'm going through a rough time right now," I sobbed. Now I couldn't tell if I was really sorry or faking it, but it sure felt good to cry—a festering boil had blown wide open.

"Behavior like that will get you detention next time," Mr. Martin said. "Do we understand each other?" Mrs. McCormick reached for the tissue box on her desk and handed it to me. With that gesture, I knew I was in the clear.

"Absolutely," I said, accepting her Kleenex.

"Don't you feel better now, getting all that out?" she asked. *Don't push it*, I thought.

"I do," I said, nodding. The truth was that in the end, sad felt better than rage—a lot better. But rage came easier. Sad felt like the world was ending.

Mr. Martin opened the door and we walked out of the counselor's office.

"Take some time in the ladies' room if you want," he said, walking back toward his office.

Mr. Martin was worried about me. He tried to call Mom, but couldn't find her. Neither could I.

That night Becky said, "I heard you cussed at Mrs. McCormick."

"Was it announced on the loudspeaker?" I asked.

"Everyone's talking about it," she said, smiling. "Your temper is a real problem."

"Good," I said, but I was flustered that everyone knew.

"I called Mom, and she sounded pretty mad," Becky said, walking into the living room.

"Like I'm even scared," I said, wondering how Becky had managed to get Mom on the phone to bust me. She was never at the apartment when we really needed her.

That spring I heard Becky talking to her friend Clare on the phone about cheerleading tryouts. As it turned out, the only thing she wanted in life was to be a cheerleader. There was no reason she couldn't make the squad; she was adorable and good at gymnastics, her long blond pigtails flipping around in circles as she did several front walk-overs in a row.

I decided that if she were a cheerleader, she'd be a happy person and easier to live with. Maybe we'd eat together and be the way we'd been when we were little, playing Dark Side of the Moon with the Whitmores. Also, I needed her to like me so she'd pick me up from practice sometimes.

Tryouts were in two weeks, so I took it upon myself to campaign for Becky during homeroom and in the hallways. "Vote for Becky Peterson," I told them. "She's great at gymnastics."

At the tryouts I sat in the bleachers nervously chewing the side of my cheek. Suddenly I wanted Becky to win because she was my sister. She'd helped me slap mud pies onto our back patio when we were toddlers, and cried along with me when a wasp stung my foot at Rocky Fork State Park. I wanted her to win because she was mine—my family.

Each of the girls came bounding out onto the gym floor one by one, yelling their cheers and flinging their arms around, ending in a high kick or a split.

Becky ran out and stood stock-still. She slapped her two hands into a fist over her shiny blond head and shouted, "Let's yell for the red, the black, and the white." She was facing to the side now, head turned toward the bleachers, where I smiled in case she saw me. She continued, moving her arms in front of her chest.

"Let's yell for the Braves, 'cause they're all right."

"Braves." (Front walk-over.)

"Braves." (Back walk-over.)

"Fight." (High jump with kick.) "Fight." (Same.) "Fight." (Straight down into the splits.)

She did it! My row erupted in applause and whistles. Becky smiled and ran off.

Twenty minutes later I saw her in the hallway with Donna Frazee and said, "You looked good," but she kept walking. Maybe cheerleading wouldn't help us after all.

The next day during homeroom, Mr. Martin came on the loudspeaker and announced the cheerleaders for what would be Becky's senior year. Becky was not one of them. After all we'd been through, what would it have hurt for her to win? She had done a great job, and now she was going to be even more miserable.

That night I was in my room studying and heard her crying. I stood in the hallway, not knowing how to approach her. Becky and I had had our share of arguments, but I had taken on the "Peterson mentality"—that we could hurt one another, but no one else could.

I walked into her room and saw her sitting on the bed sobbing into her cupped hands. When she realized I was standing there, she turned and snapped, "What are you doing in here? My door was closed!"

"Looking for a pair of gray kneesocks," I lied. I would have given anything to say something helpful, but I didn't know what to say.

"Quit wearing my stuff," she yelled, wiping away tears. "Get out of my room and leave me alone."

"You almost won," I told her without knowing for sure.

"Who cares anyway?" she said, getting up and grabbing a brush off her desk. "Get outta here." She turned away from me and began pulling the brush through her long, thick hair.

I closed her door behind me, leaving her alone. I wanted to make her feel better, I just didn't know how.

Having given up on Mom and Dad, I now looked for attention, meals, and stimulation in the outside world. I ran for class vice president and won. I won speech tournaments, and even the ones I lost were fun because all my friends were there. I spent the night at other people's houses; I was a counselor for the summer arts and drama workshops for the elementary students.

Becky became shyer and even angrier.

I fell and broke my ankle, and Mrs. Bates, who taught AV at the high school, took me to get my cast put on.

One afternoon I heard there was a rumor going around school that I'd faked my broken foot to get attention. No one would tell me who was saying it, but Julie and I asked around, and Becky's good friend, Alice Johnson, said, "Becky started it. She hates you."

I had never been handed such undiluted truth.

Besides Becky, I had another problem. Mr. Selman was no longer being coy. He actively pursued me, kissing me on the mouth while I tried to shove him off me, and leaving love notes on my locker, signed "S." Mom and Jim, lost in their love bubble, weren't any help.

I thought of talking to Mr. Martin. I was sure he would help me, but I couldn't imagine creating a huge scandal. Plus, I liked Selman when he wasn't hitting on me. I was embarrassed, grossed out, and more than a little pleased to be getting some attention. I flirted with him, even while I cringed at the thought of him touching me.

I decided to deal with Selman in my own way.

One night I broke into Selman's apartment with Julie, who knew he'd been pursuing me. It was one of the craziest things we ever did, but we hauled all his furniture out onto the lawn and set up his living room outside.

He left us a note the next morning written in red ink and taped to Julie's mailbox: "REVENGE WILL BE MINE."

We shrieked and ran around in circles. We were excited and horrified by all the possibilities.

"What's he going to do?" Julie wondered.

"God only knows," I said. "Probably slobber on us."

When we got to school, he'd covered the outside of our lockers with shaving cream.

Julie and I turned up the intensity of our attacks, breaking into his car, releasing the emergency brake, and rolling it down the small hill beside his house. I pushed, and Julie steered it right into an alley. The next morning he was disheveled and late to class.

"What's wrong?" I asked.

"Someone stole my car," he panted, shoving his briefcase under his desk.

"Are you sure?" I asked.

"It's not where I parked it last night, so I'm pretty sure," he said.

"What if it accidentally rolled down the hill?" I asked. Selman turned to look at me with his good eye. He was starting to smile.

"Is that what happened?" he asked.

"I'm just saying it could happen. Maybe the brake wasn't on," I said.

"Peterson, if you took my car, I'm gonna kill you," he said.

"I can't really say for sure," I said.

"I'll expect my car to be in front of my house by four thirty p.m. today or I'm calling the police," he said. "You're lucky. If I hadn't gotten up late this morning, I'd have called them already."

Maybe he was harmless after all. He was a great distraction and was funny as hell. I wasn't attracted to him, but at least someone was watching me closely.

He had admitted he loved me. Told me that after I graduated, we could date. I didn't know how to tell him that was never going to happen.

But I loved him as a friend, and if he was inappropriate with me, I was doubly inappropriate. I shattered a window at his house while Julie and I were breaking in to change the outgoing message on his answering machine and steal all his silverware, I stuck extralong maxi pads all over his front door when I knew he'd be bringing home an attractive date, and I mooned him out the back window of a bus, my bare ass pressed firmly against the glass. Clearly, I was begging for his attention.

JoAnn was the only one who took it for what it really was. She threatened to drive to Elk Grove and kick his ass. Every time we talked on the phone, she was sure to ask about him.

"Is Selman still messing with you?"

"Not too much," I'd say.

"Damn it. I'm going to kill that man. He'd better keep his hands off you." JoAnn called often and sometimes came up and got me so I could spend a weekend at Ohio State with her.

When I was still fifteen, Julie rushed into my bedroom one sunny Saturday morning. Her eyes were red and swollen and she was talking fast.

"Wendy's dead," she said.

I wasn't even awake yet. "What?"

"Wendy's dead. She shot herself after the ball game last night."

I sat up. "Shot herself where?"

"In the chest," Julie said.

"And she's dead?" I asked.

"Dad picked her up around midnight."

Julie started crying again. I couldn't move. All of a sudden my cozy pink room felt cold and spooky. All I could think of was Wendy holding those baby rabbits.

The phone rang. Our friends were starting to call. We decided to meet at Pizza Palace at eleven thirty. None of us were hungry.

Wendy didn't get her picture in the *Elk Grove Courier*. Only an obituary that read:

WENDY JOHNSON

Miss Wendy Johnson, 15, RR 1, Elk Grove, died at home Friday night. She was born in Cincinnati on September 15, 1962, and is the daughter of Carl and Marianne Johnson.

Miss Johnson was a sophomore at Mason County High School and a member of the Elk Grove United Methodist Church. Her activities at school included choir, cheer block, speech club, and Spanish club.

She is survived by her parents.

Funeral services will be held Monday at 2:00 p.m. at Kilner and Sons Mortuary.

At school Monday, I unlocked one of the glass showcases lining the hallways. As class vice president and a friend of Wendy's, I felt I should do something to memorialize her. I put in a vase of red roses I'd picked up that morning and pictures Julie had brought me from Mrs. Johnson. Just as I was finishing the showcase, Mr. Martin walked up behind me.

"What's this?" he asked.

"It's for Wendy," I answered. Mr. Martin put his hand on my shoulder and squeezed.

"Take it down," he said.

"What?"

"Take it down," he repeated. "We do not honor little girls who kill themselves. I don't want an epidemic on my hands." He turned and walked away.

What did he mean, "an epidemic"?

I took it down quickly, just as Mr. Martin had asked. I looked at the empty showcase, and thought, *Wendy is courageous, and I'm a coward*.

Just as Sarah Keeler had taught me that children die, Wendy taught me that you don't have to wade through the insanity; you can get off the bus. This scared me so much that a sweaty panic swept over me. From that moment on I knew it was possible (and easy, with all the guns in my house) to end my own life.

Part IV

DRIVING WITH DEAD PEOPLE

Chapter Fourteen

The fall I turned sixteen, I spent Saturday afternoons in the high school cafeteria watching films of violent car accidents far more grisly than the ones Dad had filmed. For Mr. Meese, my driver's ed teacher, this was his favorite part. Nothing pleased him more than one of us passing out cold on the cafeteria linoleum after seeing some teenager's head lying on the side of a country road, his torso still in the driver's seat. An eerie voice-over explained that he'd been drunk, driving more than one hundred miles an hour, when a deer stepped in front of the car. The impact hurled the deer through the windshield, decapitating the kid.

One day a boy ran out of the room to puke after seeing a film of an EMT opening the door of a compact car and revealing a blood-covered teenager shoved halfway through the windshield, her butt off the seat, and her arms, mangled and bloody, dangling at her sides. The camera panned to the front of the car where the top of her head had been sliced into sections from the shattered windshield, the skin on her face hanging in shreds.

Each film had running commentary on the dangers of not wearing your seat belt, driving while intoxicated, or speeding.

After the gruesome films, Mr. Meese would sit in the passenger seat, with me behind the wheel of the white driver's ed car. I'd steer us toward the pharmacy to practice my parallel parking. After a few weeks and several harrowing attempts to enter the line of traffic on Interstate 75 around Cincinnati, I earned my driver's license.

Before I was allowed to drive alone, I practiced in Mom's car on weekends. The tricky part wasn't negotiating the road, it was that every time I stopped, her loaded handgun slid out from under the driver's seat and lodged itself under the brake pedal. She called it the "pea shooter."

"This gun keeps getting stuck under here," I finally told her.

"Kick it back under the seat," she said, so I did—over and over again.

Like JoAnn, Becky decided to attend Ohio State University that fall. JoAnn didn't exactly welcome Becky to college. She had been struggling with depression so severe, she was finding it difficult to get to her classes. She wasn't sure what was so debilitating, but she didn't want Becky (or any of us) to know.

Mom made Becky leave her old red Mustang. (There wasn't parking available to freshmen anyway.) I'd finally have mobility and could leave the school bus, and my anxiety about catching a ride to Galesburg, behind.

I never thought I'd miss Becky, but I did. At least when she was home, the lights were on and someone was there. Now all the rooms were empty but mine. She was hateful, but she was home. Now I was all alone.

We had our licenses, so Dave told Julie and me that we could drive the Kilner and Sons hearse. He would pay us five bucks an hour to drive to the Cincinnati airport and pick up bodies that had been flown in from out of state. We'd drive a fully loaded gold Cadillac (they had traded in the black one) with an excellent stereo system, make money, and spend all our time together. It was the perfect job.

Julie and I felt mature getting to drive the hearse, and it was true that we'd finally lost the ugly awkwardness of puberty. She was busty with beautiful dark eyes and straight white teeth, and I was tan and lanky—not the types that usually showed up in a hearse at the cargo hold of the airport.

On the day of our initiation, Dave tossed Julie the keys and we drove over to the coin-operated car wash on Eighth Street, plugged in four quarters, hit the switch, took out the metal wand, and sprayed the hearse top to bottom.

"Are there towels in the back?" I asked Julie.

"I don't think so," she said, swinging the back door open. "No towels," she reported.

"Now we're gonna have water spots." I was aggravated.

"Let's get in and drive like hell so the water blows off," Julie suggested.

We climbed in and sped out onto Highway 50 toward Cincinnati, water droplets vanishing behind us.

We stopped in Jennings Falls about ten miles west of Elk Grove to buy a pack of Virginia Slims and two Pepsis at the Sinclair station. We never smoked without Pepsis. A cigarette tasted nasty without the sweetness of a Pepsi chaser; plus, if I didn't have something to drink, I coughed the entire time I smoked.

We weren't technically allowed to smoke but, luckily, several of the other hearse drivers were heavy smokers and the cab already smelled like an ashtray before we even lit up.

Julie put in a Dire Straits tape and fast-forwarded to "Sultans of Swing." With our windows down, our Virginia Slims lit, and our Pepsis cold, we were feeling pretty smooth. It didn't bother us that people on the highway looked at us suspiciously as if maybe we had stolen the hearse.

The only glitch for me was arriving at the Cincinnati airport to actually do our job. I felt a rush of apprehension as we followed signs to the cargo area.

Grabbing the clipboard lying between the seats, I looked to see whom we were picking up: "Everette Linville. Eighty-two years old. Coral Gables, Florida."

I was glad he was old. "It was his time to go," as Granda would say.

Once we arrived, Julie enjoyed whipping the hearse around and speeding in reverse toward the loading dock, causing everyone to scatter. She kicked her door open.

"We're here from Kilner and Sons Mortuary," she announced in a deep, authoritative voice. "You have a body for us?"

The guy working the loading dock wore navy coveralls with RAYMOND stitched in white across the top of his pocket.

"Shouldn't you guys be wearing dresses or something? Most guys picking up bodies at least wear suits," Raymond said.

"I didn't know there was a dress code, did you?" Julie asked, turning to me, in my denim cutoffs and peasant blouse.

"Didn't know," I said.

"She didn't know. Next time we'll be in our Sunday best. Where is this guy?" she asked, handing him the clipboard.

Julie took on a whole new personality at work. She was "don't fuck with me" brilliant. Authority brought out what I thought was the "Julie of the future." I could easily see her running her own company or becoming principal of a high school someday.

Raymond spoke into his walkie-talkie, and two men rolled out a cardboard box shaped like a coffin, lying on a gurney. Julie and I jumped onto the dock while the men unclipped the four black belts wrapped around the box and sliced open the clear packing tape running down the center.

"Expensive casket." Julie nodded, looking inside. Raymond was opening the coffin.

Regardless of how many bodies we would eventually pick up, I'd never get used to the popping sound the casket made when it was unsealed, or the lid opening to reveal a human lying there. Mr.

Linville wore a brown suit and a gold tie and had thick white cotton covering his face.

"What's the cotton for?" I asked Julie.

"It holds their features in place while being jostled around on the plane. It also keeps the makeup from smearing and absorbs liquid that might seep out of the nose or mouth."

Liquid seeping out of the nose or mouth? Disgusting.

We looked at the body. Julie pulled off the cotton, and Mr. Linville looked really good. No liquid.

"Shitty makeup job," Julie commented. I looked at him again. He still looked pretty good to me. We checked his hands and clothing, making sure his shoes, jacket, tie, wedding ring—all the items listed on the manifest—were there. They were. Raymond placed the ten-by-ten piece of cotton back on Mr. Linville's face, and I wanted to yell, *He can't breathe!* and snatch the cotton away. But I was working, so I just stood there.

Raymond sealed the casket again and rolled it to the edge of the loading dock. Julie backed the hearse closer, and an iron lift attached to the dock lowered Mr. Linville down. We all grabbed the handles on the sides of the casket and shoved him into the back of the hearse. Dead people were heavy. Julie slammed the door.

"Well done," Julie said. She turned to Raymond. "Later, Tater," she said, changing back into her casual self as we hopped in and drove away.

On the way back to Elk Grove, we always stopped at the Hardee's drive-through, where Julie asked for fries, "for the guy in the back." This killed us laughing, even though the girl with the vacant eyes working the window never reacted.

Our new job suited us, but there weren't enough people dying out of state to make it lucrative. We picked up a body only once a month, and sometimes not even that often. The real problem was that people needed to be picked up during the week when we were in school. Neither one of us could handle a full-time job with all the studying and extracurricular activities we had going, so we took whatever Dave could give us on the weekends.

When money became hopelessly tight, I called Mom in Dayton. "How am I supposed to pay for my books and gas and everything?"

"Ask your dad," she said, as if it were obvious.

Mom didn't give me money, even though she finally had a small income from Wright State, where she was now doing some teaching. She'd also received a good amount of money in the divorce settlement. But I was off her radar.

Whenever I needed money, I waited until the last possible minute when my gas gauge was approaching empty or I couldn't afford lunch that day, and only then did I drive to Dad's store, my gut soured from worry.

When he saw me pull in, he knew why I was there. By the time I got inside, the divorce papers were spread out on the counter, immediately putting me on the defensive.

His customers (who hated Mom and us for throwing poor Dad out on his ass) were sitting at the counter.

"What is it this time?" he asked. His customers chuckled, their fat asses hanging off the backs of the stools, their overalls covered in dirt.

"I need money to attend the Ohio State Speech Finals in Cincinnati," I said, shoving my hands into the back pockets of my Levi's. "We're spending the night. I won both Sectionals and Regionals and have a shot at going to Nationals now."

"Well, let's see if that's something I have to pay for." He took his time running his thick finger up and down the clauses and sub-clauses while I stood awkwardly on the other side of the counter.

Finally he declared in a loud, pleased voice, "I don't have to pay that. That's your mom. Good-bye." He waved his fat hand, shooing me away, my face burning red.

"Forget it. I should have known." I turned to leave.

"Cry to your mom," he scoffed.

"Mom doesn't care, Dad. I won't go to the state finals even though I have a chance to win a trip to Texas. . . . This is bullshit."

"Your mother walked out on me. I didn't make this happen."

"You didn't make this happen? You made everything happen. Why are you taking it out on me? I'm the one still standing here."

"With your hand out," he screamed. "I'm tired of beggars!" Dad tossed the divorce papers back under the counter and stormed off to the back of the store.

I reached over the counter, pounded the cash register with my fist, and took all the twenty-dollar bills.

One of the assholes on the stools yelled, "Glen, I think you better get out here."

By the time Dad made it back up front, I was in my car with the doors locked.

I could've killed someone. I was a great student, a conscientious person who never drank or got in trouble. I succeeded in everything I set out to accomplish, and they didn't give a shit.

I rolled down my window just as Dad stuck his head out the front door.

"I'm going to find a way to compete at the state competition, and I'm gonna win," I yelled.

I turned on the car and saw Dad laughing through the large front windows of his store.

I threw the car into reverse, backed right up to his front steps, put it in drive, and floored it. I struggled to keep control of the wheel as the car skidded in the gravel. I heard a satisfying spray of tiny rocks peppering the front window and saw him bolting for the front door.

"I HATE YOUR GUTS! I HATE YOUR GUTS!" I screamed as I sped away, tears streaming down my face and onto the front of my shirt.

Twenty-dollar bills scattered all over the floor on the passenger side. Meaningless. Everything was meaningless. Especially me.

I drove around crying until the sun went down. There was nowhere to go. I finally went home to a dark, empty house.

Two weeks later, I felt a painful, pressing feeling in my lower back. I had chills and there was blood when I peed. Mom had driven down from Dayton to pick up some clothes, and when I saw her headlights pull in, I was relieved. She might be obsessed with Jim, but she usually came through when we were sick.

"I think something's wrong," I told her when she walked in. Julie and I were sitting on the stairs leading up to my room. "I feel terrible, light-headed and hot. There's blood when I pee."

"You're probably catching the flu. You need to get rest. I can't stay. I'm just getting a couple of things," she said, walking into her bedroom.

Julie and I looked at each other in shock. I rubbed my forehead with the palms of my hands.

"I might need to see a doctor tonight," I said in a loud voice so she could hear me from her room. She came storming out.

"How do you manage to pick the most inopportune time to come up with this shit?" she yelled.

"I don't try to," I told her. The truth was, I was frightened. I'd never felt so ill and it wasn't a familiar feeling. It wasn't the flu or a bad cold. It was worse.

Julie stepped in. "Don't worry, Mrs. Peterson. I'll call my mom and she can take Monica to the emergency room."

Mom was furious. "Right. I'm going to make Joan drive all the way out here and then wait in the emergency room with her." She turned her back, let out an aggravated sigh, grabbed the phone off its cradle, and dialed.

"Jim? Listen, Monica is sick or something so I guess I'm stuck here for a while." She slammed down the receiver and turned to me. "Get in the car."

I sat in the backseat with Julie. We dropped her off at her house and drove to the hospital.

In the emergency room they took my temperature and a urine sample. I was lying on a gurney when the doctor came in.

"You have a temperature of a hundred and five and a kidney infection," he said. "I'm going to do an examination. Let me know if you feel any pain where I'm touching."

He pushed into my back. I flinched. "Why'd you punch me?" I asked, shocked.

"I didn't punch you. I placed my hand over your right kidney and it hurt so much, you thought I punched you. That's not good."

He walked over to the nurses' station, picked up a white phone, and said, "I need a bed." He looked over at me. "You're staying."

I was in the most pain of my life but happy to finally be in someone's care. I was relieved. Relieved there was something wrong. Relieved I finally felt as rotten physically as I did emotionally. The physical part could be monitored, controlled, and healed. Unlike my depression and feelings of being completely on my own or in the way, a kidney infection was obvious. Not a secret.

I wished there had been obvious signs of destruction on all of us kids: bruises or burn marks, something that indicated how violent our house was, but words and neglect don't leave visible marks. And that confuses even the person who knows better.

That night Mom hated me for needing her, and I hated her for the exact same reason.

The next morning while I was lying in bed on an IV drip, a nurse came in and asked me who my guardian was.

"What?" I asked.

"Who is responsible for you?" That was a very good question. When I didn't answer right away, she rephrased it. "Who takes care of your insurance?"

"My dad," I said.

"We're going to need to call him," she said. "Can you give me his number?"

I didn't want to, but she insisted.

I turned my head toward the wall. Dad was going to be furious.

I needed to figure out a way to get by financially until I graduated the following year, but I felt too rotten to think about it. I would try to sleep and think of a plan tomorrow.

The following week when I was feeling better, I drove to Dad's store on my lunch break from school. I parked in the alley until I saw him leave for lunch, then jumped out of the Mustang and walked inside.

Doug Miller worked the tool counter when Dad was out, and he was staring right at me.

"Hi, Doug," I said.

"Your dad's not here," he said, ready for a fight. Doug had been there when I'd peeled out and scattered rocks at the window. I smiled.

"I just have to use the bathroom," I lied, and walked over to the beige door. I could feel Doug staring at my back. I waited inside until I heard a customer come in. As soon as Doug went into the back to retrieve whatever piece of hardware the guy needed, I walked up front and swiped the divorce papers from under the counter.

I quickly drove to the public library, where I made copies for myself at ten cents a page. When I drove back to Dad's store, no one was at the counter. I could hear Doug running water in the bathroom, so I furtively returned the papers and ran out to my car. I'd made it.

That night I studied those papers line by line. I sat on my bed with my little green lamp directed right at them. After all I'd been through, the papers seemed benign—no wrath or fury. There was nothing about Dad throwing furniture or Mom stealing money from Dad's truck. Instead, it was dull and wordy, full of phrases I could barely negotiate my way through. I did understand two things: He was required to pay for my college education and my medical bills.

After that I made sure I needed money only for medical purposes. A doctor's appointment usually cost around seventy-five dollars, so after asking for that, I didn't need money for at least a month. Then I needed money to get my teeth cleaned. That was fifty dollars and lasted a while.

I didn't go to the doctor or get my teeth cleaned, but I had money to live on. I didn't ask too often or for more than I needed.

Julie and I had just picked up Kimberly Sanders from the airport in the hearse. She was only two years older than us, but had died of cancer anyway. She flew in from Phoenix in a Carrington cherry wood casket with eggshell crepe interior. It was the fanciest (and most expensive) coffin Julie and I had ever seen.

Kimberly had always had curly red hair, but when they opened the casket to check her and removed the ten-by-ten swab of cotton from her face, she had no hair and no eyebrows. Only freckles.

We were driving the hearse up and down Main Street, when I saw my dad in the Valley Inn Restaurant. He was sitting at the counter alone, his head bent over a bowl of chili. His shoulders were rounded and his glasses had slid halfway down his nose. Earlier at the store I'd overheard him say he had a dinner at the Elks Club. I wondered why he wasn't there.

We drove by at least four more times, thinking Kimberly might enjoy one last night of cruising Main Street, and Dad was still sitting there, drinking a cup of coffee and looking around.

We unloaded the hearse and parked it at the mortuary. After throwing Lowell the keys, I drove Julie to her house in the Mustang. On my way home I drove through town. Dad's truck wasn't at the restaurant, so I decided to stop by the Elks Club just to see if he'd ended up there. I ran into a couple in the parking lot who'd known Mom and Dad when they were married.

"Hi, Monica," the woman said.

"Oh, hi." I didn't know what to say so I said, "I'm looking for my dad."

"Oh, we don't see much of him anymore," the woman said.

"Why not?" I asked.

"He tends to overstay his welcome, if you know what I mean." She smiled.

"No kidding," I said, not understanding.

"Your father is funny for about five minutes, until you realize he's all surface, no depth."

I hated my dad, but I could have punched this woman. Her husband took her arm and said to me, "I'm sorry, she's had a few too many." As he was escorting her away, she turned and said, "What I'm trying to say is, your father doesn't wear well, does he?"

They wandered to their car and I stayed put. Maybe Dad wasn't such a big shot after all. Maybe people had him figured out.

When I got home, I was hungry so I poured a bowl of Rice Krispies and sat down at the kitchen table. I caught my reflection in the small-paned windows. There I was, head down, shoulders rounded, eating a bowl of cereal alone. Dad and I looked nothing alike physically, but our lives were similar. I ate alone, I exaggerated stories, and I didn't let people see the depth in me. Maybe *I* didn't "wear well" either.

I pushed the cereal down into the milk with the back of my spoon and thought back to the day when Dad was a good guy.

When we bought our house, I was six years old. Our back-yard was mostly a marsh swollen with stagnant water that swirled in the spots where dragonflies and mosquitoes lit. Dad kept saying, "I'm gonna turn that mess into a grassy backyard and build a gazebo back there."

Every day he came home on his lunch hour, hauling load after load of dirt and leveling it with Papaw's red Farmall trac-tor. One Sunday, I was climbing up to the crossbars of our metal swing set, where I could sit and watch Dad rolling back and forth on his tractor. I was wearing a red-white-and-blue-ruffled bikini because we were going to Rocky Fork State Park to swim when Dad was done.

I managed to climb to the top of the swing set but lost my balance and fell smack on the ground, directly onto my back. I couldn't get up and I couldn't breathe. The fall knocked the wind out of me, which had never happened before. I lay there panicked, not able to make a sound. Dad must have seen me fall, because he jumped off the tractor, leaving it running, and ran across the yard to get to me. He swept me up in his arms and ran into the house. I was still not breathing.

"Come on, Monica, let some air in there," he said, pounding on my back. I couldn't make a sound and my skin was covered in a thin layer of sweat. He laid me on their bed, saying, "It's comin', don't worry, it's comin.'" He wasn't kidding: I sat up and projectile vomited all over the bed.

The vomit brought a rush of air, and my lungs sucked in as much as they could get. I was so relieved that I grabbed Dad around the neck and hugged him tight. He patted my back. "You took a big fall," he said, stating the obvious. I was cry-ing now from the relief of breathing again. "You saved me," I told him.

I stood up from the kitchen table and put my cereal bowl in the sink.

The phone rang. It was almost eleven o'clock. It had to be Mom. I walked over and picked up the receiver.

"Hello?"

"Monica?"

"Yes."

"It's JoAnn. Were you sleeping?" she asked.

"Are you kidding? I just got home." I pulled the phone cord around the corner so I could sit on a kitchen chair. "How's it goin'?" I asked, tucking my feet up under my butt.

"I was just making sure you were home and eating," she said.

"I just had a bowl of cereal," I told her. "I'm eating."

"The last time I saw you, you looked really thin," she said. "How much do you weigh?"

"I have no idea," I said. I'd never actually weighed myself except when the doctor did it.

"Make sure you eat," she said.

"Okay. Is that why you called?" I asked.

She laughed. "That's why I called."

I slept better that night knowing JoAnn was thinking about me.

That Thanksgiving, I asked Dad where he was going for dinner. He grunted something about staying home since Mammaw and Papaw were in Florida on vacation.

I couldn't get it out of my mind that Dad was eating alone on a family holiday—that no one had invited him to their house. I kept picturing him eating that bowl of chili.

Maybe it was because he gave me the "medical" money without a fight, or maybe it was because I knew how sad it felt to be alone, but I fixed a big plate of food from Thanksgiving dinner at Mom's and drove it eighteen miles down to Lake Hiawatha. He was surprised to see me, and I was surprised to be there.

"I brought a plate of food," I offered, shrugging. "I thought you might be alone."

"Well, thanks," he said awkwardly. I half-expected him to smack it out of my hand and call me an idiot, but instead he smiled. I saw his teeth for the first time in years.

We walked into the dining room, where he set the plate down on a plastic woven brown-and-orange place mat.

"White and dark meat, dressing, mashed potatoes," I said. "It might not be warm anymore."

"Mmmm," he said, "this looks pretty darn good."

I sat across from him while he ate. We didn't say anything. It was awkward and oddly rewarding. It was the first time in my life I had offered something to my dad. I hadn't realized it, but I'd never thought to bring him anything before. I'd treated him like Mom had—he gave, we took.

Looking around, I saw for the first time the home Dad had set up for himself. I noticed a large green macramé plant holder hanging from a hook in the living room ceiling, and a clock made from a shellacked cross section of a cypress tree trunk, placed over the stairwell. There was a plaid upholstered recliner right in front of the television and enormous lamps with seashells plastered on their stems and bases. Dad's decor would have sent Mom into a coma, but I was fascinated.

Here was who Dad really was. Mom's cherrywood dining room set and gorgeous slip-covered couches had nothing to do with him. His rust-colored wraparound couch and wagon-wheel coffee table were just his style. I didn't know he'd had it in him to create such a cozy home. His kitchen was fully stocked with pots and pans hanging from a square wooden frame over the sink, and matching plates and silverware. The house was spotless.

The music playing on his stereo was soft country. Mom hated country music. I had never heard it in our house.

Taking in the place, I felt sorry for Dad because I realized none of us had ever really known him. Part of the reason was his cruelty, but part of the reason was that Mom had obliterated everything in the house that Dad would have liked, as if she were ashamed of him.

Glancing over at Dad, his white paper napkin spread across his lap and his head bent over his plate, I decided I would try to be nice to this monster. I would try to understand him a little; after all, soon I would be at college and gone forever.

On December fifth I called Dad and invited him to go Christmas shopping. It was the first time I'd ever called without asking for money. He was hesitant, but accepted. The following Sunday I rode along with him to Cincinnati. It was always harrowing to be in the car with him, so I pretended he was someone I didn't know. I'd decided to start over.

Dad wore a red sweater and a tweed Bing Crosby–style hat. I tried to look festive too, in a green-and-white-plaid jumper with a white turtleneck underneath. We rode along without speaking, Christmas carols playing on the radio, a cold rain peppering the windshield of his pickup.

I learned how he shopped. He liked to pick things up and really look them over, especially the price, and more often than not, he wouldn't buy it. I decided to forget my urgency to finish my own Christmas shopping and follow Dad around instead. He even treated me to a sandwich at Denny's.

Maybe the divorce had been good for him. He was definitely changing, softening. He spread the divorce papers on the counter a few more times, and then just started giving me the money.

I also found a job working after school and on Saturdays at Photography on Main to supplement my meager hearse-driving income. This helped both of us feel that we were on more equal ground—that I was making an effort to take care of myself.

One day when Julie and I ran into the Valley Inn Restaurant to buy a Coke, we saw Dad sitting with Dave Kilner and a couple of other men.

"Aren't you proud of Monica for becoming a member of the National Honor Society?" Dave asked Dad. Dad didn't know what he was talking about. He sort of grunted.

"I'm going to be initiated into the National Honor Society on Friday night," I told him. And responding to Dave's expectant look, I said, "You can come if you want." I knew Dad wouldn't come to any goofy event of mine.

"Okay," Dad said, slurping up a spoonful of vegetable soup.

"Okay?" I asked.

"I'll come," Dad said, not looking up. I looked at Dave, who winked at me.

"Okay," I said.

Dave walked Julie and me out to the parking lot. When we got to the car, he put his hand on my shoulder and said, "Kid, you gotta start somewhere."

One thing Mom and Jim never missed were my awards ceremonies. They liked taking credit as "my parents" at these happy, prestigious functions. Mom was furious when she saw Dad walk into the room in a suit.

"What's that *thing* doing here?" she asked, nodding in Dad's direction.

"I invited him," I said.

"Why would you do that?" she asked.

"Because he's paying for the pin they gave me and the new shoes I needed for the ceremony," I snapped.

"Jim is the one who provides for you," Mom said.

"What?" I burst out laughing.

"You don't appreciate what Jim gives you?" she asked, and I

swear to God, I thought she was joking, but she gave me this peculiar look, like she'd smelled something nasty.

"You *can't* be serious," I said.

"It would kill Jim if he knew you felt this way," she continued, "after all he's done for us."

"For *you*," I said. "All he's done for *you*."

"You ungrateful little shit," she said, storming off to find her table.

Ten minutes later my name was called. I walked onstage angry and confused. Was I crazy, or was she?

CHAPTER FIFTEEN

During the fall of my senior year, I went to a basketball game in Harrisburg with Julie and some friends. We were eating popcorn and cheering on the Elk Grove Braves when I noticed a tall, skinny blond boy with shoulder-length hair walking in front of the bleachers. He had light blue eyes and the look of a kid who'd seen too much—a little sad and definitely interesting.

The second time he walked by, he looked right at me and smiled. I smiled too, and when I did, a flush started in my chest and ended (surprisingly) in my crotch. I shivered.

I watched the boy climb into the stands but lost track of him in the crowd. The ball game was still going (with Elk Grove losing) when the kid tapped me on the shoulder. He was leaning in from the aisle. I turned around and he waved a finger for me to follow him. I was intrigued—especially by that flushed feeling.

"I saw you in the stands," he said. Up close he looked pale, almost anemic.

"Right," I said, completely flustered. Suddenly I didn't know what day it was, my favorite album, or my address.

"Could I take you on a date sometime?" he asked. No one had ever flat out asked me on a date without knowing me.

"Okay," I said, feeling awkward. He seemed about ten years older than me, but he couldn't have been.

"What's your name?" he asked. I laughed, realizing I'd accepted a date from someone who didn't know my name.

"Monica. What's yours?"

"Adam," he said. "Let's find a piece of paper so you can give me your number. I'll call you this week." I tapped Julie on the shoulder and asked if she had paper in her purse. She only had the back of a deposit slip, so I used that.

My writing was sloppier than usual because I was sure that life was about to become a lot more stimulating. I handed Adam the paper and he winked at me. The body flush came back.

As I watched him walk away, I decided that if he *was* trouble, I wanted it. He wasn't like Phil Robinson or John Mitchell from my high school—with short hair, Future Farmers of America jackets, and glasses. And he sure as hell wasn't like Keith "Mom's a Homosexual" Phillips. He walked like Mick Jagger, loose and sexy.

That was the word; Adam was sexy.

None of my friends had ever heard of Adam. In Elk Grove that was unusual.

He grew up about twenty miles east in Greenville but was attending college at Otterbein College in Westerville. He was twenty-one and had come to the ball game with a friend who'd moved to Elk Grove. I was seventeen and ready for a huge distraction.

On our first date we went to see *Breaking Away* in Cincinnati. In the parking lot of Northbrook Mall, Adam gave me my first romantic, sexy kiss. Suddenly nothing mattered more than Adam and that kiss.

He drove me home in his light blue 1973 Ford Galaxy. It was a goofy car, but I didn't care. I was so mesmerized, he could have picked me up on a John Deere tractor. When he walked me to my door, he said he'd pick me up the following Friday at seven o'clock. He didn't ask, he told me.

The next Friday we drove to Rocky Fork State Park and kissed on a picnic table. He laid me down on top of it and pushed his hand under the waistband of my jeans. Fear leapt into my throat but I didn't stop him.

Suddenly, and to my surprise, lying on the picnic table under a million stars, I had no worries. I was connected to Adam in a way I'd never been connected to anyone. I decided it was real love.

Sitting in his car at the park, I asked, "How do you know what to do with me?"

"I've been with lots of girls," he said, pulling out a pack of Marlboros.

"How many?" I asked.

"I don't know, plenty," he said, lighting a cigarette.

"Did you have sex with them?" I asked.

He blew smoke out of his mouth as he laughed. "Yes, I had sex with them."

"Will you have sex with me?" I asked, shocking myself.

He flicked his cigarette out the window, took my chin in his hand, and kissed me. "I would love to have sex with you. When you're ready."

"I'm ready," I said quickly.

"You're not ready. *I'll* let you know when you're ready," he said. He drove me home, kissed me good-bye, and headed back to Westerville. I listened to the forty-five of "My Sharona" over and over that night.

Adam made me wait three more months. I used that time to drive to Planned Parenthood in Manning, where no one would know me, and got on the pill.

Finally, we had sex in his friend's trailer. If I hadn't been so hell-bent on doing it, I would have opted for a more romantic place, but I would have done it on top of the Galesburg water tower by the time Adam finally agreed.

He went slowly and gently, but it didn't matter. Sex was a colossal letdown, the biggest lie I'd ever been fed—not only from friends (including Susan and Julie)—but from my girl manual, *Seventeen* magazine. Who the hell was actually enjoying *that*?

It was the most searingly painful, bloody, hideous thing I'd ever experienced. It wasn't romantic, it wasn't pleasant, it wasn't even humane. I was beyond pissed.

"That's the way it is the first time. Didn't anyone tell you that?" he asked casually.

"No," I said, looking for my panties.

"Then I'm sorry," he said, pulling me close to him. "I should've told you. You'll see. It'll get easier."

"I can't imagine *ever* enjoying that," I said. He laughed and lit a cigarette.

"You'll love it, trust me," he said.

"When?"

He looked up at the ceiling, dragging on the cigarette. "In less than two weeks, it'll feel great." I smiled.

It took less than two weeks—it took more like three days, and it didn't just feel great, it was life-altering, mind-boggling, perfect. My faith in *Seventeen* was restored.

Adam drove back and forth from Westerville to Elk Grove on weekends, but we decided we wanted to see each other during the week too. His grandmother had an apartment in Cincinnati, so he picked me up after school and drove me to Cincinnati.

During the week I'd stay in Cincinnati and he'd drive me down in time for school the next morning. No one was keeping track of me anyway.

I couldn't imagine loving anyone more than I loved Adam. I even understood, for the first time, how Mom must have felt about Jim.

Adam and I continued like that through the fall of my senior year. He drove down, sometimes I drove up, and we had sex all the time. We couldn't even sit through an entire movie, instead leaving in the middle of it to rush to his grandmother's apartment to attack each other. She stayed in her room the whole time. I'd never even seen her.

One night he told me that his grandmother was schizophrenic and he thought he might be as well. That would explain his occasional erratic behavior. I'd sometimes find him on the couch completely spaced out or giggling to himself. Sometimes he became very quiet and would then make weird faces at me. I always got the feeling he enjoyed scaring me. That it was deliberate, made up.

I stayed with Adam. I was in love with him and he was separate from Galesburg, Elk Grove, and my family, which only made him more attractive. And there was the mind-blowing sex, which trumped his probable insanity.

Also, I wouldn't have broken up with him; I'd never been in love before and wasn't sure it would happen again. I wasn't sure someone sane and straight would even date me.

For New Year's Eve of my senior year, Adam told me he was going to Westerville with friends but would drive down New Year's Day to see me.

When my friends and I walked into a New Year's Eve party in Elk Grove, Adam was on the couch with a brunette sitting on his lap. I stayed long enough to see him kiss her on the mouth.

I swallowed my humiliation with Mr. Boston ready-mixed screwdrivers and drove seven of my friends to the elementary school parking lot to do about a hundred doughnuts in the snow. There was no one home at my house, so my friends told their parents they were staying with each other and stayed with me instead. These were the nights it was great to have no parents. At my house we drank more vodka, smoked Virginia Slims, and threw bottles at our back fence. Then everyone picked a bed and slept until noon.

I woke up feeling hungover and heartbroken. I played Air

Supply's *Lost in Love* album on the downstairs stereo. Julie woke up and wandered into the kitchen.

"You should kill that music," she said. "It's only going to make it worse."

I was sobbing, mascara from the night before running in long Alice Cooper–like streaks down my face.

"Why would Adam do that?" I asked.

"He's an asshole," she said. "Maybe he wants to break up but didn't know how to tell you."

"Why would he want to break up?"

"I don't know," she said, opening the fridge and staring inside. Julie appeared to be more hungover than I was.

I started a pot of coffee.

Adam pulled into my driveway two hours later. I still hadn't showered or brushed my teeth. I met him at the door.

"What the hell, Adam? Why are you here?" I asked.

"Looks like you had fun last night," he said, laughing.

"Are you going to act like you didn't see me at the party, you fucking asshole?" I was standing in the doorway.

"What party?" he asked.

"Oh my god, I'm going to kill you," I said. "The one where you were kissing that girl."

"She's just a friend who I kissed because it was almost midnight. Don't be so possessive," he said.

"Possessive? You said you were going to be in Westerville. If you were in Elk Grove, you should have been with me, right? WE ARE DATING, RIGHT?"

"I'm gonna let you cool out. I'll call you later in the week," he said, turning to leave.

I stood in the doorway and watched him back out of the drive-way. I slammed into the house, walked to the stereo, and lifted the needle on the turntable to "All Out of Love." When the intro began, I burst into tears again. Julie was making scrambled eggs.

That week I found out from several people at school that they'd seen Adam with a bunch of different girls over the last few months; they just hadn't known how to tell me. But since we were close to graduation and I had caught him anyway, they thought I needed to know what a creep he was.

Girls in Elk Grove had seen him with me and had gotten his phone number. I found out who these girls were. I knew them, had gone through school with them, but they weren't friends. They were the "wild" girls, and I acted like a "good" girl, which was probably the reason they felt okay screwing me over.

I felt worse than duped, not to mention that my heart was broken.

I pulled out the phone book and looked up Stephanie Knox. I sat on my white leather beanbag chair and dialed her number.

"Is Stephanie there?" I asked when her mom answered. She put down the phone to find her. I waited.

"Hello?"

"Stephanie?"

"Yes."

"This is Monica Peterson. I just called to thank you for screwing my boyfriend."

There was silence on the other end.

"I'm sorry, Monica. But he, you know, he came after me. I wasn't looking for it."

"That makes me feel SO much better. I hope this happens to YOU someday so you'll know how I feel," I said.

"Oh, it's happened to me. Twice," she said. This threw me. Stephanie was a sad case.

"Didn't you learn from that? What the hell's wrong with you?" I said.

"Adam's really, really cute," she said.

"NO SHIT! That's why he's MY boyfriend." I was fighting tears now.

"I know. I'm sorry," she said again.

"Do me one favor, since you already fucked me over. Don't tell Adam I know. I'm going to tell him myself this weekend. And then he's all yours."

"Can I take him to the senior prom?"

"What?"

"Would you care if I took him to the prom?" she repeated.

"Oh my god, this is a nightmare." I hung up.

I didn't call the other girls on the list.

Tuesday night, Adam called.

"Hi, sweetie, have you calmed down?" he asked.

I bit my tongue and said, "A little."

"Can we have a date and I'll make it up to you," he teased.

"Friday night," I said. "Pick me up around six."

"Where do you want to go?" he asked.

"I don't even care," I said.

"I love you." I didn't say anything. "I can't wait to see you," he added.

"Okay, see you Friday." I hung up and burst into sobs again. I put on Barbra Streisand's album *Guilty* and put the needle on "What Kind of Fool." Adam had sounded like he always did. I loved him and wanted to have sex with him at least fifty more times. But that wasn't going to happen.

I told him to come to my house because I wanted him to make the long drive to Elk Grove so I could break up with him and send him back to Westerville. The phone was too easy.

The following Friday, Mom and Jim drove to Columbus for dinner. When Adam pulled into the driveway, I put on my gray wool coat and walked outside. He stepped out of his car and leaned down to kiss me. I pulled my head back.

"Are you fucking crazy?" I said.

"What?"

"I know about those other girls. I spoke to Stephanie Knox. Get back in your car, and get the hell out of my driveway. We are *over*."

He stood there for a moment, and then punched me in the face. I felt a blinding pain below my eye. Before I could react, he grabbed my left arm and pulled me toward his car. I fought to get away, thrashing and grabbing his hair, but he was stronger. He pushed me into the passenger seat. I was screaming, but he hit me in the face again and told me to "shut the fuck up." I couldn't believe this was happening.

"You're driving," he said as he shoved me over and took his place in the passenger seat. He grabbed a rifle from the backseat and propped it on his lap, aiming it straight at me. He opened the glove compartment and pulled out a box of Winchester rifle cartridges. Then he opened the box, shook a few shells out into his hand, and dumped them into the pockets of his jeans.

"Head to Cloverdale, and I'll tell you where to turn," he snapped.

My hands were shaking and I was trying to figure out if anyone could see what was happening. Would one of the Whitmores call the police? God knows they'd never missed me smoking a joint in the driveway. Mom always got a call when *that* happened, but today, perhaps for the first time in the eleven years since we'd moved next to them, they were minding their own business.

Adam forced me to drive to an abandoned train trestle and told me to get out of the car. I didn't budge. It was snowing by then and I sat there glued to the seat with fright. I would rather have been shot in a car than out in the frozen woods, where it would take forever for someone to find me.

I thought of a recurring dream I'd had as a child: a man

kidnapping me and killing me at a train trestle. Maybe it had been foreshadowing.

Adam grabbed the keys out of the ignition, got out of the car, and disappeared into the thick woods that surrounded us. I was positive he was either going to blow his own head off or shoot me through the windshield.

I sat in the car trying to make a plan for myself to get out of there. I thought about running, but what if it pissed him off more? He'd definitely shoot me. Plus, we were so far out in the country that there was no place to run, especially as cold as it was.

It was getting dark and I didn't have my watch. Then I heard a shot in the woods. I took a quick intake of air. The hollow sound of the gun ricocheted off all those trees. He'd done it. He'd shot himself. I didn't know what to do.

I strained to hear something, anything, but the snow was keeping everything still and quiet. If he were alive, I'd hear him moving around, unless he'd run off and left me there.

If he'd shot himself, I'd have to find his body and get the keys to the car to go get help. And if he hadn't shot himself, maybe he was trying to get me out of the car so he could shoot me. I had never been so petrified in my life.

I rubbed my hands together. I didn't have my gloves and I was freezing; I couldn't feel the tips of my fingers.

Suddenly, I felt the car bouncing. Adam had jumped onto the back bumper and was jumping up and down. He was fucking with me, and I was fucking furious. I kicked open my door and lunged toward him.

"Give me the keys," I said.

He held them above my head, with the rifle waving around in his other hand. He was smiling.

"Shoot me or give me the fucking keys!" I yelled. He threw them into the snow.

While I was down on my hands and knees looking for them, he randomly fired shots into the woods. I grabbed the keys and made it to the driver's door, but I wasn't quick enough to lock it before Adam was inside as well. He smiled. I was thinking of ways to save myself.

"We're both tired," I told him. "We need to think things over." I put the key in the ignition and Adam didn't object. I flipped the key and turned on the car. I was so cold by then, I couldn't bend my fingers. Adam held the rifle between his legs, pointing up.

"You're not breaking up with me," he told me.

"I was just angry about that girl. You know I love you," I said. I was getting out of this mess no matter what.

"You're just saying that," he said, his hair wet from the snow. I didn't know if he was selfish, crazy, or both. I didn't care.

"Have I ever left you?" I asked.

"No," he said, smiling, looking down.

"Exactly." I touched his arm. "I'm backing the car out of here. I'm starving. Let's go to the house and I'll make us something to eat."

He nodded. "I knew you'd come around," he said, pulling a cigarette out of the glove compartment and flicking his lighter. "I knew you would."

"Put the gun in the backseat," I said.

"No." He blew smoke out.

"I'm not going to forgive you and make up unless that gun's in the backseat," I told him, backing onto the road.

"What, this?" he said, pointing it directly at me. I threw the car into drive and shoved my foot against the gas pedal. He was still holding the gun. I watched the telephone poles zipping by and wondered how I could crash the car in such a way that Adam would take the hit. I was starting to believe I'd never make it home, when he finally tossed the gun into the backseat. I didn't even look at him.

"It's in the backseat," he said, scooting closer to me. He leaned over for a kiss. I wanted to bite him. I gave him a peck and drove to my house as fast as I could. I pulled into my driveway and saw the lights were on. By some miracle, Mom and Jim were home.

When Adam saw this, he told me to pull back out, but I was already out of the car and running up to the side door. Adam must have shoved over into the driver's seat, because his car squealed out of the driveway and sped away.

I ran into the house.

"Mom? Jim?" I screamed. They both came running from the kitchen.

I was sobbing. Jim put his arm around me.

"What happened?"

"I broke up with Adam and he took me to a train trestle and held a gun on me." I could barely get the words out. "He punched me in the face."

"I'll call the police," Jim said, heading toward the phone.

"The gun's in the backseat of his car," I told him.

"Maybe we shouldn't call the police," Mom said. I looked at her in disbelief. "Do you want the whole town to know?"

"What if he comes after me again?"

"She's right. We need to call the police," Jim insisted.

"I doubt he'll try this again," Mom said.

"But he knows I'm alone in the house a lot. He knows my schedule," I said.

No one said anything.

I went into the bathroom to see if my eye was black from the punch I'd taken. It was red and puffy from crying and it was sore— but it wasn't black. As usual, there were no obvious signs. And it would be a secret that my boyfriend had punched me in the face and terrorized me with a rifle for two and a half hours—because it was more important that Mom keep up appearances than keep her children safe.

❦   ❦   ❦

The next morning I threw my birth control pills into the trash. If sex meant possible death, I didn't need it, but I did need to get out of Mason County. If Adam was still gunning for me, I wasn't going to be sitting there, waiting.

I packed Mom's cloth flowered suitcase and drove to JoAnn's apartment in Columbus. During the two hours it took to get there, I continuously checked my rearview mirror. I was positive Adam was following me.

I imagined him jumping out at the next rest stop and shooting me in the face. When I did stop to pee, I ran in, peed standing up, didn't wash my hands, didn't check myself in the mirror, didn't buy a Coke, unlocked my car as quickly as possible, jumped in, locked the doors, and sped away. If he were following me, he'd have to be quick.

Even though Becky lived near JoAnn, I didn't tell her I was coming down. She'd met Mitch, her new narcissistic boyfriend, and they lived in a posh gated community outside Columbus on Griggs Reservoir. She was now in her own love bubble. I wouldn't have chosen her to lean on anyway. It would have been the equivalent of leaning on an electric fence. We tried to be nice to each other at holidays and birthdays, but it was strained.

JoAnn was welcoming and beyond furious about Adam.

"I could kill that bastard. He better NEVER come near you again. I'm serious. I'll kill that son of a bitch." JoAnn usually didn't curse. I hugged her.

I was exhausted. I lay down, closed the door to her bedroom, and fell into a deep, safe sleep with my sister right outside.

When I woke, I rummaged through my suitcase, searching for a pair of warm socks, but there weren't any. I stuck my head out the door.

"Can I borrow a pair of socks?" I asked.

At home I'd begun raiding Jim's sock drawer. He had white Goldtoes that were extra large and cozy. The socks were warm, but mostly I liked that they were Jim's. He was starting to grow on me.

"Top drawer," JoAnn said.

I closed the door and padded over to the dresser. When I opened the drawer, I saw there was a book, *Bisexuality in the Arts*, lying just below her dress socks. I glanced at the inside flap. "Essays on being gay or bisexual in a creative community." I was startled. I quickly stuck it back under her socks, put on a pair of white tube socks with two green rings around the tops of them, and walked into the kitchen, where JoAnn was making a plate of hummus and pita for us. Her roommate, Stacy, was at work.

I sat on the wooden bar stool at the counter and studied JoAnn with her straight brown hair and no makeup. She was wearing Birkenstocks, a tie-dyed T-shirt, and baggy blue hospital scrubs as pants. Maybe she was gay.

"Your eye looks black," she said.

"Really?" I walked into the bathroom to take a look. It was black, all right.

"Do you want some ice?" she yelled.

"Actually, it's not sore, but thanks," I said, poking it with my finger. It *was* sore.

I stared at the bluish purple half-moon under my eye and the small dot of bright red blood on the white part. There was finally physical evidence that something violent and wrong had occurred. I didn't put ice on it.

That weekend JoAnn laughed and sang along to Judy Collins on the stereo. She and I picked up her roommate from work and went out for pasta at Noble Romans. JoAnn hung on Stacy's every word, leaning forward to "brush" Stacy's black curly hair off her forehead as she talked. I twirled my spaghetti onto my fork and paid attention. Something was going on.

I drove back to Elk Grove without asking JoAnn about the book.

❖ ❖ ❖

A couple of months later I heard Stacy was moving back to Cleveland. I called JoAnn.

"How are you?" I asked.

"Not bad." I heard her dragging on a cigarette.

"You don't sound great," I told her.

"Yeah, well, that's the way it's been lately," she said.

"Did Stacy move out?" I asked.

"She's pregnant. She's getting married," JoAnn told me, her voice cracking. There was a long pause. "I get to be a bridesmaid."

"I'm sorry," I said.

"Why?" JoAnn asked. I was thrown by this. If she didn't want to tell me, I wasn't going to "out" her.

"You sound sad," I said.

"I'm tired. I gotta go." JoAnn hung up.

Two months later I saw pictures of JoAnn wearing a lacy peach bridesmaid dress and a forced smile, walking down the aisle toward a pregnant Stacy, who was marrying her high school boyfriend.

For the next four months JoAnn slumped into a bad depression. Becky saw her in Columbus and told Mom that she was sleeping a lot, not eating, and barely making it to classes.

I called JoAnn.

"Listen, I just want you to know I don't care if you're gay," I blurted out. She laughed. I waited for a reply.

"When I get up off the floor, I'll be able to actually say something," she said.

"It doesn't matter if you're gay. It only matters that you're happy. You have to pull yourself out of this depression," I told her.

"I'd like to," she said.

"I'm coming down this weekend and we'll see what we can do," I told her. My hands were shaky as I hung up the phone. I thought about Bill Lawrence and their prom picture. I thought about Keith Phillips and our prom picture.

Things were never the way they seemed, and it was happening more and more.

What would being gay mean for JoAnn's life? What would people say and how would they treat her? Whatever it brought, I'd be there to help. JoAnn had become the sister I'd always wanted, and I wanted more than anything to be a good sister too.

On Saturday, I drove to Columbus. JoAnn had her shoulder-length hair cut to less than two inches all over. Her head looked like a baby chick's.

"You're not just coming out of the closet. You're standing on the porch waving a flag," I told her.

"To hell with it," she said. "I'm tired of being someone I'm not."

"Fucking right," I said. "You've hidden it long enough." But inside I wasn't sure. The idea of someone being gay didn't bother me; it was just that I wanted JoAnn and me to be alike. Now, standing next to her with my long permed hair and painted fingernails, I knew just how different we were. I hoped that wouldn't keep us from being close as she began a new life.

When I got home, it was senior week.

Julie and I went to a party at our friend Dawn's house. Her mother and about one hundred and fifty high school kids were there. A makeshift bar was set up on a picnic table in the backyard, and it seemed like the same joint was being passed from eight till midnight without a time-out. We smoked, drank, danced, and saw Dawn's mom making out with our class president, Richard Hastings.

I graduated on an eighty-degree afternoon in May, and Dad was there, waiting for me outside the gym. He gave me a card with two hundred-dollar bills inside. I hugged and thanked him. I wanted to invite him out to the house, but Mom would have killed me.

Mom and Jim gave me a huge party. They invited my friends, teachers, neighbors—everyone I'd ever known came. There was ham, potato salad, deviled eggs, green beans, rolls, sodas, iced tea, and a huge cake that said CONGRATULATIONS MONICA on top. Mom surrounded the cake with all the trophies I'd won throughout high school, at the White Creek Players, and on the speech team. It was the best party I'd ever had.

Ironically, I was sad about leaving home, mostly because I was terrified of the future. I never trusted that things would get better. I believed in treading water, staying in the lousy, lonely, crappy place where everything was familiar. Change scared me more than a thousand Adams or Dads or empty houses.

Later that month I stopped by Dad's store to see how he was doing. I was heading up to Columbus to see JoAnn and his store was on the way.

I didn't think twice about stopping in at Dad's nowadays. If I had a few minutes to kill, instead of driving the eight miles to Galesburg I'd stop in at Dad's and use the bathroom or make a call. Sometimes he and I would lean against the counter watching the cars drive by or stand in his front window checking out the western sky for any approaching weather. We hardly ever talked; we just hung out. If he heard a siren, he ran out the door without so much as a good-bye. I understood.

The other kids didn't see much of Dad. Becky didn't see him at all.

The year before, when Jamie, JoAnn, and I were already waiting in the car to go down to Dad's for Christmas dinner, Becky walked out to the driveway and announced, "I'm not going down there ever again." And she didn't. She hadn't seen him since.

"Does it bother you that you don't see Dad?" I asked one day.

"Why would it bother me?" she asked. "After all he's done, he's nothing to me."

I was amazed and impressed by her ability to cut someone off like that. At the time, I didn't realize that a person could walk away from a parent. It seemed like an impossible thing to do, and something that would send you straight to hell when you died.

Jamie still wanted Dad's approval and saw him on every visit, but Dad was silent and mean when Jamie was around. JoAnn put up with Dad. But he and I had found our footing.

Before heading to Columbus, I sat at the counter and drank a Coke with Dad.

"I'm going to see JoAnn," I told him.

"Here," he said, banging open the cash register. "Give her this. Maybe you could take her to dinner or something." He handed me a hundred-dollar bill.

"Why?" I asked, taking the money.

"I got a call from Mitch Nolan. He said JoAnn's dating her roommate, if you know what I mean." I was in shock. Besides being narcissistic, Mitch was homophobic. Becky's boyfriends were almost as bad as mine. She must have told Mitch, who had then taken it upon himself to call Dad. What an asshole!

"Mitch is a jerk," I said.

"Yeah, but he might be right about this one," Dad concluded. He looked almost happy—and Dad hated homosexuals, made fun of them all the time with jokes and slurs. It didn't make sense.

"Okay, I'll give her the money," I said. "I'm sure she could use it."

"She's still family, and we have to love her just like we always did." He'd never told any of us he loved us. What was going on?

I left the store thinking JoAnn was going to crap her pants, but when I handed her the hundred-dollar bill and told her what Dad had said, she replied, "Wow, a hundred bucks. That's pretty cheap for my sexuality."

CHAPTER SIXTEEN

I was eighteen when I walked into the theater at Kenyon College for my freshman audition. My hands were sweaty and my shoulder-length feathered hair was sprayed stiff with Aqua Net Extra Super Hold hair spray—this was the moment I'd prove myself ready for college theatre. My monologue was from Shakespeare's *The Winter's Tale*, and my sheet music from *Chicago* was tucked under my arm. Nothing could break my concentration—except that boy standing right over there. He was as relaxed as I was nervous. I watched him leaning against the wall, smoking a cigarette, and reading the *Kenyon Review*. He looked up as his name was called over the PA system: "Patrick Romano, please report to the stage." He was next.

After taking one last drag off his cigarette, he stubbed it out in the ashtray and sauntered onstage. I watched from the wings as he cursed his way through a tense monologue from David Mamet's *American Buffalo* and then, in a soft and clear tenor voice, sang "Metaphor" from *The Fantasticks*.

He ended his perfect song with a smile, did a quick bow of his curly brown head, and thanked the director. He meandered offstage looking directly at me. I was terrified of the audition and titillated by Patrick. "Hey, don't worry. It's a walk in the park out there," he said, giving my arm a little pinch.

"Monica Peterson, please report to the stage."

Luckily, my audition was not hindered by nerves and, afterward, as I happily ran offstage, Patrick was standing there clapping. "You and I are going to rock this department, Monica Peterson," he said. "You and I." He turned and walked toward the door. My breath was coming in short spurts. He wore blue jeans, tennis shoes, and a gray T-shirt. He looked delicious.

I had just moved into Bradford Hall, the only coed dorm on campus, but Patrick was renting a house. This immediately set him apart as cool and mature.

I saw his funky run-down place for the first time after the annual theatre department football game the following week. He had a party after the game, and invited me by tucking a small piece of paper with his address on it into the back pocket of my Jordache jeans.

Arriving at his house, I smelled marijuana wafting across the lawn. Everyone was hanging out on his creaky front porch, playing guitars and wearing moccasins. We had missed the sixties and seventies hippie scene, but it was being reenacted there on Romano's front porch.

Patrick walked up behind me and whispered, "Hello, there" in my ear. I spun around and smiled. Patrick was sexy in a Robert Downey Jr. sort of way. Drugged up sometimes, playing his guitar and singing Neil Young sometimes, and bathed sometimes. He was tall and thin with thick black eyelashes and smooth olive skin.

I didn't know who Neil Young was, nor did I own a pair of moccasins. Still, this guy intrigued me.

"Do you have a boyfriend, Monica?" he asked.

"No," I said, wanting to kiss him.

"I have an awesome girlfriend. Her name is Isabelle." (I wouldn't be kissing him.) "She's amazingly beautiful, but she's three hundred miles away. You can read her soul just by looking into her eyes." (I tried to picture that.) "I transferred here from American University. I'm actually a sophomore. Isabelle is still back at school." His eyes misted over. I wasn't sure what he wanted me to say. "It's rough, you know?" he added, prompting a response.

"Sure," I managed to say, feeling confident he wasn't reading my soul in my eyes.

I left the party deflated but relieved. Patrick and I did not belong together. He seemed silly and overly dramatic but sexy. It was best that he had a serious girlfriend. After my sexy but insane boyfriend, Adam, I needed someone "normal," preppy even.

Unfortunately, Patrick's dating status and our obvious differences did not stop my physical response to him. Monday morning I saw him walking by the library and wanted to jump his lanky body right there in the quad. Even in theatre history class while listening to Dean O'Malley's lecture on the Roman theatre and taking copious notes, my body kept distracting me, reminding me that it desperately wanted Patrick Romano, two rows over.

A month into school, Patrick, knowing I lived near Cincinnati, offered to drop me off at home for the weekend since he was driving down to see his brother and to "score some pot."

"You could ride along and I could get to know you better," he offered.

I agreed. It was a five-hour drive.

He picked me up at my dorm around seven p.m. and I threw my small duffel bag into his trunk. By the time we hit Highway 56 south, he had his hands down the front of my khaki shorts. His girlfriend with the soulful eyes didn't matter, religion didn't matter, and the fact that I had to straddle a console between the seats didn't matter. I was obsessed with this boy.

Patrick pulled the car off onto a small side road and threw it into park. By now the windows were completely steamed up, and I had on white Reebok tennis shoes and that's about it. We bungled our way into the backseat. I stopped.

"Do you have a condom?" I asked, panting.

"No," he said.

"I don't either. We can't have sex without a condom, but we can do something else," I said, attacking him again.

"We don't need condoms," he responded.

"I'm not on the pill," I said.

"No, what I mean is, I don't carry them because I'm sterile. I had radiation two years ago and it made me sterile."

"Are you sure?" I asked. "How do you know you're sterile?"

The sex skidded to a stop. He took a deep, dramatic breath.

"I had a rare kind of bladder cancer and needed radiation. The effects of it left me sterile. Now I'll never see the faces of my children." Long pause. "That was taken from me." Tears started rolling down his cheeks. I was embarrassed to be witnessing this.

"Wow, I'm really sorry," I said. "We shouldn't be doing this anyway. You have a girlfriend, and I'm not usually like this."

"Oh, I hope you usually are," he teased, his tears vanishing.

"No, this is new to me. I don't usually attack boys I hardly know who are involved with other people," I said. "Hey, no harm done." I was climbing over the front seat to grab my clothes. I felt really naked all of a sudden.

"I hope what I said didn't freak you out," he said.

"It did not freak me out," I said.

"Please don't tell anyone. Okay?" he asked.

"Of course not," I said, trying to imagine any conversation where it would be appropriate to interject, "Romano's sterile."

He joined me in the front seat and lit a cigarette. He turned on the car. "I love you in just your white tennis shoes." He smiled.

"Thanks. It's my new look." We laughed and drove the rest of the way with the radio blaring and his hand on my knee.

That weekend I saw a Judy Collins concert with JoAnn, who had just started dating a new girl, Jenny. When I saw them together at Union Hall on the campus of the University of Cincinnati, they looked adorable, and JoAnn seemed to be doing much better.

"How's college?" JoAnn asked.

"I don't know yet. I'm still getting used to it," I said.

We went inside and watched the concert, JoAnn holding Jenny's hand. I was impressed she would do that on such a conservative campus. She was able to be herself.

Patrick's emotional display in the car along with Judy Collins singing, "You can live the life you dream," and songs about "Women who are strong and free" had cooled my jets over him anyway.

When Patrick picked me up to head back to Kenyon, I was dressed in sloppy sweatpants and a white T-shirt. For the entire five hours back I stayed in my seat with my hands in my lap. I felt no urges.

Instead of taking me to my dorm, he pulled into the driveway of his house. He looked over. "Would you like to join me on the porch?" he asked.

"We said we weren't going to do this," I said.

"I didn't hear anyone say we weren't going to do this. And we don't have to do anything. Come on, I'll get some wine." He got out of the car and headed into the house. He had on those great jeans again.

I had the same feeling then that I had as a child when I wasn't supposed to ride my bike around the firehouse parking lot but did it anyway. This no longer felt right, but I wasn't sure how to stop it.

We had sex on the wooden glider on his front porch. It was impersonal and quick; not at all like the passion we'd experienced in the car and not at all what I had been picturing every day since I'd met him. Afterward I asked him about Isabelle. "We're free to see other people. We've moved on," he said. As he drove me back to my dorm, I wondered what had happened between the two of them.

I would have to give this time and see how it unfolded. I really liked him, but something had shifted and I wasn't sure what.

The following week I walked into the theatre and saw Patrick with his arm around a beautiful girl with long black hair. They were laughing, and I knew before he even said it: "Monica, this is Isabelle."

"Oh, nice to meet you," I managed to choke out.

"Monica is an amazing actress. You'll *love* her," he told Isabelle.

"Great," she said, but they were obviously more wrapped up in each other than in talking to me. My stomach felt as though a cement brick had been thrown at it. It was my own fault; I had known about her and I should have stayed away from him. It made my face flush to think that he probably knew of her visit before having sex with me. It wasn't as if he owed me anything, but it just wasn't a decent thing to do.

I decided to forget Romano. I snagged a great part in the fall play. It would be in competition to attend a festival at the prestigious Kennedy Center in Washington, D.C., and I was the lead. Mr. Whitfield, the head of the theatre department, was the director and Patrick was on the crew designing sets.

Isabelle flew back to American University, and within two days Patrick was walking with his arm around Cynthia, another black-haired, blue-eyed beauty. She was hanging on his every word. At rehearsal that night Patrick walked over with his arms out to offer me a hug. "Hey, no thanks," I said, and walked onstage.

He smiled. "I bet I get a hug out of you by the end of the evening," he teased.

I looked at him. "I doubt it," I said dryly, as I began leading the actors through warm-up stretches.

I was glad the sex had been bad. I was glad I hadn't invested much in Patrick. I concentrated on the play and tried not to notice Cynthia's disappointed face as she watched him walk down the hall with his arm around the waist of Rebecca. Oh my god, a serial dater. I was glad no one knew about us.

A month into rehearsals I came down with the flu. My hair wasn't washed, my face was pale, and I couldn't have cared less. I felt lousy.

Three days later at the theatre, we did a full run of the play. My character was dying of tuberculosis and one of her lines was, "I was so much stronger before I got pregnant. Before the baby, I was strong." And that night, when I said those words, with Patrick standing in the wings, I knew with absolute certainty that I did not have the flu. I was pregnant.

The next morning I rode my twelve-speed Schwinn to Planned Parenthood over on Fairview Road. I peed in a cup and lay down on the examining table, placing my legs into two stirrups that were covered in tube socks to make them more comfortable. The doctor did a pelvic exam. On the ceiling directly above me was a poster that had a cartoon of a cobra with bugged-out eyes tangled up in the branches of a tree. It read, "Things could be worse; you could be in my position."

The examination was surprisingly painful. My head was pounding. The nurse walked in with the urine test results, and I said, "I'm pregnant, aren't I?"

"You most definitely are," she replied.

The room buckled in on me. I pulled my legs out of the stirrups and sat up. "How far along?" I asked.

"Four or five weeks," she said.

I couldn't believe it. I was too smart for this. I turned to the nurse. "I can't keep this pregnancy." (I could never have said "baby.") "I have to stop this from happening. What are my options?" She told me I'd be talking to a counselor as soon as I got dressed.

My mind was racing as I pulled on my black tights and pleated gray skirt. Patrick was definitely not sterile. How could I have been so fucking stupid?

The counselor sat across from me at a small metal table. She laid out three pamphlets: "Having a Healthy Pregnancy," "Terminating Your Pregnancy," and "Giving Your Baby Up for Adoption." I stared at them numbly.

"How was it that you had unprotected sex?" she asked.

"I slept with someone I didn't know very well and he told me he was sterile," I said.

She put her hand on top of mine. "That's the oldest trick in the book."

Motherfucker. I was going to kill Patrick Romano. What about his tears? What about the faces of his never-to-be-realized children?

I remembered my friend Sandy Webster in high school having three abortions. I could never imagine taking it so lightly. This would never happen to me a second time. I would spend the rest of my life protecting myself.

The counselor went over different options.

"You can have the abortion without anesthesia. This can be uncomfortable and traumatic. You could also have it with anesthesia. It would be easier on you psychologically. The problem is that it's expensive—five hundred dollars."

I put my head in my hands. I was totally fucked.

"The only place with anesthesia is in Louisville, Kentucky. They won't do it in Ohio if you're under the age of twenty-one without parental consent." (Louisville was five and a half hours away.) "You have to wait three weeks to make sure you're absolutely doing the right thing. That's our policy."

"Three weeks?" I gasped. "I can't wait three weeks."

"Well, you'll have to. Usually they're booked up three weeks in advance anyway," she said.

I wanted to die. All I could think was: If I ignored what was inside me, it would grow into a person. I didn't feel like I could wait one more hour, let alone three more weeks. I scheduled the proce-

dure with the anesthesia for three weeks to the day and left .
Parenthood in a stunned haze.

I pedaled my bike into traffic, not caring about the horns honk-
ing or the rain that was now peppering my face. I was in a panic to
get to Patrick. He would tell me this wasn't possible, that it was some
kind of mistake. I rode my bike up his driveway, walked into his
house, opened the door to his bedroom, and straddled his sleeping
body, pinning him under the covers.

"You lied to me."

"What?" He was trying to focus his sleepy eyes.

"I'm pregnant. You told me you were sterile."

"I did not," he said.

"Yes, you fucking did," I replied. "You fucking cried about it on
my fucking shoulder."

"Whoa. I'm not sterile? Well, that's good news for me, I guess."
He rubbed his eyes and tried to sit up, but I still had him pinned
down with my legs.

"I'm totally fucked, Patrick. I don't know what the hell I'm
going to do. I need five hundred dollars by the end of this month and
someone to drive me to Louisville." He rolled me off him.

"We'll think of something," he said. "We'll work this out. Don't
worry. I'll talk to my brother. Meet me in front of the admissions
building after theatre history and we'll talk then."

I stopped my bike three times to puke in the gutter as I rode back
to my dorm to grab my books. Each puke reminded me of what I
didn't want to know. I ran upstairs, threw some toast in the "community" toaster, and went into my room to change my clothes. When
I came out, the toast was burnt. I ate it anyway. Then puked again.

In class I heard nothing of the lecture, just noise coming out of
Dr. O'Malley's mouth, like the grown-ups in *Peanuts* cartoons.
Patrick had not shown up for class. Finally, after theatre history, I
walked to the admissions building. No Patrick. I stood there for ten

minutes. I finally threw my notebook on the ground and sat on that, still waiting. Forty-five minutes later, I realized he wasn't coming. I went to my room knowing I was on my own.

I hated myself; I hated everything about me. I was a smart person and yet I'd gotten myself into this situation in the dumbest, most obvious way, all for a one-night stand.

I jumped into the shower and glanced down at my stomach. I expected it to be sticking out even though I was only four or five weeks pregnant. Instead, it was concave from all the puking. I put my face under the hot shower and let the water run into my eyes and nose and mouth. Everything was a blur. I needed five hundred dollars, a car to drive to Louisville, Kentucky, and someone to sign me in so they'd give me anesthesia. I was fucked. There was no one in the world I would tell about this . . . no one.

I couldn't even imagine telling JoAnn. As close as we were, the pregnancy seemed too seedy and irresponsible to disclose to the one person I'd always looked up to and emulated. I wanted her to believe I was an upstanding person—smart and independent. The shame and embarrassment overruled my asking for support.

That night I showed up at the theatre, pale and terrified. I ran into Patrick in the hall. "What's going on?" I asked.

"I can't help you. I talked to my brother and he thinks you're framing me. It's probably not even mine. I won't help you." He walked away and began talking to a group of friends who were standing outside smoking. I watched him through the glass doors. I wanted to slit his throat.

I couldn't focus on him, at least not until I found the money and had the procedure. Once this was out of my body, I would deal with Patrick. I had other things on my mind. It was opening night.

I walked into the theatre. Mr. Whitfield smiled at me. "Monica, you're doing a beautiful job. Your character really seems like she's dying. Not easy to pull off," he said.

"Easier than you'd think," I quipped, and walked past him to the dressing room.

Mom and Jim had just arrived to see the play. I had to give a great performance and then spend the weekend with them, puking and showing them the campus. It was going to be a nightmare.

The show opened and, in front of Mom and Jim, I said again, "I was so much stronger before I got pregnant. Before the baby, I was strong." I wanted to stop the play right then, step out of the stage light, and tell them how scared I was and what a mistake I'd made and how the world was ending. I wanted them to comfort me and tell me they still loved me and that I would get through this. But instead I pretended to die of tuberculosis. The play ended with a standing ovation.

I wish I could have told them. Jim would certainly have understood; he would have been supportive. But my mother was now in direct competition with me morally and academically. She'd brought her report card down to show me that she was still a 4.0 student. "And what's your average?" she asked. Mine was a 3.75. "Must be hard competing with a genius," she teased. I was too nauseous to care.

At the opening night party I won an award for my performance. I threw the trophy into the garbage after my family left, because I knew it would always remind me of being pregnant. Plus, this was the beginning of my punishing myself. I stopped eating real food, choosing crackers and water instead. I would not allow myself to watch television or go to a movie. I refused invitations to parties or dinner. I worked out day and night, jogging, lifting weights, and abusing the StairMaster, trying to get the baby to die. I wanted it dead, gone, away from me. Regardless of how nauseous I was, I punished myself, driving my body into the ground.

That week I ran offstage in the middle of a scene and puked in a trash can. Mr. Whitfield grabbed my arm after the performance. I was mortified.

"You feeling okay?" he asked.

"Flu," I said, walking quickly to the dressing room.

Three days later, he called me into his office.

"Monica, I think there's something going on. Do you want to talk about it?"

"No."

"I've been watching your work, which is outstanding but really raw. I wish you'd let me help you with whatever you're going through."

Tears welled up. I felt like a child. "I got myself into something monumentally stupid, but I'm taking care of it."

"Are you pregnant?" he asked. I hesitated. "You know you wouldn't be the first person this has happened to here," he said, encouraging me to talk.

I nodded.

"Is the person who did this with you helping?"

"He told me it was my problem."

"Do I know this person?" he asked.

"No. He's on the soccer team," I lied. Patrick was helping with the play and I didn't want to put Whitfield on the spot.

"I'll help any way I can." He grabbed a box of Kleenex and handed it to me.

"I don't need help," I assured him. "My parents know and they're being supportive."

"That's good," he said. "Remember, if there's anything I can do, I'll do it." I attempted a smile. He placed his hand under my chin and gently kissed my forehead, just as a father would do.

The next day I didn't get out of bed. I didn't get out of bed the following day either. I called school to say I was ill. The third day when I couldn't get out of bed, I called Planned Parenthood and asked for my nurse. I had weighed only 105 to begin with, and had then lost eight pounds.

"Hello?" she said.

"This is Monica Peterson. I can't wait another week for the abortion. I'm suicidal. I can't get out of bed and when I do I want to die. I have to move my appointment. I have to have the procedure sooner."

"I'll talk to Louisville and call you back," she said. I hung up.

There was a surge of energy that was going to propel me through. I was going to push up the date of my appointment, find the money, and get out of this excruciating mess.

I picked up the phone and called Dad. I hated to do this to him, since he was already paying for college—even though he reminded me constantly that he was only paying because the divorce papers ordered him to do so. Still, I was mortified to have to ask for anything more.

Dad knew I had health issues. My kidney infections would lean in my favor.

"Hello?"

"Dad?"

"Yes."

"It's Monica."

"How's the weather up there? It's raining here, about forty-three degrees outside."

"It's cloudy. Dad, I've had an emergency come up and I'm going to need a minor medical procedure, but they won't take my insurance. I have to pay up front and then send in the insurance form. Could you maybe loan me some money?"

"How much do you need?"

"Five hundred," I said without leaving a pause. "I need five hundred, Dad. I'm really sorry. I wouldn't ask unless it was a real emergency, which it is."

"That's a lot of money." (My heart sank.) "I don't know if I have that much lying around." I waited silently.

"I'll send you a check in the next couple of days," he finally said. I felt tears starting down my cheeks. "It's not your kidneys again, is it?"

"No, Dad, it's not my kidneys," I said.

"Well, do what you have to do," he said.

"Thanks, Dad. I can't tell you how much this means to me. I'll pay you back by the end of the semester. I promise."

I'd won an acting scholarship, which was supposed to be used to travel during the summer, but I would give it to my father now. I didn't care.

I hung up the phone just as Planned Parenthood called me back. I was having the abortion in three days. I needed that check to make it to me by then. I called Dad back.

"Dad, I'm really sorry to ask you this, but could you put the money directly into my checking account down there? I don't think I can wait for the mail."

"What's all the hurry?" he asked.

"Please, Dad, just put it into my account. I'll pay you back. Thanks." And I hung up the phone. I was a despicable person, but I was desperate and I needed that money.

On the morning of the abortion, I got up at four thirty a.m., dressed in gray sweatpants and a white sweatshirt, and grabbed my backpack with my wallet containing five hundred dollars in cash plus an extra twenty for gas or food. The bathrobe and slippers they told me to bring were shoved into a brown grocery bag.

I rode my bike over to Patrick's. He had said I could borrow his car, but his car wasn't there. He was at his new girlfriend's house. I rode over there. Nothing was going to stop this day. I banged on the door, and Patrick finally opened it. "I need your car, asshole. If you don't give it to me, I'm going in there and telling your girlfriend why I need it." He turned and walked back into the house. When he came back, he threw his keys at my feet.

"Fuck you," I said, walking away.

I had never driven five and a half hours by myself. I felt much younger than eighteen, and the morning was so dark. I was petrified and my hands were freezing and shaky, trying to grasp the steering wheel.

Patrick's piece of shit car rattled to a start and I pulled out onto the road. All I could think was, *When I see this road again, I will not be pregnant anymore. When I see this road again, I'll be okay.* His gas tank was empty.

I got gas and then followed the written directions I had figured out the night before. I was terrible at reading maps. Thoughts kept racing through my head: *What if I die during the procedure and my parents don't know where I am? My great-grandfather's sister, Great-Aunt Nettie, bled to death after an illegal abortion. What if it doesn't work and I'm still pregnant afterward? What if God holds this against me the rest of my life?*

I arrived at the clinic five and a half hours later. I was exhausted and strung out from no sleep and fear. I needed someone to sign a form saying they'd take me home so I wouldn't drive after the anesthesia. I looked around the waiting room and picked a guy with a kind face. "I need you to sign me out, please." I stared straight at him. "I need you to say you will drive me home, but you won't need to drive me home. I have to have someone sign." He actually did it. I don't know why, but he signed for me.

I sat down in the waiting room. There were no other hurdles blocking the abortion. I was there, I had the money, I had a person say he would sign me out—it would be over today. A brunette nurse called my name and I walked into the next room.

I looked around. There were women and young girls sitting in bathrobes and slippers, their hair in green shower caps. They were reading *People* and *Reader's Digest* as if they were waiting for a massage or a facial. Soon I was sitting among them in yellow slippers and the white terry cloth bathrobe Mom had given me for my birthday. I wasn't the youngest one. I picked up a magazine and pretended to read, but tears were already starting to fall.

My name was called and I was led into a smaller room. This time I lay down on a gurney. There was a girl on the gurney next to me. She already had an IV in her right hand. While the nurse was putting an IV into my left hand, I winced. I'd never felt so alone or so ashamed. I kept thinking, *How did I let myself end up here?* and *Please don't let anything happen to me.*

I looked over at the girl next to me. She had huge green eyes and black eyebrows. She was looking at me, too.

When the nurse left, I whispered to my neighbor, "Nobody knows I'm here."

"My boyfriend's waiting for me. But he's the only one who knows."

She was the first person since it had all begun who knew what I was feeling. I was so grateful she was beside me. I reached over and held her hand.

"I'm scared," I told her.

"I'm scared too," she said, and looked up at the ceiling. Tears began rolling into her hairline.

"We're going to be fine," I said, hoping it was true, even as tears started down the sides of my own face.

"I hope so," she said. The nurse injected something into our IVs and, with our fingers intertwined, we went to sleep.

I woke up to a nurse saying my name over and over again. Everything was blurry. The first thing I asked was, "Is it over?" And she said, "It's all over." I began to cry again, my shoulders shaking with sobs.

When it was time to get dressed, I realized how hard it was going to be to drive five and a half hours after being under anesthetic. I listened to the nurse rattling off the "at home" instructions and groggily walked out the door to the waiting room. The nurse at the front stopped me.

"Is someone driving you home?" she asked.

"Yes, he's pulling the car around," I said. She smiled and let me go.

It was evening and dark outside again. I was having bad cramps and was very sleepy, but I needed to get back to Kenyon. I would not have thought to get a hotel room, not that I had the money to pay for one. I just wanted to be back at the dorm with my warm quilt and my toothbrush. I wanted to be eighteen and starting college again. I wanted to start over.

I turned on the car and rolled down all the windows, even though it was thirty degrees outside. I hadn't thought to bring my coat. I needed the air to stay awake. In the five and a half hours it took to get back, I only stopped three times to get caffeine and take care of all the bleeding.

Patrick was furious that I got back so late with his car. I was so exhausted I didn't care what he thought. I threw his keys onto the front porch by the wooden glider. I couldn't imagine sitting on a bicycle seat, so I walked it home, my backpack over my arm. My cramps were getting worse.

I spent the weekend in bed but felt terrific by Monday morning. The relief I felt at having my life back, at being in control again, at surviving the worst thing I'd ever been through, was monumental. I absolutely knew that if I couldn't have had an abortion, I would have killed myself or done what my great-aunt Nettie did in 1922—I would have found anyone who would perform one, and I would have prayed they knew what they were doing. She picked the wrong person, and died at the age of thirty-one.

I saw Mr. Whitfield. "You look great," he said.

"I feel better," I said. He smiled and gave me a big hug. I hugged him back.

Patrick saw me that afternoon and said, "You kept my car just to fuck with me." I swung around and shoved him hard in the chest. "Stay away from me. Don't say anything to me; don't even come near me. You are a lying piece of shit."

I walked away knowing I would never get over that experience. I would carry it with me the rest of my life. I'd always be grateful that I'd had a choice, that my life hadn't been derailed. I vowed to try to let other people help me the next time I was in serious trouble. I vowed to always be smarter than the person I was dating. I would work on trying to forgive myself, and I would ask others for forgiveness too.

That summer I spent time at Dad's lake house, and one day when he was flipping steaks on the grill, I said, "I can finally pay back the money you loaned me."

"Don't worry about it," he said, not looking up.

"But it's five hundred dollars," I said.

"We all get a little short sometimes," he said, leaning down to blow on the hot charcoal.

I felt tremendous guilt. I wanted to tell him what I'd done, to make sure he still would have given me the money if he'd known, but I just stood there, looking at his profile. I wanted to say that my life had almost been ruined but he'd helped me.

"Thanks, Dad," I managed.

CHAPTER SEVENTEEN

The fall of my sophomore year, Becky was going to marry Mitch, who more and more reminded me of the old, cruel Dad. She walked away from Dad, only to marry his doppelgänger. They were having a big wedding at a church in Cincinnati and a fancy reception at his father's country club. His family had a lot of money and, once again, we were the hicks.

I'd landed my first professional acting job at a summer theatre in Vermont and had gotten the lead in two of the plays. I was thrilled, until I received a call from Becky.

"We're moving the wedding to July," she said.

"Why?" I asked.

"Mitch will be starting school in the fall, so we're having it this summer," she said.

"But I can't make it," I said. I didn't have the money to fly home.

"I know," she said. "Gina Burns is taking your place. She's the same dress size as you."

Each time our relationship was revealed as the empty, hateful thing it was, I was caught off guard. I hung up the phone as quickly as possible. With Becky, I was always convinced I'd done something unforgivable to her that I just couldn't remember.

I talked to Mom later that week. "Becky doesn't want me in her wedding."

"She doesn't want you taking all the attention," she said.

"I wouldn't do that," I said.

"You're the center of everything," Mom said. "You make sure of that."

Stunned, I slowly walked back to the rehearsal for *Oliver*.

One month later Mom placed a picture of Becky in her wedding gown, JoAnn in a fuchsia bridesmaid's dress, and Jamie in his gray tuxedo, on the buffet table by the front door, where it sat for years.

A reminder that for one day at least, it was exactly the way she'd planned: three children.

When I got back to school, I started dating Joel, a bisexual magician. He was wholly original, introducing me to sushi and teaching me Ashtanga yoga. He was the funniest person I'd ever met. He wasn't "normal," but neither was I.

Mom loved him, Jim tolerated him, and Dad just shook his head in disbelief at my incredibly bad choice. I didn't care.

It ended in disaster, but not until I participated in at least forty magic shows performed out of the back of his Audi hatchback. The final saw through my middle was Joel sleeping with Patrick Romano. The ultimate betrayal.

Joel eventually had a nervous breakdown, barricading himself in his apartment. His parents, who were Baptist ministers, shipped him off to South Dakota to convalesce.

After Joel my sophomore year became less about studying and more about parties.

My roommate and I threw a luau in our dorm room, and I woke up the next morning to find vomit right outside my door. I nearly stepped in it when I walked out to pee.

"Who the hell puked in front of my door and just left it here?" I bellowed down the hallway, where several doors were open.

"You did!" came a voice from one of the rooms.

I ducked back into my room and gingerly closed the door.

Looking in the mirror over my dresser, I could see my hair was mangled and tangled with leaves and small twigs. *What the hell happened last night?* I had no memory of even going outside.

I looked over at my roommate, who was still sleeping. She had wavy brown hair all the way down to her waist—only it was also tangled up with dried leaves and twigs. I shook her awake. When her eyes opened and she saw my hair, she started laughing.

"What the hell happened to you?" she asked.

"The same thing that happened to you," I said, pointing to her head.

She got up and looked in the mirror. "Oh, shit," she said, fingering the mess.

"There's vomit outside the door," I told her. "Apparently, it's mine."

"What did we do last night?" she asked.

"I have no idea," I said. "I'm terrified."

We didn't find out how the foliage had gotten into our hair or what had gone on at our party, but I did discover that I'd written a check for eighty dollars to Pizzaroni's delivery for nine muffulettas, which apparently fed our entire floor. Not exactly luau cuisine. There were cigarette butts in my spider plant.

I decided to take my acting seriously and settle down. I didn't want to end up like Jamie, who was still in Salt Lake City, with no college degree, and only booze to distract and comfort him.

My junior year at Kenyon started with Mr. Whitfield calling me into his office to discuss my having a nose job.

"How was it singing in 'Annie Get Your Gun'?" he asked.

"It was great. The only problem was that some of the notes were too high, and I couldn't belt them. I have to develop my upper range—from scratch."

"What about your breathing?" he asked.

"My breathing?"

"You've been complaining over the past two years that you can't breathe through your nose. Is it bothering you?"

"It bothers me, but it's not keeping me from singing," I told him.

"I think you should consider having a consultation with a plastic surgeon I know," he said.

"Probably too expensive," I told him.

"If there's a medical problem, insurance will pay for it. I'll set up the appointment."

Mr. Whitfield drove me to that appointment and when we were in the examining room, he told the doctor about my breathing and then pointed to the bump in the center of my nose.

"This is what I'm interested in getting smoothed out," he told the surgeon. "Is it possible to get this nice and straight as well as narrowing down the bridge?" he asked.

"That's no problem," he said.

I was watching them go back and forth as if I weren't in the room. I wanted to breathe through my nose, I wanted to look prettier, but I hadn't planned on surgery.

"When can we schedule the surgery?" Whitfield asked, turning to me.

My eyebrows flew up. "I have to talk to my mom and dad first."

"Well, let's book a date. We can always move it." Whitfield turned to the surgeon. "Should we shoot the 'before' picture?" Clearly Whitfield had done this before.

That January I had my nose straightened and my deviated septum fixed. Insurance paid. As soon as the swelling went down enough to reveal a lovely straight bridge on a very narrow nose, Whitfield was talking about fixing my teeth.

"They stick out," he assured me, as if I didn't already know.

I steered clear of Whitfield's office for a while. Sitting in the costume shop with my friend Bella, she asked me about the nose job.

"Whitfield thought it'd be better for my career if I could breathe through it," I told her.

"He's always trying to get girls to have plastic surgery," she laughed. Bella had been a student in the department for almost five years, taking a couple classes each semester. She'd seen a lot of girls come through.

"Why does he want girls to have surgery?"

"He wants all women to look like someone he could fuck," she said, not even looking up from her sewing. I could feel the shock and embarrassment moving up my neck in a steady red wave. I excused myself and went for a two-hour bike ride. I needed some air.

The summer following my junior year at Kenyon, I was accepted to the Chautauqua Institution in upstate New York. Teachers from Juilliard gathered for six weeks of acting workshops. I was proud to be accepted. Acting was usually the place I felt strong and self-assured. But once I arrived, I had an unexpected crisis of confidence.

Most of the students came from the East Coast, and I came straight from the cornfields. My teachers tried to change the way I spoke ("You have a Midwestern drawl with an annoying nasal quality. It's difficult to listen to"), the way I walked ("Please stand with your head directly over your shoulders and try to walk as if you were poised"), and the way I breathed ("You breathe very high. Have you ever thought of breathing from your diaphragm?"). Until I arrived at Chautauqua, I'd had no idea what a mess I was.

I worried myself to death, rehearsing every line, every dance step, every breath I took, and where in the monologue I was supposed to take it. I didn't sleep, I didn't make friends, and I didn't do good work.

I figured if I couldn't cut it at Juilliard, I couldn't cut it at all, which only brought on more angst.

Several messages from Mr. Whitfield came in that summer. "Give me a call when you get a chance." Finally, I walked to the pay phone.

"Hello?" he said.

"Mr. Whitfield, this is Monica."

"Monica Peterson—you finally called me," he said.

"It's hectic here. I'm completely miserable, by the way. You might as well know, there's no way I'm getting into Juilliard for graduate school. They think I'm retarded, and they might be right."

"Don't worry about that now. You have all next year to worry about that."

"Instead of coming back to Kenyon, I'm enrolling in beauty school and learning to perm hair."

"I wanted to ask you something," he said.

"Go ahead."

"I've been sensing something from you, and I thought we'd get it out on the table." I heard him shut his office door.

"What?" There was nothing he could say to upset me at this point in the summer.

"Are you attracted to me?" he asked. I was wrong—there was something he could say to upset me. Mr. Whitfield was forty-two years old and married. His daughter was four years younger than I was and he was ten years younger than my father.

He took another approach. "Do you feel any attraction toward me?" I didn't, but I was mortified and he kept waiting for an answer, so I finally said, "I guess so."

"I feel the same way," he said, and hung up the phone.

I stared at the number pad on the pay phone. What was that?

I took my time walking back to my dorm, sitting by the lake, watching the sailboats bobbing in the sparkling water. I was in this magical place where everyone was focused and talented and the scenery was picturesque, and yet I felt just the opposite. With my call to Whitfield, my problems just got bigger.

❦ ❦ ❦

When I returned to Kenyon in the fall, it was my senior year. Whitfield cast me as Ariel in *The Tempest* and had the costume designer put me in a white unitard. The set designer said my butt looked like "two little bears in a bag wrestling." I knew who the unitard was for.

After rehearsal one night Whitfield asked if he could drive me home. And that's how it began—the thing I couldn't picture—my professor and me having sex. It was seedy and obvious.

Worst of all, it was mind-blowingly terrific. If it had been terrible, it wouldn't have been a problem to stop, but it was like nothing I'd ever experienced before. Rifle-toting Adam was a novice compared to Whitfield, who was interested in what my body could do and how many times it could do it. I was surprised to see that my body could do quite a few things, quite a lot of times.

Boys asked me on dates, but I was busy with Whitfield, in the lighting booth, on his desk, in the costume shop, and in his car. His only attempt at being noble about his marriage was his refusal to kiss me.

"This is not a romantic relationship," he once told me as he pulled up his jeans, "it's physical."

So, when he'd call and I'd be curling my hair for a date with someone else, I'd tell him, "I'm trying to find something physical *and* romantic." We wouldn't speak for a day or so, and then back to the lighting booth we'd go. We became obsessed with each other and stayed that way throughout my senior year.

When it was time for graduate school auditions, I chose an acting conservatory as far away from Whitfield as I could get: San Diego, California. UCSD was affiliated with the prestigious La Jolla Playhouse regional theatre, which was the combination I wanted—a professional theatre and a focused acting program. When I told Whitfield, he kissed me on the mouth and begged me to go to NYU.

He would have easy access to me in New York, since he frequently traveled there. I wanted to focus on attaining my master's degree and fall in love with someone who hadn't been alive during World War II. I couldn't have Whitfield calling and visiting. The closer I got to graduation, the more he wanted to kiss.

The summer after I graduated from Kenyon, Whitfield drove down to Elk Grove because his elderly mother owned a farm there and he was helping her sell it. He and I met at Bullard's Drive-In but immediately went to Dad's lake house instead. Dad was at Mammaw's trailer in Florida, wining and dining his girlfriend, Laura, so Whitfield and I partook at Lake Hiawatha. We were having a wild powwow, clothes thrown all over the living room, when I heard a car pull into the driveway. Dad was home two days early!

We dressed—fast—and by the time Dad hit the doorway, we were sitting in the living room, Whitfield in a chair, me on the floor, pretending to have a conversation. My bra was unhooked, my Conair vibrator was shoved under Dad's plaid recliner, and I was flushed and breathing hard. My legs were like noodles, but Dad was oblivious.

I introduced Dad to Whitfield. "Dad, this is the head of my department at Kenyon, Mr. Whitfield. You met him last spring." Dad shook Whitfield's hand and nodded. "His mom is selling property near Elk Grove," I added, hoping that would keep Dad from suspecting that Whitfield was having sex with his daughter. Turned out, I needn't have worried.

"Glad to see you," Dad said. He walked into the kitchen and prepared three cups of homemade hot chocolate with miniature marshmallows bobbing on top. I sat in the living room watching the two of them sitting side by side with matching green-and-white mugs in their hands. The wrinkles on their foreheads and their soft tummies were a thwack to the side of my head.

What was I doing with Whitfield? He looked like my dad.

With that thought, I got all squirmy and grossed out. I excused myself, set my mug of cocoa on the kitchen counter, and went into the bathroom to rehook my bra. I looked at myself in the mirror. What the hell was wrong with me? The list was endless.

Whitfield and I said good-bye to Dad and drove back to Elk Grove. When I dropped him off at the only hotel in town, I saw his white-haired mother opening the curtains in their room and waving to him. Trying to find any dignity in the situation was hopeless.

After Whitfield left, I visited the Kilners, my family-away-from-family. We were watching *Ghostbusters* in the living room when a call came in. Julie's younger sister Liz picked up the phone, grabbed a white pad of paper, and wrote down the details. When she hung up, she said, "Business calls, ladies."

"Who's dead?" I asked. Liz was the new undertaker at Kilner and Sons, having just earned her degree. She was also running for Mason County coroner.

"A guy from Harrisburg. I'm meeting them at the mortuary. You want to come?"

I was so excited. It had been years since I'd last played in the mortuary, and after the craziness with Whitfield, I needed some good, clean fun. I was going to see a dead body.

I glanced at Julie, who looked bored. "Will you come too?" I asked.

"I'm not gonna sit here by myself," she said, pulling herself up off the couch. I could always count on Julie.

The three of us squeezed into the cab of Liz's shiny black pick-up and headed into town, smoking and laughing.

We pulled into the mortuary and Liz unlocked the doors. Julie and I turned on the lights and went into the office to find cookies. Ten minutes later an ambulance pulled up to the side of the building.

"Dead man on blacktop," Julie yelled to Liz. They started laughing. I flinched.

"Are you gonna be able to handle this, Mo?" Liz asked.

"I think so," I said.

"Don't be a pussy," she said, referring to the time I'd called her a pussy when she was only in fifth grade and refused to put her hands up in the air on the big roller coaster at Kings Island.

"I'm no pussy," I said, but suddenly I wasn't sure.

Liz walked outside and signed for the body. As I watched from the office window, the EMT helped her get the gurney into the body elevator.

I turned to Julie. "He's coming down."

"I'll alert the *Elk Grove Courier*," she said dryly.

"We can leave if you want to," I said.

"I'm gonna call Jay on the office phone so we can have a long conversation for once." Jay was Julie's new boyfriend and he was a long distance call away. Julie's phone bill was enormous and she'd been warned by Dave and Joan to cut down on "Jay" calls. She picked up the mortuary phone as I headed downstairs.

It took a lot of strength to lift the corpse onto the white porcelain embalming table, but I didn't offer to help. I couldn't bear to touch the man. Once they had him in position, the EMT pulled the gurney toward the elevator. The dead guy looked youngish, with black hair, and was wearing jeans and a blue-and-white flannel shirt. I imagined him sitting in front of his television watching *60 Minutes* and suddenly dropping like a stone.

"See ya, Liz," the EMT yelled from the elevator.

"See ya," Liz hollered back.

"Do you want to undress him, Mo?" she asked, winking at me.

"No thanks," I said. "I can get that action on any corner in Elk Grove." I walked out and sat on the steps. It wasn't dignified to watch a dead man being undressed.

A few minutes later she yelled, "He's naked, Mo."

"I'm on my way," I said, walking back into the room.

He was naked all right, except for a white terry cloth towel covering his crotch. He looked too young to be dead, but he definitely looked dead. His skin was a yellowish bruised color, his eyes were shut but sunken, and his fingernails were blue.

Liz put on a white plastic apron and threw one to me.

"Am I gonna get shit on me?" I asked, worried.

"You never know, Mo. Be prepared for anything," she said, giving me the two-fingers-over-the-eyebrow Girl Scout salute.

Liz enjoyed torturing me. She pushed a button on the boom box sitting on the shelf behind her, and AC/DC's "Back in Black" started playing. I loved "Back in Black," it helped me relax, but I looked at the guy on the table and wondered if the song was relaxing to him. He didn't appear to be in his body. Still, I felt a little sorry that we were jamming.

Liz uncoiled a clear plastic hose and began spraying the body.

"Disinfectant," she said, over the beginning drums of "Back in Black." I nodded as if I'd always known that morticians sprayed humans with disinfectant.

I wasn't going to freak out. I'd waited more than eleven years to finally have a look at what Max had been doing behind the big wooden doors. I wasn't going to blow it now. It might be my last chance.

After Liz sprayed the disinfectant, she didn't dry him off. I knew it wasn't irritating his nose or stinging his eyes, but I still wondered.

Once he was hosed down, Liz lifted his heavy head onto the head-block and crossed his stiff, thick hands over his stomach, hand over hand.

"Once they're embalmed, you can't move 'em," Liz explained. "I make sure everything's in place before the formaldehyde gets into the tissues." I nodded.

Liz held up two plastic discs. "These are going under the eyelids," she warned. "Can you deal?"

"I'm good," I said, wondering what a dead person's eyes looked like. I guess you could no longer see their souls through their eyes, since their souls had, hopefully, departed to a "better place."

AC/DC started singing. *Back in black, I hit the sack, I've been too long I'm glad to be back.* Liz rubbed cream onto the eye caps, opened the man's eyelids, and placed one on top of each eye so quickly, I couldn't see his actual eyes. When the eyelid folded back over it, his eyes weren't sunken anymore.

"Amazing," I said, pulling up a metal stool, my stomach less tight. The plastic eye caps helped depersonalize the embalming. This was a job with tricks and tools, just like any other job—only there was a large naked dead man lying there.

I wondered who he was. He looked to be around forty, so I imagined his parents were still living. Who'd called them tonight? *I've been looking at the sky, 'Cause it's gettin' me high, Forget the hearse 'cause I never die.*

"What killed him?" I asked.

"Heart attack," Liz said.

"How old is he?" I asked.

"Forty-three," she said. He was Whitfield's exact age, and in much better shape than Whitfield.

Liz took a piece of suture string with a curved needle and stuck it through his lower gums. Then she pulled it up through his upper gums, right through his nostril, crossed it over to the other nostril, and threaded it back down through the gums on the other side. I was slapping the top of my thighs and squirming on the stool.

"What the hell, Liz?" I gasped.

"Can't handle it?" she asked.

"You're never doing that to me," I said. "It looks beyond painful."

"Doesn't it?" Liz smiled.

"If I die, you can play AC/DC, but you can't stick a needle

through my nose." I silently contemplated cremation.

"I'm setting his mouth," she said, adding a plastic mouth former under his lips, using white cream to hold it in place. She rubbed a clear wax on the outside of his lips to keep them from cracking. His mouth was done.

I had a headache.

"Back in Black" was over and the four bells at the beginning of "Hells Bells" were chiming.

Liz dumped two plastic bottles of chemicals into the glass embalming machine that looked like a Waring blender with a clear hose attached. AC/DC sang: *My lightning's flashing across the sky, You're only young but you're gonna die.*

She took a scalpel and held it up for me to see. I gave her the thumbs-up and she cut a small incision in the man's shoulder near his collarbone and used a small metal hook to pull up an artery and a vein. After cutting through both, she inserted a tube into the artery and another tube into the vein. The hose in the artery was attached to the embalming machine. When Liz switched the machine on, embalming fluid gurgled and pumped into the artery, forcing blood he would never need again to drain out of his veins. The reddish maroon liquid emptied into a canal along the edge of the embalming table, and then swirled into a drain below.

Within a few minutes his skin took on a peach-colored hue and his blue fingernails turned pink. It was magical and unsettling.

Liz stitched the artery and vein closed, pushed them back into his shoulder, and stitched up the incision.

I was less than twelve inches from the body. It was so shocking that I felt detached—floaty.

"You'll love this," she said, picking up a long metal tube with sharp blades on the end. The other end was connected to a hose. She held it up. "Cavity treatment." She grinned.

"I'm very afraid," I said.

She pierced the skin by his belly button and poked the metal tube inside, jabbing around inside him. A suctioning sound rose above AC/DC. It was the same sound I'd heard coming from behind that door through all the years I'd sat outside this room.

"What are you doing?" I asked in horror.

"Draining the organs. If you don't, gases build up, and you know what happens then," she said, and laughed. "Explosion."

She inserted the metal prong back into his body, filling the organs with special cavity fluid. When she was done, I swear she took a plastic screw and screwed it right into the hole by his belly button. I couldn't believe it. Again, cremation for me.

She hosed down the body to clean him off.

I stood up and stared at him. He looked peaceful, and yet he'd been through hell.

I'd been right, even when I was in fourth grade and saw Sarah Keeler lying in her coffin: When you're dead, no one can hurt you.

I had a new respect for Liz Kilner after seeing what she had to do every day. She was no longer just Julie's little sister; she was strong, unflinching, and, best of all, a certified mortician.

A few weeks later, before I left for California, Julie and I drove to Kenyon so I could say good-bye to Whitfield. He and I had one last fling in the costume storage attic, but when we walked out the back door of the theatre, his wife was walking in, pushing a baby carriage. Whitfield flew into full panic mode. He mumbled something and ran back into the building, leaving me standing there with his wife.

I was appropriately mortified as I excused myself. He called me later that day to say everything was okay. He told his wife that I'd confessed to being in love with him and he had turned me down. For a moment I envied that guy on the table at Kilners. It was my turn to hang up on him.

Suddenly, change didn't scare me like it had before. I was looking forward to the four-hour plane ride that would separate me from Ohio and expose me to the West Coast. After twenty-one years of dead bodies, bad choices, and lousy love affairs, I was finally getting out.

I was leaving for California.

Part V

I Didn't Know I Was Falling Until I Hit the Ground

Chapter Eighteen

The University of California, San Diego, sat on the bluffs of La Jolla, overlooking the ocean. I'd never seen anything as mesmerizing as the sun setting over that water. I met the nine other actors in my program and we stuck together that first week. None of us were from San Diego, so we rode our bikes to the cliffs every night during the first month, to do what would never become routine for me: watching the round orange sun dipping into the luminous Pacific Ocean.

In our first acting class our teacher, Stanley Brooks, who was a genius and the reason we were all sitting there, talked about the importance of courage in acting. The next day for our acting scenes, four out of the ten of us came out completely naked. I was not one of them. It hadn't even occurred to me. I decided right then to get my body into really good shape—just in case parading around naked was part of graduate school.

I talked to Stanley.

"I'm not courageous enough to be nude."

"You don't have to be nude to be brave," he assured me.

"I'm not sure I'm brave at all."

"What do you want to be?" he said.

"I want to be normal," I answered. I was done with eccentric and reckless.

"How about being strong," he suggested. "I can get you into a weight-lifting program where you could start exercising your body.

You'll be surprised how strength on the outside focuses you inside, and vice versa."

Weights were torture. I couldn't lift them for very long without my spaghetti arms giving out on me.

I cursed at my trainer. "Why the fuck am I doing this?" I asked, but he didn't answer. I was holding up a two-pound weight, saying, "Is this really fucking necessary? Damn. This is killing me."

I hated my trainer and I hated how I felt afterward, sore and exhausted. Stanley assured me this was "normal."

He was right; I became strong. I now had the stamina to run three miles, as opposed to three feet into the door of the 7-Eleven for a Big Gulp.

Strangely, whenever things slowed down at school, which wasn't often, I would be nudged by that dark depression and fear I'd fought in Ohio. It crept in when I was singing alone at the piano, or followed me across campus at night when I was positive I'd be raped or strangled, though there were plenty of lights on and other students around.

I was happier than I'd ever been, with friends and teachers who stimulated and excited me, and yet that feeling of dread was right at my back.

Partly to avoid that feeling, I bought a motorcycle. I fantasized that it would be difficult to be depressed with salt air blowing around my body and sunshine warming my knuckles as I sped along the sandy rim of the Pacific. Plus, I was in desperate need of transportation since everything in southern California was so spread out. I could actually afford it. My student loan finally arrived, so I had enough money—four hundred dollars.

It was an aqua blue Honda 250. Small enough to be safe, big enough to be hip. It was fun as hell too. I drove it along the Pacific Coast Highway with my newly blond-highlighted, shoulder-length hair blowing out the back of my white helmet.

When I bought it, I'd imagined myself speeding by in a cool black leather jacket, pants, and hip boots, but those things were expensive. Instead, I looked like a homeless person layering on everything I owned—a red hooded sweatshirt under my green wool sweater with an orange wool scarf wrapped around my throat that Granda had sent me. I pulled thick pink sweatpants on under my yellow peasant skirt to protect my legs from the chill and the hot metal pipe.

At stoplights I happily pulled up my face guard and breathed in the salt air.

I usually had one of the other actors riding with me. One afternoon I pulled out of a deli on La Jolla Village Drive with my friend Madeline on the back, but when I got to campus at the top of the hill, she was no longer back there. I sped back down, arriving just as she was stepping onto the curb. The macaroni salad I'd asked her to hold for me was splattered on the front of her.

"I slid off the back when you tore off," she said, picking macaroni noodles off her denim jacket.

"I'm sorry, Maddie," I said, pulling up next to her. I stifled a laugh.

"No, don't you laugh. You aren't allowed to laugh," she said.

"I'm really sorry," I managed to sputter out, again.

"If you hadn't needed this stupid salad, I would have been hanging on to *you* instead of *it*, and I wouldn't have fallen off," she concluded.

"Bad choice on my part," I said.

"My ass is going to be killing me now."

"I'll go slower."

"I'll hang on this time," she said, swinging her leg over the seat.

✦　✦　✦

That first summer at UCSD, Dad flew to Los Angeles with the Shriners and took a train to San Diego to visit me. I watched as his train pulled into the San Diego Amtrak station, and among the passengers climbing off were fifty middle-aged men wearing maroon fezzes. Dad was one of them. I could see him waving at me from the middle of the crowd.

I'd rented a tiny car because I'd thought it would be just the two of us. He'd forgotten to mention that he was bringing his girlfriend, Laura, my dad's uncle Warren, and his wife, my great-aunt Caroline. I offered to trade my little rental for a bigger one, but they said it would be fine as they squeezed into the white Ford Escort, shoulder overlapping shoulder. Being Shriners, riding in tiny cars must have been second nature to them. We were on our way.

I was anxious driving. It was the first time I'd been in a car with Dad when he wasn't behind the wheel. Also, I wasn't familiar with the layout of San Diego, having spent most of my time on campus, but Hertz had given me a map. I'd circled places I thought they might enjoy.

Laura and Aunt Caroline picked Old Town San Diego. It turned out to be a good choice, not only because it was beautiful, with the sparkling white Hacienda Hotel and purple and pink bougainvillea draped on almost every porch, but because we sat down to the most delicious lunch—enchiladas and margaritas. I was starving, and the margarita helped me relax.

"There are no bugs on the windshields out here," Dad said. "There aren't any bugs anywhere."

"There are cockroaches in my apartment," I said.

"Oh, Monica, get yourself some Black Flag spray, honey," Laura said. She was always offering good and caring advice.

"Back home, I'm scraping bugs off my windshield every day," Dad reiterated. "I don't get it."

"There are a lot of bugs back there," Uncle Warren agreed.

"What degree are you getting, Monica?" Aunt Caroline asked.

"Master of fine arts," I said.

"Oh, your master's. That's great." Aunt Caroline was a celebrated schoolteacher back home and appreciated education.

As we toured the "Birthplace of California," Dad took the map to figure out our next stop. "How about La Jolla Cove?" He pronounced the *J*, just like I had at first.

"It's gorgeous," I said. "There are sea lions sleeping in squirmy piles on the sand."

We squeezed back into the Escort and headed up Interstate 5. I missed the La Jolla exit three times in a row and thought Dad would be furious, but he was busy filming out the passenger window with his Super 8 movie camera. "These idiots out here build houses right on the side of a hill," he said, indicating a pink house built on stilts, the foundation sticking out over the side of the mountain. "The whole damn thing's gonna fall," he said, shaking his head.

"But if one does fall, you'll get some good footage," I said.

When we got to the cove, Laura and Aunt Caroline wanted to see the shops, and Uncle Warren and Dad lay down on a patch of grass with the dazzling Pacific Ocean spread out before them.

I wanted to stay with Dad, but the ladies convinced me to go with them. There were tacky, expensive galleries and clothing stores in La Jolla and I felt out of place in my Kmart khaki shorts, but we laughed and had fun.

By the time we met back at the cove, it was almost time to head back to the train station.

"Can we drive up the hill so I can show you my school?" I asked.

"Sure," Laura said. I drove up curvy Torrey Pines Road, but we were so packed into the car that no one's head even moved. I showed them the theatre department and the La Jolla Playhouse, where I'd been understudying all summer. We swung by my apartment building and I pointed to my balcony. My motorcycle was sitting in front of it.

"That's a good way to get yourself killed," Dad said.

"What is?" I asked.

"That motorcycle. It's a death machine." He glanced at my apartment. "Pretty nice," he said, but he didn't film it.

"And cheap," I told him as we sped off.

Dad didn't know the motorcycle was mine. Older people were scared of new things, but I wasn't going to let him scare me. I was embracing change.

We arrived at the train station just in time.

As I watched them pull out, that depression began creeping in again. Their train rumbled away just as another one was pulling in. I had an unexpected urge to step right in front of the oncoming train. The impulse was so strong and sudden that I sat down on a stone bench to protect myself from stepping onto the tracks.

Once that train stopped and began unloading passengers, I jumped up and hurried to the Escort. My heart was racing and it was difficult to breath. In fact, breathing made my chest hurt worse. I climbed into the car and laid my seat down. I tried to slow my breathing, but I couldn't. I felt light-headed and my vision was blurry. I worried I was having a heart attack. After about ten minutes my heart rate started slowing down and my head felt clearer. I was drenched in sweat.

I needed to get to Hertz, so I pulled onto Interstate 5.

When I told my friend Madeline what had happened, she said I'd had a panic attack. I'd thought panic attacks were what occurred when I thought I had a twenty-dollar bill in my wallet but couldn't find it when I was next at the checkout counter. I didn't think it was my heart practically exploding out of my chest.

What had provoked it? I was happy now. Why was I still so fucked up?

That winter Mom called. Jamie had had a serious accident. He was rock climbing in Utah and fell thirty feet off the side of a mountain.

He broke his back, his wrists, and his pelvis. I assumed he was either drunk or stoned at the time. When I talked to him later, he confirmed he was both, saying, "I didn't even know I was fallin' until I hit the ground. If I hadn't been so relaxed, I woulda killed myself." If he hadn't been so messed up, he wouldn't have plunged in the first place, but that was lost on him.

Jamie was—not so passively—trying to get himself killed. Every broken bone represented a time when he felt too stupid or worthless or sad. His two front teeth were chipped, and his nose, which had been broken several times already, was broken again. Jamie was a tenderhearted person, but when he drank, he became so violent that I knew he was capable of hurting one of us. My darling brother was in pieces.

In an uncharacteristic moment of compassion, Becky flew out to help Jamie. He reciprocated by getting drunk and sawing off his own casts with a handsaw and threatening her with a hunting knife. That was the first and last time Becky ever became the cavalry for any of us.

I vowed to continue becoming stronger. I wasn't going to let the "You're a hopeless loser" tsunami that pounded and enraged Jamie catch up with me. I would stay ahead of it until I was strong enough to face it—whatever "it" was.

Dave and Joan Kilner sent me a plane ticket to fly home for Julie's wedding. She was marrying "long-distance Jay" and wanted me to be her maid of honor.

I was a terrible maid of honor. I had no idea that I should have thrown her a shower and taken care of all kinds of things. I was poor, living on a tiny school loan, some of which I'd used for my motorcycle, and I was three thousand miles away from her until the night before the wedding. I barely got there in time for the rehearsal. She deserved someone who knew what they were doing. But I stood up with Julie, who looked angelic in her wedding gown, and watched her marry someone I barely knew.

She had a Catholic wedding, and when the priest handed her the chalice of wine, she sucked down every last drop with a loud *sssllluurrpp* sound at the end. There was none left for Jay. This sent us into unfortunate hysterics. Joan said all she could see were our shoulders moving up and down, as she sat in the pew and panicked.

"They're gone," she told Dave, shaking her head. "They're going to laugh through the rest of the ceremony."

The priest reminded us, "This is a serious moment," and we straightened up—sort of.

Dave and Joan looked happy and fancy as we danced at the reception. Julie looked thrilled and a little drunk.

I danced with Mr. Royce, my sixth-grade teacher, and thought of all the things I'd seen that weekend. Julie's family and friends stopping by with gifts and good wishes. A photographer taking pictures of Julie with Dave, Joan, and her sisters in their front yard. Julie's luggage with her new initials embroidered on it sitting in her bedroom near the toilet.

I saw Julie and Jay's new apartment in Cincinnati. It had a beautiful sofa, pine end tables, and matching wrought-iron lamps. In San Diego my apartment was furnished with plastic milk crates for end tables and a saggy yard-sale couch.

Maybe if I found someone normal and sophisticated, it would stop the pattern of recklessness and depression in my life. Maybe I could find the stability Julie now had.

I met Mr. Stability that fall. His name was Daniel and he was the director of marketing for the La Jolla Playhouse.

On our first date we saw *Julius Caesar* at the Old Globe Theatre. Every time the lights went down for a scene change, we kissed wildly, and after the play we danced in Balboa Park under a white trellis, thick with wisteria and pink roses.

One Sunday, Daniel drove me to Julian, up in the mountains east of San Diego, to see the autumn leaves and eat warm apple pie. He was adorable and had the sweetest smile. On a red flannel blanket under an oak tree with acorns scattered all around us, I fell in love with him. He was the right person, and I knew it.

I think Mom and Jim felt the same way, because when Daniel got off the plane with me that Christmas, his Brooks Brothers suit slightly disheveled, jet-black hair combed perfectly to the side, my mother whispered, "Marry this man."

Daniel came from an East Coast upper-class background, which included expensive restaurants, correct-for-every-occasion clothes, and no jumping in leaves or hugging. I was nervous about what he might think of Galesburg, with its single grain elevator north of town. Much to my surprise, he embraced it. All of it. The tiny post office, the cemetery with the sunken grave, and Whitmore's field behind our house, where we'd buried all those birds, squirrels, and murdered cats. He'd grown up in Washington, D.C., and had never seen such a rural place. Surprisingly, his new favorite thing was Christmas at Mom's.

He was Jewish, but that first Christmas Eve he insisted on performing "Silent Night" with my family at the Galesburg Methodist Church. We were an eccentric choir that year, with Christine, JoAnn's new black girlfriend, singing soprano; Jim, who was now my stepdad but who still had the stain of dishonor from living in sin with Mom for two long years, singing bass; and Daniel, the Jew, singing tenor. After our song, I ran downstairs to go to the bathroom and returned to see Daniel receiving communion. I thought God would kill him right there.

Daniel, not unlike my family, was happy to ignore any inconvenient fact—like being Jewish on Christmas Eve—for the sake of belonging. Everyone agreed I had made a good choice for the first time. Even Dad liked Daniel. "He's quiet," Dad said. "He doesn't get in other people's business."

My second summer in San Diego, Daniel and I drove to La Jolla Village Square mall and bought a diamond and sapphire engagement ring. No one could believe it. I was going to marry someone normal and successful. I moved into Daniel's condo.

Daniel worked incessantly. This left plenty of time for the actors to come over and swim in the pool or sit in the Jacuzzi at the condo, but not much time for Daniel and me to deepen our relationship. I was busy with classes and rehearsals, but Daniel's schedule was worse. Sometimes he'd be in his office at the playhouse until two or three in the morning.

One night we were supposed to meet at the Rusty Pelican for dinner, but Daniel didn't show. I drove my motorcycle to the playhouse, pulled into the "valet" zone, threw down the kickstand, and stormed into the box office. There was Daniel, sports coat off, tie flung over his left shoulder, helping someone figure out the seating system. I was furious to see how handsome my no-show was.

"Hi there," I said, standing at the door, holding my helmet under my arm.

"Just a second, Mon," he said, holding up one finger, not bothering to look up at me. "I'm right in the middle of something."

"You're always in the middle of something, and it never has anything to do with me. I don't need to be stood up by my own fiancé," I snapped.

"If you'll just wait a second, I'll be right with you."

"I'm not a patron of the theatre. I'm your fiancé, you freak, and I just spent twenty minutes waiting in a restaurant for you."

He was looking at me now. "Okay, hang on." He turned to the woman he'd been working with. "Excuse me a minute. I'm sorry." He walked out of the box office and slammed the door.

"Don't ever talk to me like that in front of someone I'm working with," he said.

"FUCK YOU!" I yelled so it echoed all the way down the lobby of the theatre, where everyone he worked with could hear it. "DON'T STAND ME UP EVER AGAIN—EVER!" I yelled. Daniel's cheeks were bright red.

"If you can wait, I'll only be a few minutes and we can sit down at dinner and talk this out," he said, trying to touch my arm. "Just a few minutes."

I nudged him in the chest with my helmet. "Take your time," I said, storming out the door.

I jumped on my bike, put on my helmet, and sped across the parking lot, only to be immediately pulled over by a rent-a-cop, who was also on a motorcycle.

"Step off the bike," he commanded into his little speaker. I threw my leg over the seat and turned to face him. "Helmet off, please," he said. Boy, was I getting pissed. I pulled off my helmet. When the cop saw all my hair, he had the nerve to laugh.

"Expecting a guy in tights?" I asked.

"You drive pretty wild on that thing," he said.

"Not usually. It's been a particularly shitty evening," I said.

I looked up and saw Daniel walking across the grass, smiling. Fuck.

"Hi, Stan," Daniel said. He knew this guy? Of course he did. Daniel knew everyone, especially campus security, because they were also security for the theatre.

"Do you know this young lady?" the policeman asked.

"I think we're engaged, but I'm not sure," he said.

"You won't be getting married if she doesn't slow down, because she's going to be riding in a hearse," said Stan.

"Not my first time," I assured him.

"Look, what can I do to help here?" Daniel asked.

"You can walk back to the theatre, you workaholic maniac," I said.

"You're engaged to her?" Stan asked again.

"We're engaged, Stan," I said, showing him the ring. I turned to Daniel. "This is none of your business, so go back to the most important thing in your life: work." Daniel smiled. "I'm glad you're happy I got pulled over."

"You should stay off the bike until you calm down," Stan said. "Driving like that is extremely dangerous, not just for you but for students and patrons walking across the parking lot."

"I'm sorry," I said. "I don't want to run over anyone."

"Then slow down." He flipped his ticket pad shut and pointed it at Daniel. "Good luck," he said, straddling his motorcycle.

"Good luck to you, STAN," I yelled behind him as he sped away. Daniel was still smiling. "Shut up," I said. God, I was crazy about Daniel.

That winter Mitch divorced Becky, and even though she hadn't wanted me in her wedding, she did want to live in our California condo now that she had no home. I wasn't thrilled with the idea but thought it might be an opportunity for the two of us to create a better relationship. Starting over in a new state might help break the cycle of hate. I hoped so.

Becky moved out of Ohio and into our place with her black-and-white cat, who shit in my bathtub and, I swear, smiled at me afterward. Becky needed to get on her feet and her cat needed a cork up his ass. His name was Vinnie, and he was not helping break the cycle of hate.

But Becky and I began enjoying sunny afternoons and sunsets at Torrey Pines beach, where she would generously set up two chairs, a blanket, and a picnic of shaved turkey, cheeses, chips, soda, and water. I would speed in on my motorcycle after rehearsals or classes. We'd sit on the beach and laugh like we used to when we played

Barbies under the piano. I didn't think it was possible, but Becky was starting to like me.

Mom graduated with her PhD that spring and was pissed off that Becky and I couldn't afford to fly out for her graduation. She thought Daniel should pay for it, but Daniel and I were just getting our footing. Unlike her, I wasn't relying on a man to take care of me.

It would have been impossible for me to leave the theatre production I was in, and Becky had just started a new job with a big insurance firm.

"I'll *never* forgive you," Mom assured us.

I'd never forgive her for missing years of our lives. We were hardly even. So why did I still feel guilty? Why did I send her money from my school loan to fly out to see us as a graduation gift? I needed that money to live on.

The following fall Daniel unexpectedly quit the playhouse to join a company that created ticketing software for regional theatres.

He moved to New Haven, Connecticut, and six months later I graduated with my master's degree. After signing with a renowned talent agent who told me to move to Los Angeles for my career, I followed Daniel to Connecticut. Becky stayed in San Diego, where she had been promoted at the insurance company and was making an excellent salary.

That summer I didn't perform in a New York play, I didn't join an excellent acting troupe, and I didn't tour the country with a Broadway musical. I worked at Camp Deer Lake in Madison, Connecticut. I spent the summer with Archery Ken, Arts and Crafts Kathy, and High Adventure Rich, tweezing splinters out of filthy fingers and gravel out of tiny knees.

I was the assistant director of a summer arts camp. After earning my prestigious degree and snagging an excellent agent, I learned to set fire to a paper bag full of dog shit and successfully convince a camper to stomp it out.

When I got home at night, Daniel was still working. I was overwhelmed by the vast future ahead of me. I had no plans. It was the first time in my life there wasn't a sure step in front of me. I was panic-stricken and embarrassed. Some of the other actors from UCSD were performing in the city. I was helping some poor kid weave a multicolored lanyard.

Finally, I came to the conclusion that New Haven, a two-hour train trip, was too far from New York and a possible career. I sublet an apartment with my friend Tina, moved into the city, went on auditions, and worked temp jobs.

Meanwhile, Daniel was consumed by his new career at the software company. I hardly ever saw him. When I did, we cooked elaborate meals together, enjoyed movies, and took picnics to Tanglewood, where we listened to gorgeous music, snuggling on our quilt. But there was something enormous missing; there was an emptiness I couldn't fill with Daniel. The longer I was out of school, the worse my depression became.

Once in a while Daniel asked me about the engagement ring I was still wearing.

"Are we ever getting married?" he'd ask.

"Sure," I'd say.

"When?"

"Soon," I'd answer.

After three years Daniel delivered his ultimatum: "Marry me or we're breaking up." When I told Mom, she said that Daniel would last (as a single man) about as long as a paper shirt in a cat fight. "Someone will snatch him up and he'll be married so fast it'll make your head spin," she assured me.

That night I drove to Barnes and Noble and picked up Martha Stewart's book *Weddings*, a fifty-dollar guide to spending thirty thousand dollars on a wedding. I didn't have a career, I didn't have financial stability. I guessed I'd have a wedding. I loved Daniel, and I ignored the nagging voice in my head that said, *Isn't this what your mother did? The very thing that screwed up all our lives?*

Against my better judgment, I opened that book and began planning our wedding.

Daniel promised we'd move closer to New York so my commute would be shorter. We looked for a place in Darien, thirty minutes from the city.

I wanted Daniel to be the one. I wanted life in Connecticut to feel as perfect as the country inns and beautiful seaports that defined the New England countryside. But, at that point, we hadn't had sex in a year and a half. We were more like siblings. I, who'd had sex in a moving car and on a professor's desk, had let go of one of the most thrilling aspects of my life. But life with Daniel wasn't thrilling; it was steady and reliable.

My roommate Tina told me at dinner one night, "You *must* have sex. It's too important. And if you aren't having sex now, what do you think will happen later?"

I knew that sex was important, but I convinced myself that love was the most important thing and wanting a great sex life (or any sex life) was asking for a perfect equation.

We set the date: November third, picturing a blue sky in late autumn with jewel-colored leaves swirling around our guests. Mom was ecstatic, hanging up on me to call her friends to tell them to hold that date. Dad seemed happy too, offering to send a check.

I booked Tollgate Hill in Litchfield, Connecticut, a large gambrel-roofed red clapboard colonial built in 1745. Fritz, the innkeeper, graciously served me a complimentary quiet lunch so I could observe the atmosphere. The clincher for me was the second-floor ballroom with an enormous walk-in fireplace.

I daydreamt about the ceremony taking place in front of the roaring fire, our guests rosy-cheeked, my veil floating in the breeze.

The next thing I know, my veil catches on fire, I fall into the fire-place, and that's when I order another glass of wine.

I shook off all bad thoughts and attended to the endless details of the wedding (shoes from Peter Fox, flowers by Country Iris) so I wouldn't worry about my decision to go forward.

Dad, true to his word, sent two thousand dollars to help with the deposit. I was grateful he was going to help us. Everything was falling into place quickly.

The wedding was the only way to stay numb, and numb was the only way to avoid the gigantic boulder of depression that had been threatening to flatten me for as long as I could remember. Daniel was steady and true, and I was nutty and unstable. This was the right decision because, at some point, maybe I'd become steady too.

With the wedding looming, I temporarily fled, taking a summer-stock job in Michigan with my favorite acting company. I'd spent two summers with them in the past and loved it there. I hoped acting would distract and center me.

The summer bumped along—no visits from Daniel, our rela-tionship was not about seeing each other, it was about knowing we were each in the world—and then my veil arrived. It represented something both spectacular and hideous—the wedding.

I called Dad from a pay phone in the lobby of the theatre, with the flat cardboard box shoved under my arm.

"My veil arrived," I told him.

"Okay," he said. "How's the weather up there?"

I glanced out the enormous tinted windows in the lobby. "Sunny with a few clouds. It was seventy-eight today."

"Sunny here," he reported.

"That's good. Are you coming up to see a show this summer?" I asked. It was a long drive.

"I have to see if I can get someone to watch the store," he said. This meant he wasn't coming. He took cruises to the Bahamas and trips to Florida. He left the store all the time. I wanted him to come because I needed someone to tell me to call off the wedding.

"Don't worry about coming up," I said. "Thanks for helping with the wedding, Dad. The veil looks really nice," I said, patting the box.

"All right," he said.

"I'll talk to you later," I said.

"Are there lots of mosquitoes up there? We're having a terrible time down here," Dad said.

"Not too bad," I said.

"Buy yourself some Off," he said. "It couldn't hurt."

"Will do."

"Bye-bye," he said.

"Bye."

I drove the veil back to my woodsy house on Lake Michigan, where the acting company was staying, and tried to bond with it. I draped it over a hanger in my room and let it float down to the floor so I would be forced to face it every day. When my housemates were at rehearsal, I wore it to talk on the phone, and I watched *Postcards from the Edge* in it.

There was a long mirror with beveled edges in the hallway, where I stared at myself. At least the veil was perfect.

All was going forward as planned until Alex Sullivan joined the company midsummer. I knew him from a previous summer when he and I had kissed passionately after I'd consumed a 7-Eleven Big Gulp filled with a little Coke and a lot of Bacardi rum.

Alex was sexy and I was celibate. I called Daniel.

"How are you?" I asked.

"Good. Good. I'm working hard." I could hear Daniel tapping his computer keys as we were talking.

"Alex Sullivan is in the company this summer. He just got here," I said. Daniel had met Alex a couple of summers before and knew I had a hopeless crush on him.

"And?" The typing continued.

"I just wanted you to know he's here—right now," I said.

"Look, if you want to be with Alex Sullivan, I can't stop you."

"I know that." Long pause.

"Let's not talk for a while," Daniel said. The typing stopped.

"We need to call off this wedding," I said, my stomach tightening.

"No. Get this out of your system and then we'll talk." He hung up.

At the company party that night, Alex sauntered over. He looked edible and I blurted, "I'm getting married."

"I heard."

"I won't be kissing you this summer."

"I understand."

"I'm not kidding."

"No problem."

"Everything is ordered, so stay back."

"I'm getting a drink. Do you want one?"

"No. No drinks, no nothing. No. No thanks." I was dying to kiss him.

He was forty-eight and had an unfortunately alluring British accent, small darting eyes, and a wife. It was the kind of ridiculous and complicated situation I craved. I felt alive when I was kicking up terrible shit around me.

Alex drove to my house one humid night and kissed me on the bed while my veil bobbed in the breeze.

The next evening, during a performance of *The Music Man*, I tripped over an intern, did an unchoreographed somersault, and broke my ankle. It was surely the hand of God striking me down. *I won't be able to have sex with Alex Sullivan with a cast on my leg*, I thought as two muscular stagehands carried me to the car for the trip to the hospital.

While sitting in the balcony of the theatre in a wheelchair the next night, watching another actress perform in my place, I received a large brown box from the mail room. The Watters & Watters silk bridesmaids' suits had arrived. The wedding wouldn't leave me alone. It was everywhere—on my message machine, on my desk calendar. It was even coming through the mail. The more wedding items I received, the more I wanted to sleep with Alex Sullivan.

I needed to release the brake on my wheelchair and roll into a different life, one that was already figured out.

I asked Alex to drive me to my house, where he shoved the unopened Watters & Watters box deep under my bed. I attacked him before he could even get the boxes situated, jerking his shirt off over his head, and unbuttoning his fly. Working around my cast was not a problem. A herd of stampeding elephants wouldn't have been a problem. I didn't realize how neglected I'd felt. There was something wrong between Daniel and me, because passion came back to me so fast, I nearly killed Alex with my enthusiasm over its resurgence.

The next day I dialed Daniel and called off the wedding with four weeks to go.

Daniel received a partial refund, Dad received no refund, and our wedding guests received a call from me. Each one going something like this:

"Hi, it's Monica calling. How are you?"

"Fine. Are you getting ready for the wedding? Are you excited?" the guest would say.

"No. Actually, that's why I'm calling. I've decided to call off the wedding. I'm having second thoughts. It's completely my fault. I wanted to call you myself."

"Oh my. Is there anything I can do?"

"There's nothing you can do, but thank you. I'll talk to you soon."

Daniel took it better than my mother, who was inconsolable. I got the impression that if it weren't for Jim, Mom would have married Daniel herself.

Dad told me it was better not to make a mistake, and that I needed someone more lively than Daniel anyway. He wasn't kidding.

Daniel helped me pack everything I owned and moved me to Brooklyn, where I settled into the basement of an old brownstone with a friend from the summer theatre.

I wasn't relieved. I wasn't devastated. I wasn't feeling much of anything. I was in shock. The thought of Daniel being gone forever was excruciating, but the passion I knew I was capable of wasn't just a sexual passion, it was a passion for life. And Daniel and I didn't bring that out in each other. He and I shared only safe things. It was the dullness I would miss, the cotton-stuffed stifling dullness.

Life was no longer dull; in fact, it became goddamn chaotic. I was about to understand why I had fought to stay numb. I was about to turn around and face the cause of my depression and panic attacks head-on.

CHAPTER NINETEEN

Three days before Christmas, my phone rang. I was in Brooklyn, throwing warm socks and brown corduroys into a suitcase for a trip to Washington, D.C., where I'd pick JoAnn up and then drive us to Ohio. My first Christmas in five years without Daniel. It was back to Hanukkah for him.

"Hello?" I said, tucking the receiver between my shoulder and chin while I rifled through my underwear drawer searching for my beige camisole.

"It's me," JoAnn said. I had to laugh. She was checking in because I was usually late.

"Don't have a heart attack, but I'm on time," I told her, finding the camisole and laying it in the suitcase.

JoAnn had been in D.C. for five years now. She'd set up an invigorating life—a studio apartment and a career in social services.

The only problem was she'd recently broken up with Christine, who'd sung in our choir that first Christmas with Daniel. Christine was a successful, gorgeous African-American woman who'd recently admitted to fabricating her entire life.

She'd told everyone that she was born in Sweden to a wealthy family and that her mother was white and her father was black. In truth her entire family, including sisters and brothers no one had even heard about, didn't live in Sweden, but in a neighborhood a few minutes away from downtown D.C.

JoAnn had moved out of their beautiful two-bedroom apartment a couple of months before.

"I wasn't calling about you being on time," JoAnn told me. "I was calling to tell you not to drive down here. I'm not going home; I'm not up for the holiday frenzy."

"Are you sure?" I asked.

"I'm positive. I didn't want to add four hours to your trip for nothing. Go ahead and leave from there." Something was up. JoAnn never missed Christmas at Mom's.

"I'm coming to see you first. It wouldn't be Christmas if I didn't give you presents," I insisted.

"Okay, but I'm not in a cheerful mood," she said.

"Be any way you want. I'm coming down." I closed the suitcase and zipped it shut.

"Okay."

"I'd better hang up and get movin'. See you soon."

Christmas would be boring as hell without JoAnn, and Mom would be furious. It was an unspoken gospel, "No one misses Christmas in Ohio."

Four hours later when I arrived at JoAnn's apartment, I saw that something *was* wrong. I hadn't seen her in over two months, and a transformation had taken place. JoAnn, who usually weighed one hundred and fifty pounds, looked unusually thin and anxious.

"Have you been sick?" I asked, setting her presents down on the kitchen table.

"Not really," she said. "Would you like a Mountain Dew?"

"Sure." She pulled two cans out of the fridge. I watched her bend over, her sweatpants sagging off her nonexistent butt.

"Are you eating enough?" I asked.

"I'm eating."

"Have you talked to Christine?" I threw my coat onto the couch.

"She called this morning." She handed me the soda can and a white paper napkin.

"That must be hard," I said.

"It's sad," she said. "It's like she's somebody else now."

"She's not the person you thought she was," I said.

"She loved me, though." JoAnn sat down on a brown rattan chair, wiping off the top of the can with her napkin.

"You loved her, too," I said.

"What wasn't to love?" she asked. "Whatever I wanted her to be, poof, she became it."

She and Christine had had a sunny apartment filled with expensive furniture and a brand-new upright piano that Christine had bought JoAnn for her birthday. Looking around JoAnn's studio, I could see that Christine had kept all of it. I curled into a brown bean-bag chair next to JoAnn.

"Nice of her to take the piano," I said.

JoAnn laughed. Her hands were shaky when she tried opening the Mountain Dew. Something wasn't right. I looked around the apartment for a clue. It was sparkling clean, with everything in place. Even the dish towels hanging on the oven door handle were meticulously pressed and folded. JoAnn was as tidy as I was disorganized.

Outside the window, a light snow was beginning to fall. It was gray and cold out there.

"I can tell something's wrong," I finally said.

JoAnn looked at the green and silver can in her hand, not saying anything. She fiddled with the metal tag on top until it came off in her hand, then she tossed it into the trash can beside her desk.

"Something's wrong," she admitted. "I can't go home because I can't see Dad."

"Oh shit. What happened?"

"Nothing recently," she said. "That's what's so confusing."

"What?"

"The reason I can't see Dad," she said.

"I don't understand," I said.

"My whole life I worried there was something unimaginable about to level me and that I'd be powerless to stop it," she explained. "I know what that is now."

I held my breath. She was describing the tidal wave of dread. "What is it?" I asked, knowing the answer would cause me to immediately turn and look directly at whatever had been threatening to obliterate me all these years. I hoped I was strong enough to face it.

"Dad molested me." My expression froze in blank shock. "He did things to me for years." She looked at her hands, which had always been smaller than mine. "Memories started bubbling up about six months ago, and now I'm flooded with them."

Was this my secret too? I panicked for both of us. Was this the tsunami—the thing that kept me feeling worthless and unsafe? Or was this only JoAnn's story? I didn't know.

I instantly remembered JoAnn crawling over to Becky's bed in the middle of the night when we slept in the same room. "Scoot over," she'd whisper, and Becky would slide over and let JoAnn snuggle in. By the time we woke up, JoAnn would be back in her own bed. The three of us never discussed it. I had completely forgotten it until that exact moment.

I turned to her. "Do you remember crawling on your hands and knees to Becky's bed every night?"

"Sure," she said.

"Were you afraid of Dad?"

"Petrified," she said. "I probably slept three hours a night."

"I don't remember anything specific," I said, my head spinning.

"I didn't either." She got up and tossed her Mountain Dew can into a trash can in the kitchen area. "I wake up every morning remembering more and more. I can't go back to Ohio because if this gets worse, I'm in big trouble."

"What kind of trouble?"

"I feel like I'm crazy sometimes," she said. "I worry I won't be able to maintain my job, my life."

"Whatever comes, you'll be strong enough," I said.

"I hope so, because I can't stop the memories from surfacing. Believe me, I've tried."

"What can I do to help?" I offered. "I'll do anything."

"I know you would." She walked over to her futon. "I need to lie down for a minute," she said, sitting on the side of it. "Just telling you makes it a hundred times worse. It's the beginning of it all coming out." She lay down and put her hands on her chest. "I don't feel very good." She closed her eyes and, just like that, was asleep.

I walked over and looked down. She was breathing deeply, but there were tears rolling into her hairline. I grabbed a blue cotton blanket out of the closet and tucked it around her.

I grabbed JoAnn's Merit cigarettes off the kitchen counter and lit one off the gas stove. I paced and smoked. I hadn't smoked since JoAnn lived in Columbus. I wanted to be numb but I was 100 percent present.

Dad and I had worked things out. It wasn't perfect, but we loved each other, and I relied on him, laughed with him too. In the summer he played *Tiny Bubbles* on his old eight-track tape player as we toodled around on his pontoon boat with the red-and-white-striped canopy. At Christmas I went caroling with him and his funny Lake Hiawatha friends. We were father and daughter.

What would happen now?

I looked on JoAnn's desk for an ashtray and saw the book. *The Courage to Heal: A Guide for Women Survivors of Child Sexual Abuse.* Holy shit.

I turned it over. The back cover read:

> [A] comprehensive guide that offers hope and encourage-
> ment to every woman who was sexually abused as a
> child—and those who care about her. Although the
> effects of child sexual abuse are long-term and severe,
> healing *is* possible.

My first reaction was that she didn't need that book. It was for
women we didn't know.

I flipped to the index, looking up and down the alphabetized list
for something to assuage my swelling anxiety. I saw "Kingsolver,
Barbara, 158." I had just read her book *Animal Dreams* and thought
it the most creative, comforting read. It was about a young woman
learning how family ties and communal living are a way to heal.
Suddenly, healing was the theme of the day. Recognizing Barbara
Kingsolver's name made the book seem less alien.

I flipped to page 158 and a poem entitled "Remember the Moon
Survives" by Barbara Kingsolver. It said, "For Pamela."

Halfway through her poem, I read the stanza that reached down
inside me so deeply, I could barely breathe:

> *The sun is all you wait for,*
> *the light, guardian saint of all the children*
> *who lie like death on the wake*
> *of the household crime. You stop*
> *your heart like a clock: these hours*
> *are not your own. You hide*
> *your life away, the lucky coin*
> *tucked quickly in the shoe*
> *from the burglar, when he*
>
> *Comes. Because he will, as sure*
> *as shoes.*

Dad, what did you do?

Picking up the book, I twisted the cigarette into the ashtray. I kicked off my snow boots, sat on the floor, and leaned against the futon.

Holding the book against my chest, I closed my eyes and forced my brain back to those days (and nights) in Galesburg.

I'm at a church picnic and I'm seven. There's a small lake and a shelter where Mom is helping the ladies lay out food. I'm running with no shoes through the cool grass when Dad is suddenly there. He grabs the back of my shorts and jerks my shorts and underpants down at the same time. I turn in horror, realizing that I'm exposed to everyone at the picnic. I bend down with both hands to pull them both up just as Dad kicks me onto my face, exposing me even more. I roll onto my side and wiggle back into my shorts. Dad is laughing. People are staring. I jump up and run in the other direction. I see a grove of trees on the other side of the lake, where I stay until the food is served. The rest of the picnic, even during the volleyball game, I hold tightly to the elastic of my shorts, expecting Dad at any moment.

I checked on JoAnn. She wasn't crying anymore, just sleeping. What else could I remember that might piece some of this together?

I thought of Mom lining Becky, JoAnn, and me up on her bed every night and slathering Vaseline on our genitals and across our butts. I needed it because I was always red and chapped from lying in urine-soaked pajamas and sheets, but Becky and JoAnn looked okay. Still, every night she'd do that.

Was she preparing us for him? Was it unconscious? Maybe it had nothing to do with Dad. I had gooseflesh. I carefully pulled a corner of JoAnn's blue blanket over my shoulders, careful not to wake her.

I tried to meditate the way Stanley had taught us at UCSD. I breathed deeply into my diaphragm, blowing out the bad air and taking in the good.

I am nine and Mom has brought me to the urologist. She asks the doctor, "Why is she wetting the bed? What's wrong with her?"

"There's nothing physically wrong that would prevent her from waking up. Bed-wetting is usually a psychological problem. Is there anything going on in your house? At school?"

"Of course not," Mom says.

In terms of Dad, I remembered small things.

Dad's reaction to JoAnn being gay was completely out of character. He seemed almost happy about it. He hated African Americans and homosexuals, and Christine was both. Yet when JoAnn brought Christine to dinner at his house, he even hugged her.

As we walked to the car, Dad told Christine, "Take care of JoAnn for me."

I stared at him, puzzled. Why would Dad be glad JoAnn was gay and not care that she was dating a black woman? In light of who he was, it made zero sense.

I am thirteen and riding with Dad in the cramped cab of his pickup from Elk Grove to Galesburg. His hand accidentally brushes the side of my leg. I am so alarmed, I involuntarily startle, jumping so high, my head hits the top of the cab.

"What the hell is wrong with you?" he yells. "You're goddamn crazy. Nervous as cats, every one of you."

It wasn't his touching my leg that disturbed me, it was my over-reaction. I was sure, as irrational as it seemed at the time, that Dad was going to do something inappropriate. Afterward, I felt exactly the way

Dad had described: crazy and nervous. Mostly I was embarrassed. He thought I was nuts, but it couldn't have come from nowhere.

When I was nineteen, Dad told me he'd slept with a young waitress in Elk Grove. He said that he "still had what it took."

But I didn't remember what JoAnn remembered.

I opened my eyes.

I wanted another cigarette. I got up and searched the refrigerator in vain for a Pepsi. I still didn't like to smoke without one, but this was an emergency so I settled for another Mountain Dew. I was already jumpy, and after more caffeine, I'd never get to sleep. I didn't care.

I popped open the can, sat down at JoAnn's desk with *The Courage to Heal*, and looked through the table of contents. "Believing It Happened," "Breaking the Silence," "Grieving and Mourning"— all of these seemed very far from us. I turned the page.

When a person speaks out about the abuse for the first time, it disrupts the family's system of denial. The family might refuse to believe her or even disown her so they can keep up the false pretense under which they have been living.

Mom would believe JoAnn, but Dad would disown her. I believed her and yet it seemed impossible at the same time. I continued to read. A woman wrote:

It's like you came home and your home has been robbed, and everything has been thrown in the middle of the room, and the window is open and the curtain is blowing in the wind, and the cat is gone. You know somebody robbed you, but you're never going to know who. So what are you going to do? Sit there and try to figure it out while your stuff lies around? No, you start to clean it up. You put bars on the windows. You assume somebody was there because the damage is there.

I thought about all the irrational fears I carried around. My entire life I'd been afraid of being in a bedroom with the door closed and a light shining underneath it. I couldn't quit staring at that light, waiting for a shadow to cross it, indicating someone was coming in. In my apartment the bedroom door had to be open.

I never entered my car without looking in all the windows first, in case someone was hiding inside, ready to attack me.

Walking across the tranquil town green in Madison, Connecticut, I was sure that someone was waiting to rape me, even though that had never happened to me before.

I had sex only with men who were married or otherwise unavailable. Once someone was loving, like Daniel, I could no longer be intimate.

I had symptoms but no evidence. Not really. Now I was really disturbed. Ashes from the cigarette I forgot I was holding tumbled onto my gray sweater, burning a small hole in it. This fucking night was just getting better and better.

A thought occurred to me. When I had sex for the first time with Adam in high school, there was no question that I was a virgin because of the pain and the blood. That didn't mean other things couldn't have happened to me, but I knew for sure it hadn't gotten to the point of penetration.

When I was at Kenyon, I had my first orgasm. I thought it was going to be mind-altering—something completely new. But when it finally happened, it was the most familiar feeling in the world—something I'd felt many times in childhood. I couldn't remember what had been going on when the orgasms occurred, but they were not new to me.

✦ ✦ ✦

By the time the sun came up, I'd read most of the book. I was exhausted and disoriented, not knowing what to think. I was not the same person—neither was JoAnn. Who were Mom and Dad? What had happened in our house?

I put on my new red wool coat and drove to the Sunshine Market to pick up two coffees and blueberry muffins. My throat was sore from smoking cigarettes. I should have left the damn things alone. When I came back, JoAnn was awake.

"I should stay with you," I told her.

"It'd be better for me if you went to Ohio. I could use this vacation from work to figure out what I'm going to do."

"I'm worried about you. You're so thin. Do you want me to pick up some groceries?"

"I don't need anything. Look in the refrigerator; you'll see there's plenty of food in there," she said.

"Do you have someone to talk to?" I asked.

"I see a therapist three times a week. If I need her, I'll call. She calls me too, just to check in."

Thank God she was being supported by a therapist who knew what she was doing, because I had no idea what to do.

I was glad JoAnn was okay with my going home. I wanted to see Ohio. Being there might unlock some of the mystery. I expected it to look different now that I knew the depth of what had happened there.

"If you need me, I'll drive straight back," I said.

"I know, but I'll be all right."

"Mom will ask about you. What should I tell her?" I asked.

"Tell her the truth," she said.

"Really?"

"She might as well know."

✦ ✦ ✦

I pulled onto Interstate 70 west with my lukewarm coffee and thought about the man who'd raised us, the good Dad and the bad. I remembered my graduation from Kenyon and how I'd spotted him up in the corner of the packed football stadium. He had stood and waved, thumbs up, happy that I'd found him in the crowd, and I had unexpectedly cried because my dad was proud of me and I was glad he was there.

I stuck in my Joni Mitchell *Blue* cassette and put on my glasses. My eyes were so tired, the road was looking wavy.

I remembered Dad taking Becky and me to the Shrine Circus when I was eight. He was mad at Mom for making him bring us, so he refused to buy anything to eat or drink the whole day. We were hungry and afraid to even ask to go to the bathroom.

I thought of all the things he had almost done: almost bought a Cadillac, almost ran for mayor of Elk Grove, almost created rain on the sundeck of his lake house by stringing up a series of flat green sprinklers from Big Lots.

I pictured him singing "Goodnight, Irene" around the campfire at the lake, his head tilted to the side, eyes closed. He cooked us Saturday night steaks on the grill even when it was below freezing, even when he hated us.

When Dad was little, he worked as Papaw's slave. Maybe he was sexually abused. It said in *The Courage to Heal* that "the abused often abuse." There was no way to know. Maybe Dad's rage was enough to cause all of it.

I pulled into a rest stop to call Mom. I should have told her in person, but I couldn't carry that secret by myself any longer. I needed to lock arms with Mom. I needed to know during the long drive back that there'd be support waiting. Mom and Jim rarely stepped in to help with anything, but this was so huge—her daughter being molested by her ex-husband—surely they'd come through on this one.

"Hello?" Mom sounded happy. Her *Greatest Songs of Christmas* album, which she'd had since I was in first grade, was playing in the background.

"Hi, Mom," I said. "I'm running late. I'm still seven hours away."

"What happened?" She was talking in her "baby" voice, wanting Christmas to start as soon as possible.

"I got a late start from Washington. Is Jim home?" I asked, making sure she wasn't alone.

"He's sitting in the breakfast nook cracking walnuts for me. I'm making fudge," she said.

"JoAnn's not coming home this year," I told her.

"Why not?"

"She's going through something difficult," I said. "Remember how depressed she's been, how depressed she was even as a kid?"

"She's sad about Christine," Mom said.

"That's what I thought, and I'm sure the breakup didn't help, but that's not what it is," I said.

Mom didn't say anything. She was holding off the inevitable. I knew how she felt.

"Well, there's no easy way to say it so I'll just say it; Dad molested JoAnn. For years." There was an excruciatingly long pause. "Mom?"

"It's not possible," she said. "In bed your dad was always gentle and sweet with me."

"*That's* your response?" I asked. My brain was about to explode.

"What am I supposed to say? Your dad didn't do this. He couldn't have."

"Why not?"

"He's not capable," she said. "He wouldn't hurt anyone."

"Wouldn't hurt anyone? Are you serious?" She couldn't have been living in the same house as us.

"He's a bully, that's all," Mom concluded.

"When Becky was in junior high, you told her to be careful around him."

"I don't remember saying that," she said.

"I do."

"He did not do this." She was getting irate.

"I hope you're right, but I doubt you are. JoAnn seems sure of it," I said. "And he was inappropriate with me, too."

"Oh, for God's sake, this is absurd," Mom said. "It's Christmas." There was a pause. "Let's at least try to have a nice holiday. We can deal with this after." I stared at the receiver as if Mom was inside it. She had already hung up.

I sat down on the cement curb and put my head in my hands. For Mom, JoAnn's crisis was just one more thing to deal with later, like taking down the Christmas tree. But for me, JoAnn's revelation had upended everything I'd ever known to be true. Who cared about Christmas?

I walked back to the car remembering the quote from the book: *The family might refuse to believe her or even disown her so they can keep up the false pretense under which they have been living.*

If JoAnn were my daughter, I'd be tearing down to Lake Hiawatha to confront the bastard who'd molested my child. But I knew Mom was just standing there, stirring the Christmas fudge.

Seeing Ohio did not make it better. Looking at the familiar—the flowered wallpaper in my bedroom, Pizza Palace, the cemetery behind the house, Whitmore's field—only made me realize how ordinary the unimaginable felt to us.

My first night there, Mom and I sat up until three thirty in the morning talking over what we knew so far about JoAnn's recollections. Actually, I talked; she sipped Earl Grey tea and busied herself stringing popcorn for the Christmas tree. I wanted to run my fist through a window and feel every jagged shard piercing my skin. How could we be having Christmas as if nothing were wrong? And yet, I didn't know what else to do.

Becky had flown home from San Diego. She'd built a great life for herself out there, and was standing on her own two feet with good friends and an excellent job. She'd bought a flute and was finally taking lessons—a lifelong dream. We had started talking on the phone regularly after I'd moved to New York, but she had recently started dating someone, so now we rarely spoke.

After Mom talked to Becky, I approached her.

"What do you think about JoAnn?" I asked.

"I don't know." She shrugged; her face was flushed. She was as scared as I was.

"Did anything like that happen to you?" I asked.

"Of course not." She was knitting the last corner of a pink afghan she'd been working on for my Christmas present.

"I can't remember anything," I said, watching her fingers push thick pink yarn around two knitting needles. "I've racked my brain, and I don't remember what JoAnn remembers." Becky didn't even look up. "Aren't you worried he might have done something to us?" I asked. "*I'm* worried."

"I can't think about it right now. I need to finish this or you won't be able to take it back to Brooklyn." She leaned down and grabbed her knitting bag.

"I'm scared something really bad is going to happen," I told her.

"It already has," she said, cutting and tying off the yarn.

"I'm going to confront Dad on Christmas night," I told her.

"Good luck," she said, getting up and gathering up her knitting. "I'm not going near him."

I watched her walk up the stairs.

In the kitchen, I loaded Mom's dishwasher, and thought about one Christmas at the old house on Main Street when we were young. Becky and I were the first ones awake, jumping from her bed to mine, waiting for Mom and Dad to wake up.

"Peek downstairs and see if Santa came," Becky dared me.

"They'll kill me if I look." I kept jumping. We weren't allowed to go downstairs until Dad had the bright lights of the movie camera focused on the stairway. Christmas morning was the one time he filmed his children as meticulously as he filmed disasters. It took forever.

"Stop jumping," JoAnn grumbled from under her covers.

"It's Christmas morning," I told her.

"It's dark out," she responded.

"But Santa came. Don't you want to get up?" Becky said.

"NO!" She kept sleeping.

Becky and I jumped quietly. I hopped off the bed and put my face against the metal register in the floor to see if I could spot the Christmas tree down there. I couldn't see it in the dark.

The register looked down into the living room and was perfect for spying or dropping small plastic animals through. If Mom or Dad were sitting on the couch below, watching TV or eating popcorn, we could see them, cut up into tiny squares through the intricate opening of that grate.

"I can see something," I said.

"What?" Becky demanded, pushing her face close to mine over the grate.

"You got a gigantic dog poop from Santa." We started laughing like crazy. She pushed me off the register and looked down.

"You got a moldy cheeseburger," she said, and laughed.

"That's exactly what I wanted," I told her.

"Good, 'cause that's what you got."

Jamie's room was downstairs next to the bathroom. He must have still been asleep. I whispered through the register, "Jamie? Jamie, wake up, it's Christmas morning." Nothing.

"He's not getting up," Becky said.

"We're on our own," I confirmed.

I poured detergent into the door of the dishwasher and closed it. I pushed the knob and heard the water pouring in. Jamie walked into the kitchen. He'd flown in from Salt Lake.

"What are you looking for?" I asked.

"A drink, if you know what I mean." He winked. He knelt down and peered into the liquor cabinet.

"If there's rum in there, pull it out," I told him.

"Now the party's finally gettin' started," he said, rubbing his hands together. After rummaging around in there, he came out with a fifth of Bacardi. "Is this what you had in mind?"

"Perfect," I said. I wiped my hands on a dish towel and opened the fridge to get a Coke. Encouraging Jamie to drink was terrible. He had such a bad problem that there were warrants out for his arrest in at least one state because of the DUIs he'd accumulated. But I needed to relate to someone, and Jamie and I loved each other, even though he scared me sometimes.

"What are you mixing your whiskey with?" I asked, pulling down two glasses.

"I don't mix whiskey," he said. "It kills the taste." He took one of the glasses and filled it with ice.

"For you," he said, handing it over.

"Thanks."

Jamie filled his glass halfway up and downed a big gulp. I was no different, filling my glass halfway with rum and chasing it with Coke. Jamie leaned on the counter and looked directly at me.

"So Dad really did this to JoAnn?" he asked. What a relief! Someone finally came right out and said it.

"Seems that way," I told him.

Jamie began pacing around the kitchen, shaking his head. "What a bastard," he said.

"Pretty much."

"I should go down there and take care of him with a shotgun." Jamie stuck his arm out and acted out aiming a rifle.

"He's not worth ending up in jail," I told him. "He's taken away enough of our lives already."

"I thought I'd gotten the worst of it, but I guess not." He downed another gulp.

"You had it plenty bad," I said. "The way Dad treated you was unforgivable."

"I guess," he said, finishing his drink. "I just can't picture him messing around with one of you girls. I really can't picture it."

"I know."

I didn't tell Jamie I was confronting Dad, because he'd insist on going with me, and someone would end up either shot or beaten to death—and it wouldn't be Dad.

The phone rang and Jamie picked it up. It was our cousin Paul— which meant Jamie would be partying all night.

After he got off the phone, he went into his room, put on clean jeans, and a white button-down shirt with a turquoise bolo tie. "I'm going out with the guys. Be cool."

"Yes, that's me all right," I said. He started toward the door, pulling on his coat. "Jamie?" I called. He turned around. "Be careful in the snow."

"No problemo," he said, heading outside.

The next night, as guests arrived for the Christmas Eve party, Christmas carols rotated on the turntable and the manger scene glowed on a cushion of spun glass near the front door. It was the first Christmas Eve we'd sing without JoAnn's piano accompaniment.

Jamie had too many beers and told Granda about Dad. Grabbing my arm in the kitchen, she asked, "Did he use his fingers or his penis?" My mouth dropped open.

"I have no idea," I snapped.

"If he used his penis—"

I stopped her right there. "Granda, I can't discuss it like this." I walked out of the kitchen. I had to get out of the house.

I threw on my coat and walked to the back fence. I had forgotten how black it got at night in Ohio farm country, especially with no moon. The myriad stars seemed to stretch into infinity and multiply the longer I stood there.

I glanced back at our house, with every window lit. People I'd always known—the Whitmores, Uncle Dale, Granda—walked past the windows with glasses of iced tea in their hands and smiles on their faces.

I knew, just as you know when someone you love has died even before you get the call, that I would leave this family, these friends, and my home forever. I was watching my last bit of life there. I was watching it from the outside in, and from then on, I always would.

I looked across the field and up again at the stars. The next day, I would confront my father.

On Christmas night Mom wanted to know why I was going to Dad's. "Why waste gas to go see *him*?" she asked, wiping the counter.

"To find out what happened to JoAnn," I said.

Mom looked skeptical. "I bet that'll go over well."

"I'm surprised it hasn't occurred to you to confront him. You're the one who married him." I turned on her.

"I'm not going anywhere near him," she said. "One day, I stood in front of the washer and decided I was done with him. Just like that, it was over between us."

"What about your daughter?" I asked.

"He's a load of hot air and always has been," she said. "He's harmless."

"Harmless?" I smacked the top of the counter. "Are you kidding me? Harmless?" I was flailing my arms around, trying to control the urge to smack some reality into the back of her head. "He wasn't harmless. He was violent and mean to all of us."

"You're the great exaggerator," Mom said, wringing out the sponge over the sink.

"I'm not the one who said Dad molested me. JoAnn said it, and I'm going down there for her sake," I said.

"Well, everyone knows you're the martyr," she said. "The Truth Patrol."

"I don't live in a happy bubble, pretending life is bliss," I assured her.

"No one would accuse you of that," she quipped.

"If you and I really get into this whole thing, our relationship will NEVER survive." I stormed out of the room.

Mom turned on the heat under the teakettle.

That night, it was snowing like hell and the pitch-black road to Dad's lake house was winding and slick, which added to my feeling of danger.

As I slid up my father's driveway, I noticed his house was decked out with Christmas lights, but not traditional lights like everyone else at Lake Hiawatha, and not like the strings of lights wrapped meticulously around the fourteen-foot wooden totem pole that greeted you at the entrance.

Instead, Dad had hung enormous white plastic bells everywhere, with multicolored lights sticking out all over them like neon porcupine quills. They were swinging on the trees lining his driveway and swaying from the eaves of his seventies-style A-frame house.

As it turned out, he'd made them himself, out of Clorox bottles turned upside down with the bottoms cut off and Christmas lights stuffed through holes he'd punched with an awl. When I got a closer look, I could see the white plastic handles still attached.

I stopped the car and saw Dad coming to the door looking squat and wavy behind the frosted glass. I was mustering strength to face him, when he opened the door, happy to see me.

I waved and popped the trunk to gather Dad's gifts, the last ones I would ever give him.

I walked toward the house, packages in hand, dreading what the evening would bring. Would he call me names, throw a chair against the wall, hit me? Maybe it'd be something I hadn't thought of. My trembling legs could barely hold me up.

When Dad walked outside, I saw that his right arm was in a plaster cast from fingertips to shoulder. His arm stuck out at a right angle, his wrist supported by a pole that protruded from a small rubber support stuck in a wide Ace bandage wrapped around his thick waist.

"Broke it playing senior's basketball," he said.

"Looks bad," I told him.

"It's not good." He laughed.

I hadn't expected him to be injured; somehow it changed things.

As we walked inside, I scrutinized Dad's profile, foolishly expecting him to look different now that I was about to bust him for the vilest crime any person could commit. But with his thinning gray hair combed to the side, his rectangular gold wire-rimmed glasses, and his narrow lips that hardly parted even with a smile, he looked just like Dad.

He took my red wool jacket and hung it on the coatrack in the sunporch. I walked into his warm kitchen that smelled of roast beef and fresh baked rolls. In the living room I could see a Christmas tree lit in the corner. This year he'd really made an effort.

The table was set for four. Clearly, Dad had been expecting JoAnn and Jamie like in past years. I felt ashamed, as if it were my fault the other kids weren't there, but resisted the urge to make up a story to ease the moment. I couldn't have come up with one anyway. Dad picked up their plates and glasses and set them back in the cupboard.

I made small talk, sitting at the kitchen table with my arms on the round plastic tablecloth, waiting for my plate of roast beef and gravy.

"I have a nice apartment in Brooklyn," I said.

"That's good," he said, throwing the unused silverware back into the drawer. He was mad about the other kids. He was going to be even madder when I told him what I knew.

"The only thing is, a homeless man slept in my car one night. I must have forgotten to lock it." No reaction from Dad. I crossed my hands to keep Dad from seeing them shake.

He opened the pantry door. I had a sudden fear he might pull out a shotgun and shoot me square in the chest. But he was just getting two paper napkins. He handed one to me. "Thanks," I said, spreading it across my lap.

Dad served me and set his plate across from mine. A red-and-white-striped candle-in-a-jar surrounded by a green plastic wreath burned as our centerpiece. I didn't know how I was going to eat with my mouth so dry, or hold a conversation the way my mind was shooting off in a million different directions. For JoAnn's sake I needed to confront him, but I couldn't. I sat there—useless.

"It was nice of the other kids to let me know they weren't coming," he said, scooping a fork of mashed potatoes and gravy into his mouth. "What am I supposed to do with all this food?" He waved his fork toward the kitchen. He sat sideways at the table because of the cast on his arm.

It was the perfect moment to say, *JoAnn would have come, but since the memories of your molesting her came up, she hasn't been hungry.*

"There's ice on the roads tonight," I told him instead. "Do you think they'll salt them before I head back?" I forced chunks of roast beef and potatoes down my tight throat and wondered why I was such a coward.

"Doubt it. It's pretty late and the trucks don't usually go out on a holiday unless it's really bad. Drive slowly and don't use the brake too much. If you need the brake, tap it. Don't lock it up, or you'll slide."

"Okay."

"It's supposed to stop snowing tonight. I bet it ends up melting tomorrow," he said, concentrating on his plate.

After we ate, we moved to the rust-colored sectional to open presents. I handed Dad my last offerings: a red plastic box containing hundreds of different flavors of Jelly Bellies, a Pendleton wool blue-and-white-plaid shirt, and a crappy cookie dough ornament with "Dad" scribbled on top in red food coloring. I'd made it last week before JoAnn's revelation had turned that word into "pedophile."

"I like those lights you made out there," I said, interrupting the silence.

"Would you like one?" he asked.

In my overanxious, exaggerated state, I'd forgotten what we were talking about. "What?" I asked.

"Do you want a plastic bell?"

I looked out the window at all of them blowing sideways in the wind. They were goofy, but I'd never wanted anything more than I wanted one of Dad's ridiculous homemade Clorox bottle bells. "No, thanks," I said. "They're pretty, though."

In previous years Dad had given gifts from his hardware store, something he considered handy. This year was no exception. The last Christmas I would ever receive anything from my dad, I got a set of yellow jumper cables and a hundred-dollar bill wrapped in Christmas paper.

"Thanks, Dad. I could really use this," I said. He was fiddling with the TV remote.

"You're welcome," he said. "You never know when your car might need to be jumped. You don't want to be stuck somewhere without cables."

"That's right," I said.

I was trying to find the words for JoAnn, but they wouldn't come. I watched him flip through channels, looking for a Johnny Carson rerun. The wool shirt I'd gotten him was pulled on over his sweater. He must have liked it.

Maybe I didn't have to say it tonight. Maybe we could have this one last Christmas before everything erupted. I settled onto the sectional couch and stared at the TV. Dad usually fell asleep after Johnny's monologue. I should probably go soon.

Despite my immense sorrow for Dad and his own horrendous childhood and despite my rage that he had repeated his history on us, I would let him go without words. Somehow I knew this would be the last time I'd see him and he wouldn't even know it was happening.

I hugged him good-bye, the yellow jumper cables dangling from my hand, and walked out into the snowy night.

I was relieved to be out the door. The problem was the next hour, the next day, the next year, the next years. As screwy as it was, I did not know who I was without him.

It was death without the body.

The Clorox bottle bells illuminated the icy deck as I drove away from Dad, his good arm waving in the frosty air.

CHAPTER TWENTY

When I returned from Christmas, I kept in close touch with JoAnn, calling her once a week. She was doing well, working with her therapist and handling her job with the same aplomb as before. It was good she didn't need me to come down, because I was busy.

After calling off the wedding, I'd accepted a full-time job with a management consultant firm in the Flatiron Building in New York City. They were called The Strategist Group and consisted of three strategic management consultants who needed office support. They routinely hired actors when the workload was heavy because they liked "creative people," and actors usually needed temp jobs to get by. It was the most fun I'd had at work.

When Elliott, the owner of the company, asked me to stay permanently, he said, "How about twenty-five thousand dollars a year?"

"Are you sure? Oh my God!" Financial stability for the first time in my life.

"I'm sure."

"Elliott, thank you so much." I smiled. "I can't believe it." I pictured myself buying a home or jetting off on Hawaiian vacations. It sounded like a huge amount of money.

Two hours later he came back to my cubicle. "How about twenty-eight thousand?"

"Why are you raising it?" I wondered.

"Because twenty-five thousand is really low, and I felt like a jerk, especially seeing how excited you were."

"Don't you think this is a mistake? I'm an actress. I don't know anything about office work."

"You'll learn. I trust you, kiddo." He walked out, and I spun around in my chair. With money, I would have a financial floor under me, and the best part was, Elliott believed in me. Acting was on hold. A steady paycheck, and working with people I adored, was much-needed emotional and financial support after Daniel. I had no idea that I'd need that steady income for JoAnn as well.

❖ ❖ ❖

In March, I sat at my desk putting together binders for a presentation Elliott would deliver the next day. I collated the sections and attached black plastic spines with a binding machine.

JoAnn was lying on a gurney in National Hospital's emergency room, watching clear liquid drip into the tube of her IV. She'd waited too long to get help, and was dehydrated; she'd stopped eating and drinking days before.

I finished the binders and ordered sushi for lunch. After taking the elevator down to the first floor, I walked to Sushi Union on Broadway and Twentieth. I picked up a California roll and three pieces of tuna and headed to Madison Square Park to eat.

JoAnn rolled up her shirtsleeve and began unwrapping the white gauze that would eventually reveal the cuts running the length of her left forearm. The agony was finally in full view of someone. The doctor was openly disturbed.

This was the first time she'd ever cut herself, and she had no idea why it had felt necessary, and yet it had. She was tired and frightened. She'd always insisted on fighting alone, but this fight was finally beyond her.

When the doctor insisted she be admitted, she was both relieved and horrified. Pulling the white overly bleached sheet up around her shoulders, she wondered what she had started. Maybe she should have kept it a secret, every last aching detail. Maybe she should go home, but then she'd be alone again.

It was five thirty p.m. I turned off my computer and walked to Live Bait on West Twenty-third. I met Josh Hunter for drinks, my first date after calling off the wedding. He looked adorable in a black turtleneck and jeans, smelling like expensive cologne and toothpaste. We laughed, ate, and then he walked me to the subway, where we kissed for the first time. I was reeling with happiness and worry, Daniel always in the back of my mind. I unlocked my door, checked messages, and went to bed.

JoAnn curled up into a ball and tried to sleep in her single room on Nine West, the code word for the psych ward. Her room was next to the locked doors that led to the rest of the hospital, where people were having babies and routine surgeries.

Over the next three weeks I left JoAnn two messages, dated Josh, talked to Daniel, and spent a week in Boston working with The Strategist Group. Life was whipping by. I assumed JoAnn was just as busy. Sometimes we didn't get back to each other for days at a time.

Over the next three weeks JoAnn went to group sessions and sat in the window of her room, watching a construction crew build a new wing of the hospital. She marked time by how far along they were with preparing the foundation; she didn't call any of us. She felt ashamed and didn't know what to say.

JoAnn experienced flashbacks, each different from the one before—a body memory in the form of vaginal pain, or a smell of stale beer that came from nowhere. It was confusing, unpredictable, and terrifying. Her dreams were so frightening that she gave up sleeping, choosing instead to walk down the darkened hallway to a community room where she'd sit quietly with others who were in their own private hells. She wasn't sure she'd survive what she'd started, but she knew it would shake her life and her family to its core.

When I returned from Boston, there was a message from Mom on my machine. JoAnn had called her. I didn't unpack my clothes. I threw the suitcase back into the car and headed to Washington.

JoAnn had been released from the hospital and was back in her apartment.

"What happened?" I asked when I saw her.

"I stopped pretending, and finally took myself seriously," she said.

"I don't understand why you cut your arm," I said. "Are you suicidal?" If I was going to help her, I couldn't sugarcoat what was happening.

"If I'd wanted to commit suicide, I wouldn't be sitting here," she said, lighting a cigarette. "Look, I'm not really clear myself. It's embarrassing as hell."

"Don't be embarrassed in front of me. You know everything I've ever done—especially since I told you about the abortion."

"Cutting is complicated and I don't really understand it, but I know that I needed to feel alive and also be in control of something. That's how numb I felt. It's crazy."

"It's not crazy, it's horrifying," I said, but I was worried that she was slipping into something crazy. None of it made sense to me.

"It is horrifying."

"Did they tell you what you can do to stop cutting yourself?" I asked.

"I met a good doctor, and she gave me medication to relieve some of the anxiety." She shook her head. "What have I started?"

"It started a long time ago," I said. "Can they make remembering easier?"

"None of this is going to be easy. It's different for each person, but it looks like the memories are so jumbled up that it may take a long time."

JoAnn was right; it wasn't going to get better. It got sufficiently worse.

I reluctantly put my clothes into my suitcase and headed toward Brooklyn. I needed to be at work on Monday. Each mile farther from JoAnn felt like a betrayal and a relief. I shouldn't have left her, but I was so overwhelmed, I needed time to process what had just happened.

I visited as often as I could. She seemed to be getting along okay—not great, but okay.

JoAnn resigned from her job in social services in June. She was worried she'd miss something and one of the disabled adults who relied on her would not get what they needed. She needed to be present and alert at work. She couldn't risk jeopardizing someone else, even if it meant putting her own life in jeopardy by giving up the money she needed to live on.

I called Mom.

"JoAnn quit her job," I told her. "How's she going to get by?"

"Good question."

"We're going to have to help her," I said.

"Maybe this will give her the time she needs to get better," Mom suggested. It was the first time since all of this had started that Mom said something real and true.

"I hope so. Have you seen Dad around town?" I asked. "He hasn't called me since Christmas. It's like he knows something's up."

"More likely, he's in his own selfish world. Does he usually call?" she asked.

"No, but I usually call him. You'd think he'd wonder if I was all right," I said.

"That's hoping for a lot," Mom said.

Still, it bothered me. I was glad I didn't have to answer any questions from Dad, but I was hurt that if I didn't call him, we'd never speak. There was no way he could know about JoAnn. I still hadn't confronted him.

I was waiting for something absolutely damning, a memory I could point to and say, "JoAnn knows you did *this* to her on *this* day when she was *this* old." But her memories were still in vague pieces. She knew it was Dad, she knew it was in our house, but she couldn't be specific about exactly what he had done.

In July, JoAnn gave notice on her apartment without telling me. She had no intention of being alive by the end of the month. She couldn't trust herself to work, and now she couldn't afford rent or food. After our childhood, where asking for lunch money in elementary school brought shame for needing to eat, she was not going to put herself through asking anyone again. But now a timeline was established.

Pulling out a blue plastic crate filled with journals she'd written since high school, she began the heartrending task of tearing out pages she wouldn't want anyone to read. After tearing several sheets together into lengthwise shreds, she placed handful after handful of paper into three black lawn bags. She stopped ripping when she saw Stacy's name, her first lover, who had made her feel more alive and happy than she'd ever felt in her life. The passages about depression and dread were ripped into tiny squares. Once she started, she didn't stop, even for the happy parts, until she was surrounded by the white confetti of her past. One more step.

I'd still heard nothing from Dad, and vice versa. Every summer I'd visit the lake house and we'd tool around on his pontoon boat and fish for bass. What did he think had happened?

I felt guilty for missing him, after what he'd done. But it was painful to think he'd just let me float away. I had thought I was the one who'd let go.

I called JoAnn from my Brooklyn apartment, not knowing that she had chosen that night to end her life.

"How are you?" I was eating Chinese food from a cheap restaurant down the street in Park Slope. Everything was excruciatingly ordinary.

"Okay," she said.

"Do you want to come up and visit? We can go into New York?" I asked, taking a bite.

"No. I'm good."

"Are you eating?" I asked. "Because I can't stop eating. I'm eating right now."

"I eat," she said.

"What have you been doing?" I asked.

"I'm going to a concert this weekend. It's on the Mall, down by the monuments."

"Sounds fun," I said. "Is anybody going with you?"

"I don't know yet."

"Well, have fun and call me next week."

"Be careful," she said.

"Why?"

"The city is crazy, and I just want you to be careful," she said.

"Okay, I'll be careful."

We hung up.

I opened my new Andy Warhol book and finished my orange chicken. Later, I brushed my teeth, talked to Daniel on the phone, and went to bed.

That night, JoAnn didn't want to leave, but she knew she had to go. She understood, in that quiet hour, things that only people who've walked to the edge know. Dying seemed almost compassionate—a way to escape the living hell.

She'd been stockpiling prescription drugs for a few months. She methodically filled all of them whether she planned to take them or not. She pulled out the shoe box hidden in the linen closet behind a stack of towels and looked inside. The supply was ludicrous.

Having heard a story from a woman who had woken up alone after taking pills, JoAnn decided that there needed to be another step. She tucked a small box of single-edge razor blades into the corner of the shoe box.

She pulled on her white sweatshirt and blue jeans, grabbed her black bag with her wallet inside, took the shoe box, and locked the apartment door behind her. It was three a.m. She decided to go to Rehoboth Beach, where she had been on weekend trips with Christine when they were together. It was a two-and-a-half-hour drive, and she would get there to see the sunrise. She would start this day and end it on her terms.

Driving away from the city, she was relieved. She'd made a decision to be in control. She would not be dependent on other people, and she would never be humiliated and scared again.

JoAnn arrived at the beach just as the sky was beginning to brighten. She parked her Subaru on a side street that ended at the beach. As the sun peeked over the Atlantic Ocean, she tilted her head back onto the headrest and laid her hand on the shoe box. She hadn't anticipated how difficult it was actually going to be.

When the sun got a little higher, JoAnn got out of the car, walked into the sand, and sat down. She picked up a stick lying by her foot and started to draw concentric circles. Her plan seemed surreal yet logical—necessary. She glanced up to see a dolphin's fin breaking the water, and it occurred to her that when she died, there might be a part of her that would float away.

She began to panic as she realized there was a part of her, perhaps a soul, that she couldn't actually kill. Her thoughts continued as the circles got smaller and closer together.

If she couldn't kill all of her, then a part of her couldn't be killed by anyone else. There must have been a part of her that Dad couldn't have touched, that not only had survived but might also still be innocent— pure.

Even with this revelation, she wasn't comforted. What if she killed herself and didn't find mercy where she was headed? What if the Christians were right, and she'd be punished for taking her own life? What if everyone who had ever known and loved her got mad at her for doing it? What if no one ever understood? She started to cry.

She stuck the stick into the sand and walked to her car. She thought maybe she was making a mistake by not going forward with it, but she could at least be sure that someone understood before the next time.

That afternoon, JoAnn made it back just in time to keep an appointment with her doctor. During her session, even though JoAnn hadn't mentioned suicide or her drive to the beach, the doctor told her about a specialized treatment center specifically devoted to working with survivors of incest. It was a psychiatric facility that had a specialized program called The Center for Abuse Recovery and Empowerment.

JoAnn drove by on her way home. It looked like any other office building along Colorado Avenue. Empowerment—she had never thought of it that way before.

JoAnn called the center. When she told the intake social worker she'd given notice on her apartment and that she had to be out in a week, the social worker told her to come that day.

JoAnn thought she might as well try this one thing. If it didn't make her feel different, she still had the shoe box and a solid plan.

JoAnn called me at The Strategist Group on Wednesday.

"Are you all right?" I asked. JoAnn never called me at work.

"I'm at an in-patient facility down here. I just wanted you to know where I was so you wouldn't worry."

"Is it National Hospital?"

"No, it's an in-patient psychiatric facility. They have a division for abuse survivors," she explained.

"Are you safe?" I asked.

"Yes. I'll tell you what happened when you get here."

"I'll head down tomorrow. Unless you need me today," I said.

"Tomorrow's okay."

"Can I have the phone number?"

"If you call, they won't tell you I'm here, but I'll leave your name on the visitor's list." She gave me directions and hung up the phone.

An in-patient facility? I told Elliott I was going for a walk, took the elevator seven floors down, and walked out into the chaos of the city. I was happy to be anonymous. My sister was in a mental institution but I was free to walk down Fifth Avenue, so I did. I walked and cried and took in the blue sky for the both of us. Everything had shifted—again.

On my way down to see JoAnn, I foolishly stopped by Super Stop & Shop and bought sunflowers, trying to normalize what was anything but normal.

When I walked into the psych ward, I was given a small cardboard box of JoAnn's possessions: dirty white shoestrings from her Nike tennis shoes; her silver nail clippers, which she always carried with her; and a black leather belt. I stared into the box and then at the nurse.

"We don't allow items into the facility that might be used to injure a person, either themselves or someone else," she explained.

"Is she suicidal?" I asked.

"She's on fifteen-minute checks. We were lucky to catch her this time."

"She's cut her arms before," I naively told the nurse, as if she hadn't seen it a million times before. "It's not a suicide attempt," I said. "It's the opposite. It helps her feel alive."

"She admitted to being suicidal," the nurse said. "She's serious about dying, and if you love her, you need to be serious about it too. Her life is in danger. She needs hope and support."

I got it. We weren't anywhere we'd ever been before. We'd moved into an emergency phase.

I left the box behind to pick up on my way out and floated through a fog of shock to another set of locked doors. On some level I knew JoAnn was suicidal, but I clung to my denial like a life raft.

I waited for JoAnn in the visitor's lounge on a blue chair with the sunflowers across my lap. I anxiously watched patients wandering in and out. A woman was standing so close to the wall that her nose was touching it, and behind her someone was pacing back and forth and patting her cheeks with both hands. I heard screaming.

"You tried to kill me!" A patient in light green pajamas was yelling at a nurse.

"We're trying to help you," the nurse responded.

"If I want to take pills, you can't stop me," she screamed. "Shoving charcoal down my throat isn't going to stop me." The nurse quickly escorted her down the hall, away from the visitor's lounge. I nervously retied the bow on the sunflowers and tried to subdue the fear that was threatening to strangle me.

JoAnn walked through the door. She was emaciated and, from the dark circles under her eyes, I could tell she hadn't slept. Her hair wasn't combed. I'd never seen JoAnn without her hair meticulously groomed, even when we were kids.

She was wearing light blue sweatpants and a white sweatshirt with long sleeves, but I could still see deep cuts on the tops of her hands. She was smiling at me, but tears were already starting to fall. I hugged her as she cried.

Everything had spiraled out of control.

I was so grateful that she was being watched over in this place.

"You're safe here," I told her.

"I hope so," she said, wiping her nose on a perfectly folded Kleenex and handing one to me. Now that was the old JoAnn, someone who carried neatly folded Kleenex in her pocket at all times.

"I brought you useless flowers," I said, smiling through tears. She nodded.

A week later when I came to see JoAnn, I asked the nurse where she was.

"JoAnn's in the smoking room."

"Where's that?" I asked.

The nurse pointed to a large picture window to her left. On the other side of it were about ten women sitting around smoking cigarettes, and the smoke was so thick I could barely see them in there.

"Oh, that's the smoking room," I said, laughing. If JoAnn was socializing, that was good, even if she was inhaling plumes of smoke while she did it. We were working on her mental health; we'd worry about her lungs later. Suddenly, the door swung open and a column of smoke billowed out around JoAnn. She looked my way.

"I don't think you're getting enough nicotine," I teased.

"I know. It was getting a little thick in there," she said.

"At least there's a place you can smoke." She wasn't allowed to walk outside.

"It helps," she said, tucking a pack of Merits into the pocket of her sweatpants. Her hair was combed, and her eyes looked brighter—more rested.

"Are you hungry?" I asked.

"No." She weighed about a hundred pounds.

"You look better," I told her.

"They're finally giving me something to help me sleep. It helps with the nightmares. Let's go into the lounge." We sat down on a small blue sofa by the windows. "I have to ask a favor," she said.

"I hope it involves picking up a Big Mac or a grilled steak for you to eat."

"I have to move out of my apartment right away. Could you put my stuff into storage? They won't let me out even for part of the day, or I would do it myself."

"Why'd you give up your apartment?" I asked. "We can still make a few more payments, don't you think?"

"I gave it up before I came here," she said. I shook my head, not understanding. "I wasn't planning on needing it anymore."

I stared at JoAnn. She was so frail that I felt like sitting her on my lap and rocking her. "Why wouldn't you need a place to live?" I asked.

"I wasn't planning on being alive this long." She didn't look up.

I didn't know what to say. I didn't know what would help.

"You planned your suicide?" I asked. She was listless, her hands collapsed in her lap. I sat back and looked out the window. I couldn't imagine a world without JoAnn in it. I turned to her and said, "Do you know I always wanted to be dead?"

"You did?" She looked at me.

"My whole life, I wanted to be dead, but I didn't actually do anything about it. I guess I didn't want to be dead; I wanted relief. I wanted to be happy and peaceful."

"That's it," she said. "It's not about dying; it's about stopping the pain."

The next day I drove to different grocery stores, picking up boxes. Banana boxes were the biggest and sturdiest. I went back to JoAnn's apartment and began carefully wrapping her dishes in newspaper and packing them away. I wrapped paintings and sculptures she had created or bought. I came across a sculpture of two women hugging, which she'd carved in Columbus. They could be pulled apart if someone visited who didn't know she was gay. Once she moved to D.C., she didn't pull them apart anymore.

As I covered each precious piece of her life in newspaper, I became more irate. That son of a bitch had ruined us. He'd taken our childhoods, I knew that already, but he was taking our futures as well. I had to be braver than I had been up until now. If I confronted him, it might strengthen all of us. Until he was held accountable, he still held power over us.

I packed Granda's brown-and-white afghan she'd given JoAnn as a birthday gift. I remembered it spread out across the back of Granda's couch when we were little.

On JoAnn's dresser was the gold ring I'd given her for her birthday the year before. It was two hands entwined. I'd written in her card that it was her and me, that neither one of us would go through anything alone ever again. Not when we had each other. I had let her down. She was going through this alone. There was no other way for her to recover but to let the memories come, and I couldn't do that for her.

I slipped the ring onto my index finger. I'd seen her wear it so many times. Sobs finally came. I didn't think they ever would. This packing up of everything she owned was as if JoAnn *had* killed herself. I wasn't sure we'd be able to keep her alive even after she got out. I wasn't sure of anything except that I felt like I was sitting in the waiting room of the mortuary alone, helplessly waiting for the body I was sure would arrive. I needed the psychiatric facility to come through for her. I needed them to save her life.

After the apartment was packed, Daniel, whom I had called to come down and help me, arrived and we moved those boxes across town and into a storage facility with long hollow aisles. After we shoved everything inside, I looked at the stacked boxes and wondered if the next time I saw them I'd be standing next to JoAnn or mourning her. For once, Mom couldn't accuse me of being dramatic.

I didn't want to close the door, but it was getting late. I still had to drive four hours to Brooklyn.

"You look terrible," Daniel said. This brought on another surge of tears. I was so grateful just to have someone looking at me. Thinking about me. I hadn't realized how much I needed someone to help shoulder some of the pressure and sadness.

"I know." I laughed, sniffing. "I bet you'd be scared if you met me now."

"You don't scare me," he said, wrapping his arm around my neck and pulling me close.

"Thanks for coming," I said. "After what I did, you shouldn't even be talking to me."

"I'll always talk to you," he said, and then he locked up JoAnn's belongings and walked me back down the empty hallway.

I followed him as we both drove north. When I saw him take the exit for Connecticut, I felt another lump in my throat. I'd backed the wrong horse. My family was nowhere to be found, but Daniel was right there. I thought, *If he and I were together, it would be incredibly comforting.*

When I got to my apartment in Brooklyn, I needed to talk to a friend, so I called Julie Kilner for the first time in a year. She had a new baby boy and sounded happy, still living in Ohio. I didn't tell her what was happening to my family.

"Are you going to Florida to visit your dad this summer?" she asked.

"No," I said quickly. He must have been on vacation. It was the first news I'd had of him since Christmas.

"Then maybe you can come out and stay with all of us in Ohio," she suggested.

"I'd love to, believe me, but I can't leave work."

We talked a little more and then hung up. Dad was in Florida.

The following weekend, JoAnn and I met with a heavyset blond psychologist at the psych ward.

The doctor asked me, "What do you think about all of this coming to light?"

"I'm in shock," I replied.

"Still?" she asked.

"Is there a moratorium on being in shock?" I asked.

"Of course not," she replied.

"I'm shocked that JoAnn's in a mental hospital," I said. "I can't believe this is happening to my family."

"This was a surprise?" she asked.

"Yes," I reiterated.

"In families where this level of sexual abuse has taken place, it's not unusual for children to repress it," she said. I wasn't sure if she was talking about JoAnn or me.

"I don't remember the level of abuse that JoAnn remembers," I explained. "Being the youngest, maybe I missed the worst of it," I said.

"But you two slept in the same bedroom until JoAnn was fifteen, correct?" she asked.

"Correct," I said, my stomach flipping over.

"And what about your mom?" she asked.

"I don't think she was involved, was she?" I turned to JoAnn.

The doctor interrupted. "Long-term sexual abuse cannot take place unless everyone in the house is following the same dynamic. It's the family dynamic that allows something this horrific and violent to occur—especially over a long period of time," she said.

"A father abuses his daughter and the mother gets blamed!" I said, incensed.

"No, I'm saying that if your mother had been a different person, the abuse could not possibly have gotten to the level it did," she said. "I know your father's a major piece in all of this, but I would suggest that when you start looking at your mother, whom you actually trusted to keep you safe when you were young children, that's going to be the worst piece. The place you'll feel the most betrayed."

"But I don't remember anything specific. I don't think this happened to me," I insisted.

"The entire family sets the scene, and there is an unspoken agreement to ignore and forget. You might not remember, but you sure felt the effects of what went on in that house. You had to have been influenced whether you were actually molested or not."

Actually molested? In my sorrow and rage for JoAnn, I'd stopped wondering if I might have my own experiences locked away. Staring at the psychologist, who was talking to JoAnn, I began to wonder, *If Dad came to her in the bedroom, and Becky and I were also there, did we see anything? Was it realistic to think that he left us alone?* Or was this psychologist messing with my head? Maybe this had nothing to do with me. Maybe it *was* just JoAnn.

"Monica, is there any way I can help you before we end the session?" she asked.

"Only if you can make this go away," I said. "Get me out of this nightmare."

I walked out of the psych ward angry, defeated, and exhausted. It was dark and starting to sprinkle. I climbed into my Honda hatchback and turned the key. I didn't know my family. Everything I'd believed to be true was washing away with the rain.

I looked at the building where JoAnn was locked up. No one walking by would suspect the horror that was being exposed in such a benign-looking place—an office building, really. I hated leaving her, but now there was no other place to take her. There was only an empty apartment, and after tomorrow, she wouldn't even have that.

I tilted my head back onto the headrest, and thought about Mom. I missed her. I missed my mom coming to take care of everything. The thing is, she never had taken care of things. That was never my mom. But I longed for her anyway.

I squeezed my eyes shut and thought of a sweet moment between the two of us.

*I was six years old, and we were sitting in the nubby orange chair in
the living room. I was nestled into her lap, and her breath smelled like
Wrigley's spearmint gum. As she held the green book open in front of us,
it seemed like no one else was in the house, but the other kids must have
been there. Mom began reading from* Now We Are Six.

> *"What would I do?" I said to Pooh,*
> *"If it wasn't for you," and Pooh said: "True,*
> *It isn't much fun for One, but Two*
> *Can stick together," says Pooh, says he.*

I opened my eyes—even a Winnie-the-Pooh story furthered the
illusion that there was someone protecting me. As Mom read to me
night after night, I believed the fairy tales. Why wouldn't I? *She*
believed them.

It was really raining now. I started the car and headed to the
Lucky Seven liquor store. I bought Bacardi rum and a six-pack of
Pepsi and drove to the apartment. Tomorrow, I would need to
clean it so JoAnn could get her deposit back. Tonight, I needed to
drink.

I was eager to obliterate reality. Maybe that's the one thing
Jamie was missing—the ability to deny—and that's why he drank.
He didn't have the protection of denial, so he had to escape another
way. Tonight, three thousand miles away from my brother, I would
join him for a drink, understanding his alcoholism for the first
time.

When I got to the apartment, I was hungry and scared. I
called Mom. I'd just paid JoAnn's car payment, so I was also
broke. I knew better than to call her, but I was still hoping for a
crumb of comfort and understanding. I wasn't ready to give up
on her just yet.

"Hi, Mom," I said.

"Hello to you," she said.

"I've been with JoAnn at the psych ward—," I started to say, when she interrupted.

"Could we not get into that tonight? I've had a terrible day, and I don't want to talk about it."

"But I need to talk," I explained.

"Call Daniel," she said.

"I don't want to call Daniel. I want to talk to you," I said.

"Then we're not talking about JoAnn." She was silent.

"You don't even know what she looks like. She's tiny, maybe a hundred pounds. She has cuts running the length of her arms," I said. "I'm in a nightmare out here."

"Well, a gold star for you. But you aren't the only one hurting," she said bitterly.

"I didn't say I was the only one hurting, but I'm the only one *here*," I said. "JoAnn doesn't want to live. She's under suicide watch."

"Jim and I are taking a short vacation," she announced.

"A vacation?" I exclaimed.

"I need to get away, so Jim's taking me to Michigan for a few days," she said.

"Mom, we need money. I can't support JoAnn and me on my salary. I have to drive four hours back to Brooklyn on Sunday night just so I can work all week and come back down here. How could you go on vacation? Send that money to JoAnn; she needs it," I urged. "I'm afraid she's going to kill herself as it is. If she loses her car, her situation will become even more hopeless. I've already emptied her apartment into a storage facility."

Mom was furious. "You will not tell me what I need and do not need. I'm going to Michigan and I'm going to get away from all of this," she said, and hung up the phone.

I opened the Bacardi.

✦ ✦ ✦

The next morning I forced myself awake, with a pounding hangover and a sore back from sleeping on the floor. I needed Mom to prove the psychologist wrong, but she was doing the opposite. I needed her to come through, but she was leaving for Michigan, probably had already left. And to make it worse, Michigan was *my* haven, where *my* friends gathered and performed shows and swam. It was the place I was the happiest. And what I wouldn't have given to go there myself.

I was beginning to wonder if my relationship with Mom would survive this mess. In books and in music, people talk about always loving your mother. What I was feeling toward her was nothing like love.

I scrubbed JoAnn's apartment clean and dropped the keys off at the management office in her complex.

Visiting JoAnn, I saw the blond psychologist in the hallway.

"How are you holding up?" she asked.

"I'd like to not become a patient here myself, if I can help it," I said.

"Are you afraid you'll end up here?"

"I had a terrible dream last night," I said.

"Come on in," she said, opening the door to her office. "Tell me about it."

I sat down in the chair across from her desk and tried to remember every detail.

In my dream, Mom, Becky, Jamie, JoAnn, Dad, and I were sitting in a pew at the Galesburg Methodist Church.

My head was bowed for a prayer when I heard a sound, muffled and steady, like someone thumping their hand on the top of a wooden bench. It was coming from the back of the church. I looked at the people in front of me, but no one else had seemed to notice. The noise was louder now. I slid my hand across the seat of the pew to discover what I already knew; my father was no longer sitting there. I turned my head slightly to my right: JoAnn was missing as well.

The pastor was droning on about tithing as I stood and turned slowly to my left. My father was in the very back of the sanctuary, holding my sister down by the back of her neck. Her yellow Sunday school dress with the big bow in the back was hiked up over her head and he was raping her from behind, each thrust sending her small head knocking into the back of the last pew—*bang, bang, bang*.

In the congregation, people started shifting in their seats. Women in small pastel pillbox hats were looking at their laps. Everyone knew what was happening, but no one turned around or made a move to rescue JoAnn.

I stood up and hurried out to the carpeted aisle beside our pew. I held out my arms as far as they would reach and began turning, around and around and around. As I turned, the sun moved backward across the window and the Reverend Morse walked in reverse away from the pulpit and back up the aisle. I was turning back time with everything a desperate child could muster—with all the strength in the universe. And it was working. I spun until JoAnn, Dad, and I were once again sitting in the pew.

I grabbed JoAnn's hand and ran out the back of the church. She was slower than I was, but I pulled her along behind me. We ran down the street and around the corner to Mammaw's house. I shoved JoAnn through the front door and up the steps to the second floor, where no one ever went and where Mammaw kept upcoming Christmas and birthday gifts piled in corners and on desks.

I pushed JoAnn onto a double bed and grabbed the quilt off a nearby rocker. I covered her in the quilt, tucking in all three sides so tight that no one could get to her. I was sobbing and sitting next to her with my hand on her heaving chest. I watched her for hours until a miracle occurred and she slept. It was starting to get dark. The whole day had gone by. We were alone on this bed, in this dark house, and I was her only protector.

I looked at the painting above the bed, where ballet dancers pirouetted across the middle of a green background, when suddenly the colors started swirling and changing. I stared at the painting. I knew that it was telling me how to protect JoAnn, but I couldn't decipher the message. I looked at her sleeping face and understood that the answers were being offered through this painting, but I was too numb or stupid to understand them.

The front door slammed shut downstairs. There was no time. Dad had found us.

The psychologist asked me a question that would change my entire view of childhood and kill my chances of ever staying in denial.

"Have you wondered if that little girl in the dream isn't JoAnn, but you?"

"No. I thought it might mean that I knew something about what had happened to JoAnn. Maybe I saw something," I said.

"Or maybe by focusing on JoAnn, you're saving yourself from the pain of focusing on yourself."

I'd read about doctors like her who put ideas into people's heads that weren't necessarily true. I wasn't sure I trusted this woman.

"I don't know anything anymore. Everything I thought to be true, isn't," I told her. "What if I never know what happened to me?"

"Your mind will let it come only when you're ready. You must not be ready," she said.

"What makes you so sure about me?" I asked.

"I'm not sure that anything directly happened to you, but I'm sure you were very seriously affected. All of you were—you had to be."

The first thing I thought of was Whitfield. Classic move of

dating your father. Was that more than just looking for a father figure? Was I looking for a specific relationship to relive with a father
figure? I had no idea. I got that same squeamish feeling I'd had at the
lake house with Whitfield and Dad.

The next day I drove back to Brooklyn, shaky and uncertain.

At work on Monday I walked into the office exhausted and
unable to focus. Elliott came in and sat down on the corner of my
desk.

"You look like you've lost your last friend," he said.

"Don't even ask," I told him, tears already brimming.

Elliott patted my back. "Let me know if there's anything I can
do to help."

"Thanks," I managed.

My family thought therapists were for crazy people or people in
emergency situations only. I didn't find help for myself. I'd seen the
kind of shape JoAnn had been in when she'd started therapy. I was
much better than that.

In September I turned thirty. There was no celebration. Mom and
Jim completely forgot it. I spent the day with JoAnn, playing cards.

She was out of the psychiatric facility and had rented a room in
a house with two other women, but I still spent most weekends with
her. There wasn't a single Sunday night, driving back to Brooklyn,
that I didn't worry she'd need me during the week, and that I'd get
there too late.

My life had become very small. I didn't see friends, and I didn't
go to plays or parties—I worked, and I drove to Washington.

On Thursday, Mom called early in the morning.

"I need you to pay JoAnn's car payment," she barked.

"What?" I wasn't even awake yet.

"Jim and I have given enough, and we are not going to pay her car payment. You'll have to figure that out." I was confused.

"I already paid that," I told her.

"You paid last month's bill, which was late. Now this month is due. They called here, threatening to tow her car away."

"I don't have the money, Mom. I just paid it, like I said." I was trying to sit up in bed, but the phone cord was getting tangled.

"Right," she said sarcastically. Mom was under the impression that I had money I was keeping from the family. I had no idea where she was getting that, but when she came to visit, she expected me to pay for everything, including her movie ticket and the restaurant bills and taxi rides.

"I can't pay it," I said honestly. "I'm still paying Granda's car insurance." I'd started paying Granda's insurance when I got out of graduate school. It was one way I could take care of her long distance.

"Then you just get on the phone and call Becky or Jamie or whoever and find someone who can. Jim and I have given enough." She hung up on me. I was still in bed.

Becky wasn't going to help. She hadn't called JoAnn or me since I'd seen her at Christmas. Becky had told Mom, "I can't afford to lose my job and become suicidal right now. I just got my life together."

Obviously, the situation scared her to death, had her convinced that her life would spiral away from her just as JoAnn's had. I remembered how she'd cut Dad off that Christmas and never saw him again. Had he done something to her? During the most recent Christmas, she'd told me she didn't remember anything, but why wouldn't she offer even a crumb of support?

Jamie would be willing to help, but he didn't have two nickels to rub together. He probably needed as much help as JoAnn, only none of us had ever bothered to ask.

I lay there for two hours trying to figure out how I'd made it this far with so little resources backing me up. If they towed JoAnn's car, she would be devastated. I couldn't worry about it right now. I had to get to work.

That weekend, I drove to Washington worrying where the car payment money would come from. It was two hundred and twenty dollars, but it might as well have been a million. I didn't have it.

JoAnn was doing much better. She and I drove to Great Falls Park with a friend she'd met in group therapy. I watched them laughing as they climbed down to one of the waterfalls.

I hadn't prayed since Galesburg Methodist, but I said a genuine prayer of thank you for JoAnn's survival and for the doctor who'd suggested the specialized program—without it, I knew for sure, JoAnn wouldn't have lived.

They had her trusting in a future. Now we had to get money to sustain her until she was functional again.

That Sunday, before I left to drive back to Brooklyn, JoAnn opened a box Mom and Jim had sent. Inside was food for her. I was glad that at least they were stepping up a little.

We opened the cardboard lid to find Lipton onion soup, Ritz crackers past their expiration date, mayonnaise, a few "Constant Comment" tea bags, and some flour. There wasn't enough of anything in that box to make a meal. Obviously, they had gone to their cupboard and pulled out whatever was in there.

I was exasperated, but JoAnn just shrugged. "One thing you can count on in this fucked-up life is that Mom is one hundred percent predictable." And even with the deep scars on the tops of her hands, she managed to laugh, and I did too.

"Someday, she'll be old and sick, and we'll mail her dehydrated Lipton onion soup as if it were a fucking miracle cure," JoAnn said. We had tears running down our faces.

"And she can split it with Dad," I said, laughing harder.

JoAnn looked so much happier now. I worried about her car being repossessed, and what that might do to her emotional state.

✦ ✦ ✦

That night, I drove to Brooklyn thinking about money and how to get it. Clearly JoAnn's unemployment would be awhile, and I was going to need the cavalry to come from somewhere. It hit me . . . it would have to be Dad. And I would be the one to ask him.

How had it come down to him—out of a whole family of people? He was the only hope left? A pedophile? And yet, shouldn't he bear the responsibility?

I waited until the following Sunday, his sixty-first birthday, to call. I thought it might help soften my request for money.

I shoved a red metal stool into the kitchen of my Brooklyn apartment and sat by the phone. The sun was out, the trees were bare now, and a chilly wind was blowing through the kitchen door. I was petrified.

I dialed Dad's number, knowing he was waiting to hear from one of us. I hadn't missed his birthday since high school. Whatever happened on the phone would determine the fate of Dad and me forever.

I heard it ringing. He picked up.

"Dad, it's me," I said.

"Well, hello," he said cheerfully. "Where have you been?" he asked.

Trying to keep JoAnn alive and functioning after all the perverted, disgusting things you did to her, I wanted to say. "Working," I said instead. "It's hard to call with the time difference."

"You can still write a note, can't you?" he asked.

I needed to focus. JoAnn needed help. "I know it's your birthday, but I don't have good news, Dad. I need money to help JoAnn. She's in the hospital. She tried to kill herself."

"Oh no," he said. "Oh my God."

"She's going to be okay."

"What the hell happened?"

"I have no idea," I said. "She's having some kind of breakdown." I was trying to lay it out so that he'd feel responsible but not threatened. I was walking a tightrope.

"A nervous breakdown?" he asked. "She's as crazy as your mother."

At that moment, everything shifted. I'd been through too much to let him blame her for what he had done.

He'd taken her childhood, her entire life away. And it was still unclear what the future held for her. He *would* take responsibility, and he *would* pay, one way or another. I'd find the money somewhere else if I had to.

I took a deep breath and set my trap.

"She left a suicide note in her apartment explaining why," I told him. "I have it here and I don't want to open it by myself." There had never been a note.

"Don't open it," he said. "She wouldn't want you to."

"It might explain what happened," I continued.

"Don't open it," he said again.

"But we'll know what happened to her, Dad."

"I never touched her," he said, panicked. "I never touched that girl."

I put the receiver in my lap and my forehead against the cool wall. He knew *exactly* what I was talking about. He denied something that no one was accusing him of doing. If he wasn't guilty, how else would he have come up with that scenario? I couldn't believe it. I couldn't breathe.

"Why would you say *that*?" I asked.

Dad was silent.

"Why did you say you didn't touch her, Dad?" I asked again.

"Don't tell your mother I said that," he said. "It would only upset her."

"JoAnn needs your help," I told him, trying to steady my trembling voice.

"I won't help her," he said.

"She's suicidal," I reminded him.

"She's weird and she always has been," he said. Again, I put the phone in my lap, squeezing it between my knees. After I got the money out of him, I'd kill him with my bare hands.

"She needs money."

"I'm not sending money." He was mad now.

"You should help her, Dad," I told him. "She needs you, and you know why."

"Bullshit," he said.

"No shit," I said.

"Not a dime." He hung up the phone.

I slammed down the receiver and walked around the apartment half bent over, trying to catch a breath. Holy shit, holy shit, holy shit. I hadn't expected it. I certainly hadn't expected that. Oh my God, on his birthday. He'd brought it up on his own. My dad.

It was over.

Chapter Twenty-one

Sitting in a DuPont Circle coffee shop with JoAnn, I told her about my conversation with Dad. I explained how I told him about a suicide note and how he blurted out, "I never touched her."

"That's pretty amazing," she said.

"There's no way he could have known what I was talking about," I said, picking up my brown Styrofoam cup of warm green tea. "If we called any father in the country and told him that his daughter was suicidal, not one of them would say, 'I never touched her.'" I sipped my tea.

JoAnn shook her head—not devastated, not relieved, and not entirely surprised.

For JoAnn, my phone call with Dad brought closure; for me it was anything but. As JoAnn got better, I got steadily worse.

Clearly, it was time for me to figure out where I fit into all of it—the sexual abuse, the neglect.

When I returned to Brooklyn, my own overwhelming feelings (which I'd put aside while trying to stay strong for JoAnn) were screaming for my attention. I tried to ignore them. When I wasn't working, I slept.

One evening after work I was standing on the subway platform, and had the urge to step in front of the number six train. I remembered that feeling from when Dad had visited me in San Diego. I saw the light from the train coming through the tunnel, and knew it would take away the grief and confusion, so I moved closer to the rim of the platform. The hot, stale wind of the train blew my bangs across my forehead as I stepped closer to the edge. Suddenly, a tall man in a wrinkled blue suit clutched my arm.

"Hey, watch where you're goin'," he said, pulling me backward. I forced a smile and gently pulled my arm away.

The train was now stopped in front of me with the doors open. I stepped inside and gripped the silver pole near the door. I usually hated crowded subways, but was oddly comforted, standing in that packed car, buffered by all those bodies, purses, and backpacks. There was life all around me, and I wanted to be a part of it, if only I could *feel* something—anything.

The train stopped at Union Square. I watched an elderly woman negotiate the platform with her walker. A young man helped her through the turnstiles. Just normal life. I couldn't imagine it.

The next morning, I found a therapist who took my insurance.

In my first session, the calm dark-haired psychiatrist sat in her Upper East Side apartment with her brown-and-white shih tzu on her lap. After hearing almost forty minutes of my painful story, she said, "I'm not sure what to tell you, really. I'm at a complete loss. First off, your dad sounds like trailer trash; I think we're in agreement there. And the other problem is that when I feel bad, I take myself to a nice dinner or a movie, but you can't even afford that." I wrote her a check and politely closed the door behind me.

If I hadn't felt so ashamed, I would have drop-kicked that spoiled dog out her twelfth-story window just to wake her up.

The next therapist was on the Upper West Side. She wore brown leather clogs and no makeup. The session began well enough, until I heard police sirens screeching up the street. The therapist ignored them, but now they were parked close enough to her office that red flashing lights were whipping around her walls. The next thing I heard was a voice booming through a bullhorn, "Stay where

you are. Someone's coming up to get you. You don't want to do this."
I stared at the therapist, who was now leaning closer to me, indicating that she wasn't missing a single word I was saying.

"Are you going to ignore what's happening out there?" I asked.

"If you want to get up and look out the window, go ahead. I don't want you to be distracted," she said.

"Aren't you distracted?" I asked, standing up.

"Not really." She shrugged.

I looked out the window. A man was crouched high on a window ledge directly across the street.

The policeman on the bullhorn said, "Sit down. SIT DOWN ON THE LEDGE. It will help you balance until we can get to you."

Three police cars were blocking the street and an ambulance was standing by—just in case.

I looked back at the perfectly composed therapist. "A man's jumping off a window ledge," I told her.

She shook her head in a very understanding way, "This probably brings up a lot for you."

I exploded. "It brings up the fact that you're ignoring a suicide attempt outside your own office. You're pretending it's not even happening. How could you possibly help *me*? You're exactly what I'm trying to avoid. You're *exactly* like my mother—like my entire family. You're what's making *me* want to jump out a window." I swooped up my coat and backpack in one hand and headed for the door.

"You owe me a check," she had the nerve to say.

"Bill me," I said, slamming the door behind me.

I walked into the street and looked up at the small, gray-haired man crouched on the ledge. It was about thirty degrees outside, but he was wearing only a white muscle T-shirt and cotton pajama bottoms.

I wanted to scream, *Don't let them talk you down! You're right! It ain't gonna get any better! Jump!*

I sat down on the curb with my backpack between my knees and watched two police officers extending their hands out the window. The old man startled and leaned forward. I slapped my hands over my ears as if stopping the sound might stop the action, giving the officers time to grab him.

Don't fall, I prayed. *Please don't let him fall.* My prayer surprised me. It was as if this elderly man in the thin, striped pajama bottoms was holding my fate in his hands. If he jumped, the hopelessness that was already sinking me would win, but if he lived, the hope that was constantly fighting to be realized, would take the prize.

A woman officer poked her head out the window of the next apartment and called to the old man. When he turned to look at the woman, the other two officers leaned out and grabbed him, pulling him gently inside.

I thought of JoAnn telling me she'd planned her own suicide on the beach. I hoped there would always be hands to pull her back in. I was beginning to worry that those hands would not belong to me. I didn't know how I was going to handle the pressure that was pushing against my own sanity.

I stood up, barely noticing the too familiar tears starting down my face and dripping onto my coat. I wanted help, was searching for it, but it was nowhere to be found.

I called Daniel from a pay phone on the corner.

"Can I come out?" I asked.

"When, tonight?" he asked.

"Right now," I said.

"It's so late. Are you sure you want to come this far?" Daniel had moved to New London, Connecticut, which was at least a two-hour trip.

"I'm sure."

"Where are you?"

"On the corner of Broadway and Seventy-eighth."

"Don't you need to get your stuff?" he asked.

"I don't need anything."

"Come on out, then," he said.

As Metro-North rumbled out of Grand Central, I placed my forehead against the chilly window and closed my eyes. It was unfair to turn to Daniel, who had always been so kind, but I couldn't think of anyone else.

Inside me, a terror had been unleashed by the man on the ledge. I couldn't face the night alone in Brooklyn.

The next morning Daniel got up for work and I didn't. I didn't get up, in fact, for five days. No eating, no teeth brushing, nothing. Daniel called his therapist, who came to the house to see me, wearing baggy corduroys and carrying a blue canvas briefcase.

After about ten minutes of sitting on the side of the bed talking to me, he sighed as he put his hands on his knees and said, "Suicidal people bore me. They're self-centered shits who need to get off their asses and do something with their lives. Now, why don't you just . . . get up?"

This added two more days to my bed vigil.

After that, my old friend Rachel, an actress I had worked with in La Jolla, called from Los Angeles. "Honey, what's going on?" I had refused to come to the phone on three separate occasions, so she'd called back, demanding to speak to me.

"I'm having some kind of breakdown, I think."

"Maybe you should come out here for a while. Stay with us until you get back on your feet," she offered. She lived with the most wonderfully smart and sensitive woman.

"I don't have any money," I told her. "I haven't been able to save anything."

"You'll get yourself a job. You always do. Come out and we'll at least get to see you," she said. It sounded good. Really good.

Daniel bought me a very expensive plane ticket, and I flew to L.A. two days later. He was relieved to have the weeping woman gone, and I didn't blame him. Maybe the cross-country distance would give me perspective.

Everyone at The Strategist Group understood I needed to leave. I hadn't shared everything with Elliott, but he trusted me. I was doing what I had to do.

Once I was in L.A., I stayed in Rachel's guest house. We'd become close friends in the six years since we acted in that play in San Diego, and now she had swooped in and saved me.

I called Mom. "JoAnn's much better, which is good, because I can't be responsible for her any longer." I didn't pause for Mom to interrupt. "I've moved to L.A. The weight of everything that's happened has finally caught up with me. I feel lost and panicked." There was a long pause.

"Why don't you call back when you're feeling better," Mom said.

I laughed as I slammed down the phone. I laughed because I was tired of crying. I laughed at the absurdity of turning to my mother for help.

If feeling better meant I'd have to call Mom back, I wouldn't be feeling better for a *long* time.

Rachel introduced me to a psychologist who was completing her training in analysis and needed a patient to work with. She was charging a small amount of money, and my insurance would cover what little she was charging. (Elliott had kept me on COBRA at The Strategist Group.)

In time, I found a job working with Daniel's cousin, Beth, at a personnel-recruiting agency in West Hollywood. This not only helped me afford therapy and a studio apartment, but gave me an opportunity to meet new friends.

While trying to understand my part in the abuse, I continued going to therapy five mornings a week and read as many books as I could on the subject.

In the books and articles, I read about cases where memories were unearthed after a person had been coerced by a psychiatrist. So I questioned myself. Would that happen to me? But in my sessions, my therapist refused to offer any of her own opinions or speculations. I talked and she listened.

The things I remembered about myself were disturbing, but nothing compared to what JoAnn had gone through.

For instance, Dad was always staring at us. Even when he wasn't home, I imagined he was watching me—even in the bathroom. When I realized I still had that paranoia, I was finally able to let go of it.

And I used to think that Dad pulling down my pants in public was to humiliate me, and that was part of it, but I now think that he wanted to see me naked; that he wanted to look, and that there was a sexual aspect to it. Even now I feel the heat of embarrassment—the shame of being publicly exposed.

When the one solid memory I had of Dad's abuse finally surfaced, it didn't happen in therapy, it happened in my dentist's office.

I was waiting to get my teeth cleaned when I picked up a magazine. I opened to an article about a young woman who had been raped on her college campus. What struck me most about her experience was that while it was horrific to be raped, she described the sex as "eerily ordinary" in the back of the rapist's car. "It wasn't violent or rough, it was clumsy and ridiculously 'normal.'" And almost as if a switch clicked on, I realized I was looking for the wrong thing.

I was trying to remember being held down and viciously raped—especially after JoAnn's harrowing journey. But it was less frequent and more "ordinary" for me. I hadn't counted on abuse feeling so chronically familiar, instead of excruciatingly violent.

I was less than six years old when it happened, because it took place in our bedroom at the old house—the bedroom with the grate in the floor.

My father was not brutal or crazy when he came in the night, he was tender and loving, making it a bedtime ritual, a silly game. He even had a name for it, but I can't recall what it was. This was by far the biggest betrayal. After he was so mean, how confusing and twisted it was to have him choose the middle of the night to say he loved me.

He manipulated love into something perverse, confusing me about what love is, causing me to sexualize friendships and relationships, teaching me without words what I was worth. Violence would have been more honest.

And with that memory, I had the orgasm mystery solved. It was Dad, and it was during the night, only I pretended to sleep while he touched me. I tried to move away from his hand, but it was pointless. After a while, I couldn't feel his hand. I couldn't feel anything, not even my arms or legs, which is why I was afraid of being immobile in my casket with Dad walking by. It's why I was afraid of his hands when he accidentally touched me in the cab of his truck. And when the orgasm finally came, it was the one feeling I couldn't numb out. It actually felt good, and there was nothing I could do about it.

And then there was Mom.

The blond psychologist at the psychiatric facility in Washington had been right about my facing Mom's role. It *was* the hardest part.

I'll never know why Mom slathered all three of us girls with Vaseline every night. It didn't make sense. Did it have anything to do with Dad? If we were chapped or red for some reason, why wasn't she curious about what was causing it?

Why wouldn't she let us wear panties to bed? I had friends who remembered their mothers telling them they needed to "air themselves out" at night, so maybe that's all there was to that. But I worried.

Mom's insistence that Dad was harmless made him more dangerous. She wasn't monitoring him—no one was.

Again, I remembered Mom warning Becky about the way Dad looked at her when she was in junior high. At least there was that much awareness on her part—but why didn't she make sure Becky was safe? Why didn't she kick Dad out right then?

I can't forgive my mother for choosing not to change, for living her life exactly as she did before the abuse came to light, whipping into a fury if I talked about it. Refusing to see what I was forced to see—through JoAnn and through my own experiences—irreversibly separated us into two different worlds. She lived in the past, and I lived for the future.

Mom chose not to confront Dad—even though they lived eighteen miles apart, even though she occasionally ran into him at the gas station or the grocery store. "He won't care," she said, not realizing that *we* cared. It would have been an attempt on her part to protect us, not just from the sexual abuse, but from the violence as well.

The worst and most unforgivable thing of all was that she declared herself one hundred percent "not responsible."

I let go of Dad first (or rather, he let go of me), and now it was time to let go of Mom.

The last time I spoke to my mother wasn't the worst talk we'd ever had, it wasn't an argument, but it was, in my mind, the end. Years ago, hearing her tell the story about Dad and how one day, when she was standing by the washer in the hallway, she suddenly didn't care about him anymore, I didn't know that was how she and I would end. Nothing dramatic, nothing came crashing down; after an ordinary phone call, I just didn't try to love her anymore.

It began with my phone ringing and then a really high voice (my mother's) going, "Say 'yippee'!"

"What?" I asked, trying to buy time. I'd had a long day.

"Just say 'yippee.' Right now," she demanded.

"Why?"

"JUST SAY IT."

"No."

"Why do you have to ruin it for me?"

"Ruin what?"

"Exactly. You don't even know why I called. Now I don't even want to share my good news with you, so there."

"Mom, I just came from the emergency room. I hit my head on the trunk of my car and got seven stitches in my forehead. I'm not in a great mood. What do you want?"

"I want you to say 'yippee.'" She couldn't stop herself.

"Yippee," I finally said.

"That wasn't even excited, that was shitty. Just forget it."

"Well, thanks for calling, anyway," I said. "Have a great day."

"It was a happy day until now." She was pouting.

I got off the phone as quickly as possible.

Mom has some version of what that conversation was, and she has some version of who I am, and I don't care what any of that is. It's not the truth. It never will be.

We hung up and I haven't spoken with her since.

Knowing there is no cavalry is much better than hoping for a cavalry that never comes. I am strong because I have to be. I am the cavalry.

EPILOGUE

It's 2006. I'm out of the worst of it, but it was in no way a "happily ever after" ending. It couldn't be. It's been the steepest climb to where I am now.

I live in Los Angeles with my beloved husband, Matthew, and my precious son, Aidan. JoAnn lives three blocks from us in California. She carries the scars, not just on her arms and hands but in her bones, in her life. We both do.

I think of JoAnn and how comfortable her life is now—how having her close by comforts me. Last week I was dropping Aidan off at her office. When we pulled up, she was already standing beside her little red sports car, impeccably dressed, talking to three colleagues. Aidan jumped out, anxious to show Aunt Jo a rock he'd found. She squeezed him tight, both of them smiling. They are the best of friends.

Becky has never come forward or tried to analyze her place in all of it. That's absolutely her right. It flipped my life completely upside down, but I would tell anyone that it was worth coming out the other side. I might not be completely free of my past, but I'm no longer paralyzed by it.

It's impossible for me to see Becky, who is still living in denial. I don't want things to be the way they were, and she can only (unconsciously) repeat what was.

Jamie is gone. I have no idea where. But he can't be part of my life as long as he's drinking and violent. I've had enough of violence

316 • Monica Holloway

and deceit. Still, the thought of Jamie can bring me instantly to tears. Whenever I hear Neil Young, I immediately think of him sitting on the floor of the condo in San Diego, his brown head bent over his acoustic guitar, strumming "The Needle and the Damage Done," as he sings quietly, "I caught you knockin' at my cellar door." And that's it, really; it's the damage done.

I'll always be damaged in a way. I had hoped that I could completely heal those cracks, but I'm starting to think the real trick is learning to live a full life in spite of them. Cracked people are everywhere, and so I can forgive myself for being overly anxious or easily frightened. But I will no longer allow myself to be swallowed by my past. I insist on having the happiest life I can muster, and I am in control of that now.

I don't see Dad. I've had no contact with him since the "not a dime" birthday call fourteen years ago.

Actually, there was one communication, but it was indirect.

Six years ago Julie Kilner was visiting me in Los Angeles and, having no idea what had happened to our family, turned to me and said, "I ran into your dad last week." I held my breath. "I asked him how you girls were, and he said, 'As far as I know, they aren't dead yet.'"

I was caught off guard by how much this disturbed me. I must have unconsciously fantasized that Dad was sorry for all he'd done. Instead, he wished us dead.

I clicked open my cell phone and dialed 1-800-flowers. I ordered a fifty-dollar bouquet to be sent to my dad's address at Lake Hiawatha on Father's Day, which was one week away. When the operator asked me what to put on the card, I didn't hesitate:

Dear Dad,
I miss you every day.
Love,
Monica

I would jog his memory of who we used to be—remind him of all he'd screwed up—so if someone asked about me, maybe he wouldn't say, "She's not dead yet." Maybe he'd remember and say nothing at all. Maybe he'd remember that I loved him a long time ago, loved him despite everything else, and wanted him to love me too. And that was where it all began—and ended.

I'm driving through Elk Grove, surprised to be back in Ohio after so many years. I came back to find the newspaper records of Sarah Keeler's accident, to visit the Kilners, and to officially say good-bye to home—not the people, the place.

Driving past the empty lot where Dad's store should have been, and a huge CVS drugstore in place of Conroy's Pharmacy, I wonder what's left of me here.

I'm staying at the Holiday Inn Express out near the hospital where I spent the night with my kidney infection in high school. The hotel is new and I'm the only guest. It's strange to be in my hometown in a hotel, and stranger still to be the only occupant.

I drive to Galesburg to see my old house. As I head into town, past Wanda's farm, I'm stunned to see the gigantic maple trees that lined our street are gone. Galesburg is now three blocks of small houses in the middle of a flat, leafless field.

The biggest shock is our house. It's empty with a FOR SALE sign stuck in waist-high grass. The windows are broken and there's a deep sag in the worn roof. A dead plant hangs from a dirty white plastic hanger on the front porch, where the blue paint is peeling and the porch swing dangles by one rusty chain. The shrubs surrounding the house have been pulled.

I turn into the driveway that is now a crumble of cement, gravel, and dirt, and I'm suddenly the kid who wet the bed and rode my bicycle up to the cemetery to see the sunken grave. My knees might as well have scrapes and bruises on them for how young I feel.

I walk to the backyard where our climbing trees once grew. There are no trees at all, except for the small maple we planted in the west corner when I was nine, the year my hip was dislocated. That tree is now grotesquely huge, reminding me how long I've been gone, and Sarah Keeler longer still. It doesn't seem possible that that much time has passed, but the wrinkles across the tops of my hands tell me otherwise.

The white rail fence in the back is gone now, allowing Whitmore's field to spill into the backyard. Nothing separates one from the other. Standing back there, I can see Alton Cotterman's old house. His rusty metal glider, from where he fired all those shots, is still sitting on his back patio. He died more than eleven years ago.

I walk toward our house and check the doors—they're locked. No one locked houses when I lived here. We didn't even own a key. The danger was inside, not out.

I push my head through an opening in one of the broken windows. There's maroon paint randomly splashed across the dining room walls and an old box spring lying on the floor. In Jamie's room green wallpaper has been ripped off the walls and hangs in jagged strips. There's shattered glass on the faded red carpet where he worked on his model cars.

I walk around to the front porch and peek in through another broken window, where I see the living room. I've never seen my house without our furniture. Mom moved out long after I was gone.

What happened here? I wonder, scanning the overgrown trash-riddled front yard. But I know what happened. There's just no pretty facade to hide it now.

I move to the front sidewalk and look across the street at the Galesburg Methodist Church. It looks exactly the same. The stained glass window with Jesus's face is visible from where I'm standing. I still miss the Sunday mornings when, for forty minutes, we sat as a family and sang "We Gather Together" in unison. We didn't know, sitting in our Sunday best, that for reasons too tragic to imagine we would not end up together.

I climb into my Hertz rental and drive around the block. Someone is living in Mammaw and Papaw's old house. I wonder if the root cellar under the pantry is still there.

On down the street, I notice that Granda's trailer, like Granda, is gone. Granda died with my arms wrapped around her tiny failing body. I held her gently but firmly just as she'd held me throughout my childhood. I helped Dave Kilner lift her carefully onto the stretcher in her white short-sleeved nightgown and cover her with the black velvet drape embroidered in red. I stood in the snow without my coat, watching them drive away together.

The garage where she killed her cat still stands. It looks rundown and unsteady. I feel like kicking it over.

Down the street I see the blinker light still flashing, and the Galesburg Tavern, which is not only still in business but has a sign nailed to the front door that reads KARAOKE EVERY SATURDAY NIGHT. Uncle Ernie quit drinking years ago and died suddenly last year of a heart attack. So I know he's not in there.

I drive back to Elk Grove, past the Rotary Club where I met Julie Kilner for the first time. It's still there, only now the sign reads PIONEER ENGINEER CLUB, and when I crane my neck, I can still see the dirt tractor-pull track where Papaw competed.

Julie and I had dinner at Pizza Palace last night, ordering a taco pizza and a pitcher of Pepsi. We needed to catch up. She and Jay are planning their twentieth wedding anniversary and raising two handsome boys.

As she sped away in her Honda, I could hardly believe how many years had gone by since we'd lain in coffins.

I make a left into Maple Creek Cemetery and park in the back.

Walking down the newly paved road to a grave I haven't seen since I was twelve, I pull my glasses out of my purse and wipe the lenses on my sweatshirt. I'm looking for Sarah Keeler. I forget the color of her headstone but not the location: section fifteen, tenth row back.

The last time I saw Sarah, she was by herself back here. Now there's another stone to her left. It's gray, like Sarah's, and has a cross with a flower wrapped around it just like hers. I instinctively hope it's her mom, so she won't be alone anymore.

I slip on my glasses and lean down to read the names on the stone. It's her mom and dad, who both died recently, within three months of each other. I'm not sure what I believe happens after death, but I am comforted that they might all be together after thirty-four years.

I pull a crumpled blue Kleenex out of the pocket of my jeans, realizing I'd imagined Sarah's mom to be all the things mine wasn't. I'd pictured them as the perfect mother and daughter, senselessly separated. Now that I'm forty-three, I know that's not realistic. They would have gone through their own highs and lows, hopefully faring better than Mom and I.

I look at Sarah's stone and feel compelled to leave flowers or something meaningful to thank her for secretly sustaining me all these years. For being the dead girl so I could be the live one.

But it doesn't feel appropriate.

I look up to see a line of cars snailing around the bend of the road. Liz Kilner is driving the new black hearse, leading the way. I don't wave because she's working, but she gives me a thumbs-up, so I wave after all.

I turn back to Sarah Keeler and sit in the grass. The cars stay for five or six minutes, and then Liz Kilner leads them back out the gate. I look over and there's the tiniest casket sitting there. It's a baby.

I remember Mom saying, "Babies aren't people until they're two years old." I bet these grieving parents don't feel that way.

A thin man in overalls jumps down into the grave, and another man in a brown canvas jumpsuit carefully hands the casket down.

The man in the hole gently takes it and I can't see it anymore.

Dried leaves blow across the winter grass and I pull my hood up over my head. Purple and yellow crocuses are starting to push through the black Ohio dirt.

I can see Wendell's grave, where Tim gave me my first kiss and presented me with the plywood stop sign that hung inside my childhood closet until I was almost twenty.

Another headstone stops my heart. It's across the narrow road, a rust-colored stone with the names David and Joan Kilner engraved on it. I hurry over. I spoke to them an hour ago, but in my heightened state of nostalgia and anxiety I worry they've been buried since then. It's enormously reassuring to see the death date blank for both of them.

I look to see what section they're in, and the small black-and-white marker reads SECTION 14.

I hike across Highway 64 to the cemetery office. A big-bosomed woman in black stretch pants wants to know what I want. Being in the plot-selling business, she knows everyone in Elk Grove, and I am an outsider.

"Are there plots available in section fourteen?" I ask.

She walks to her computer. Standing behind her chair, she holds a pair of broken glasses up to her eyes with one hand and taps the keys with the other. Dropping the glasses onto her chest, where they swing from a silver chain, she declares, "Looks like it."

"How much is a plot?" I ask. Judging from the sigh she expels, I assume I'm taking up too much of her time.

"Five hundred," she huffs, handing me a card with a phone number and a picture of the entrance to Maple Creek Cemetery on it. I head out the door and can feel her watching me as I cross the small gravel parking lot.

Five hundred dollars isn't that much. I open my cell phone and call Matthew in Los Angeles. I'm interrupting him. He's either writing a script or hanging out with our eight-year-old son and his friends.

"Hello?" Matthew's voice sounds just right to me. Like home.

"I'm at the cemetery," I say.

"Sounds like you're having a fun vacation," he teases.

"Plots at Maple Creek are only five hundred dollars," I tell him. "There's room with the Kilners. Maybe we should get four and then we'd have them—just in case."

"Four?"

"You, me, JoAnn, and Aidan," I tell him.

"I don't want to be buried in Elk Grove," he says. "I don't know anyone there."

"Where do you want to be buried?" I ask.

"I haven't thought about it," he says.

"Think about it, because I want to be with the Kilners, not with Liberace or Bette Davis under the burning fake sun at Forest Lawn," I say. "I want to be under an oak tree covered in rain or snow."

"You said you'd never go back to Elk Grove. It makes you sad," he says.

"There's part of me that still belongs here," I tell him.

"Aren't you getting cremated?" he asks. "When we got married, that's what you told me."

"That was twelve years ago," I say.

"You told me if you died first, I had to carry you around in a satchel."

"Especially if you're dating," I say. "Carry me on all your dates."

"We can talk about this when you get home." He laughs.

"Okay, but if I die before I get home, put a little of me in the satchel and a little of me next to Dave and Joan," I tell him.

"I will," he says. "I promise."

It's cloudy and a soft spring breeze is blowing across the cornfield as I make my way back across the highway to Maple Creek. I'd forgotten the smell of Ohio, but here it is: damp soil, freshly cut grass, and burning wood coming from somewhere on the other side of town.

❧ ❧ ❧

I leave the cemetery and drive through Elk Grove on my way to the Cincinnati airport, where, luckily, I won't be picking up a body at the cargo hold. Sitting at the four-way stop on the corner of Orchard Street and Highway 64, the corner where Dad's store burned and where Pizza Palace still sits, a brown car stops across from me.

I can't see the person's face clearly, but I instinctively know—it's Dad and he's staring right at me.

I don't step on the gas. I don't do anything. And neither does Dad.

Dad destroyed all of us, and yet he's heading to the Valley Inn Restaurant or maybe to the grocery store to buy steaks for the lake house, normal things. He lives without consequences.

Dad moves first, driving slowly through the intersection, approaching me on the left. I look right at him. Unlike JoAnn and me, he isn't afraid of showering at night or walking to his car in an open parking lot. He doesn't constantly look over his shoulder or startle at the smallest sound. He gave his fear to us, and we took it and moved away.

If he recognizes me or makes any effort to stop, it'll be a huge showdown right here on Orchard. My adrenaline kicks in as I put my left hand on the door handle.

Dad taps his brakes, and I move my other hand to the gearshift, ready to shove it into park if he wants to tangle. But Dad drives by, glancing at me without a flicker of recognition. I'm a forty-three-year-old woman in a baseball cap and glasses. The last time he saw me I was twenty-nine.

He looks exactly the same.

I glance at myself in the rearview mirror and see the wrinkles around my eyes. They're from laughing. I'm glad I don't look the same; there's no way I could. I'm happy now.

I step on the gas and head out Highway 50 toward Cincinnati. I have a plane to catch.

ACKNOWLEDGMENTS

Elizabeth Kaplan, my smart and savvy agent who took me under her wing, thank you for believing in me.

To the wise and incomparable Tricia Boczkowski, editor extraordinaire. Your fierce loyalty and fine eye served as my backbone throughout the writing of this book. How can I ever thank you for your unflinching support and for caring so deeply? There is no book without you.

Thank you to Jennifer Bergstrom for your great ideas, sense of humor, and ardent support.

Cara Bedick and Katherine Devendorf, thank you for your careful and tireless work. Thanks to Bara MacNeill, a terrific and smart copyeditor, and to everyone at Simon & Schuster who supported and enriched *Driving with Dead People*. I couldn't have been luckier than to have landed at Simon Spotlight Entertainment.

Eric Raymond, thank you for being so smart and guiding me so thoughtfully toward the end.

To my husband for his unfailing confidence in me, even when I was positive I couldn't write another word, and for reading this book in all its many forms—many, many, many times. Thank you for how incredibly smart and patient you are, and for still being attracted to me even after I crawl out of my office unbathed, wild-eyed, and behind schedule. I couldn't have dreamed you up if I tried.

My son, you are a priceless gift and my greatest joy. I had given up on unconditional love until I was utterly blessed with you. You restored my faith in all things. You are my life.

My precious sister, your strength and wisdom constantly remind me to be courageous myself. You came out of the worst storm imaginable with such aplomb. You are my inspiration every day.

Hope Edelman, there are not enough words to thank you for all you've brought to my life. Your confidence and steady guidance over the years have given me the confidence to follow my dream of writing. I am dazzled by your talent and your extreme generosity.

Jennifer Lauck, you are a shining star who gathers up all who love you and shows us exactly where the light is. I am profoundly blessed for finding you just when I needed you most.

Liz Berman, your friendship and steady hand on my back throughout the writing of this book has been an infinite source of inspiration and support. I am grateful for your enormous heart as well as your exceptional talent.

Leslie Morgan Steiner, you shepherded me through my first professional writing job, becoming not only my mentor, but my trusted friend and confidante. You are one of the smartest, most talented women I know.

Barbara Abercrombie, friend, teacher, and grooviest of humans, you are an extraordinary teacher and writer who inspires all who are lucky enough to know you.

Jo Ann Beard, your miraculous book, *Boys of my Youth*, sent me racing to my computer to put my own story on paper. My profound thanks to you for showing me I was ready.

Beth Schachter, for encouraging me all those years ago to tell my stories and for sharing the tiniest living space possible in New York City and still loving me, I thank you. You are a true friend.

Steve Wall, I met you at a crucial juncture in my life and you changed the way I would feel about myself forever. I am eternally grateful.

To the precious Ceballos family, who took care of everything and everyone while I was in my office pounding the computer keys.

To my aunt and uncle who still live across from the old Methodist church. I love you and thank you for standing by me when no one else in the family was willing.

To my incredible circle of friends who bless me with their love, their undying support, and lots of snacks.

To that quirky, fabulous funereal family with whom I spent some of the happiest times of my life. Thank you for allowing me to write our story.

And lastly, thank you to the people of my hometown who took good care of me when all was not well, whether you knew it or not.

Photo by Russell Baer

MONICA HOLLOWAY is an actress turned writer whose essay "Red Boots and Cole Haans" was described by *Newsday* as "brilliant, grimly hilarious." This is her first full-length book. Learn more about the author at www.MonicaHolloway.com.